Yours
In
Struggle

THREE FEMINIST PERSPECTIVES
ON ANTI-SEMITISM
AND RACISM

Yours In Struggle

THREE FEMINIST PERSPECTIVES ON ANTI-SEMITISM AND RACISM

Elly Bulkin

Minnie Bruce Pratt

Barbara Smith

Firebrand
Books
Ithaca, New York

Early versions of the essays included in this book originally appeared as follows: Elly Bulkin's "Origins," "Extensions," "Threads," and "Separations" in *Conditions;* "The Male Enemy/The Left Enemy" in *New Women's Times;* and "Breaking a Cycle" in *off our backs.*

Portions of Minnie Bruce Pratt's "Identity: Skin Blood Heart" under the titles: "White Women, White Terror" (*WIN*) and "Who Am I If Not My Father's Daughter?" (*MS*).

Barbara Smith's "A Rock and a Hard Place: Relationships Between Black and Jewish Women" in *Women's Studies Quarterly.*

Originally published by Long Haul Press, this edition (1988) is published by Firebrand Books.

Book design by Chaia Lehrer
Cover design by Betsy Bayley
Typesetting by Diane Lubarsky

Printed in the United States on acid-free paper by McNaughton & Gunn

Library of Congress Cataloging-in-Publication Data

Bulkin, Elly, 1944-
   Yours in struggle.

   Reprint. Originally published:
New York, N.Y. : Long Haul Press, 1984.
   1. Afro-Americans—Relations with Jews.   2. Antisemi-
tism—United States.   3. Racism—United States.
4. United States—Race relations.   I. Pratt, Minnie Bruce.
II. Smith, Barbara, 1946-   .   III. Title.
E185.615.B79   1988   305.8'00973   88-24411
ISBN 0-932379-54-0 (alk. paper)
ISBN 0-932379-53-2 (pbk. : alk. paper)

ACKNOWLEDGMENTS

We would like to thank the Astraea Foundation for a grant which helped with production costs for this book. We are also very grateful to the individuals whose generous donations and pre-publication orders helped to cover printing costs. We want to express our deepest appreciation to Diane Lubarsky for the dedicated typesetting that helped us meet our printing deadline; to Chaia Lehrer for the design and layout of the headlines; to Anna Bulkin for work on promotional mailings; and to Jan Clausen, our publisher, for all her work to bring this book into existence.

ELLY BULKIN: Many people contributed to my work. The editors of *Conditions* who read its opening sections: Dorothy Allison, Cheryl Clarke, Mirtha Quintanales, Nancy Clarke Otter, Rima Shore, and Adrienne Waddy. Those who read drafts of parts of this article at different stages in my writing: Rita Arditti, Joyce Bressler, Lawrence Bush, Renée Franco, Jewelle Gomez, Barbara Kerr, Diane Lubarsky, Judith McDaniel, Minnie Bruce Pratt, Mab Segrest, Cris South, Aida Wakil. Particular thanks are due Cherríe Moraga and Barbara Smith for being there during a difficult winter/spring and thereby helping to make this work possible; Sherry Gorelick, Chaia Lehrer, and Shelly Weiss for consistently challenging and encouraging me; Ana Oliveira, acupuncturist extraordinaire, for keeping me healthy; Stacy Pies, an editor's editor, a writer's therapist, for worrying about my logic, my politics, and my topic sentences; Anna Bulkin for bearing with me; and Jan Clausen for things too numerous to be listed.

MINNIE BRUCE PRATT: I would like to acknowledge that much of the work for this essay grew out of the work, conversation, friendship, and political analysis of the women with whom I co-edited *Feminary* magazine. I also thank Joan E. Biren for her loving support and for her hope in the struggle.

BARBARA SMITH: I would like to thank all of those individuals whose practical and emotional support made it possible for me to complete this essay, especially Dorothy Allison, Nancy Bereano, Akilah Blakwomyn, Renée Franco, Jewelle Gomez, Barbara Kerr, Raymina Mays, Judith McDaniel, Betty Powell, Beverly Smith, and Aida Wakil. I would also like to thank Cherríe Moraga for her invaluable editorial help and for her continuous faith in me as a writer.

CONTENTS

April 13, 1984

To Our Readers:

Initially *Yours in Struggle* was to have been one essay, which Elly Bulkin started in the summer of 1982. The original conception expanded a few months later, however, when Elly and Barbara Smith decided to do a joint publication, after Barbara had been invited to be on the plenary panel on racism and anti-Semitism at the 1983 National Women's Studies Association conference. After the NWSA presentation, Barbara and Elly asked Minnie Bruce Pratt, who was also on that panel, to be a contributor to this book.

Yours in Struggle grew out of the three of us having known each other for several years. We are all lesbians who have worked together politically and respect each other's work. This book happened because we were able to talk to each other in the first place, despite our very different identities and backgrounds—white Christian-raised Southerner, Afro-American, Ashkenazi Jew. Each of us speaks only for herself, and we do not necessarily agree with each other. Yet we believe our cooperation on this book indicates concrete possibilities for coalition work.

We are writing as part of a growing dialogue among women whose backgrounds and political perspectives are far more diverse than our own. We are aware that a great deal more can be said about anti-Semitism and racism than we can possibly say here. And we are particularly aware of how much more needs to be *done* about these issues. As activists, we hope that our writing will support the organizing being done by women in our communities. Difficult as it was to complete our essays, we know that what we each have learned in writing them will have a strong impact on our future political work.

Yours in struggle,

Elly Bulkin

Minnie Bruce Pratt

Barbara Smith

IDENTITY:

SKIN   BLOOD   HEART

BY
MINNIE BRUCE PRATT

IDENTITY:

SKIN   BLOOD   HEART

I live in a part of Washington, D.C. that white suburbanites called "the jungle" during the uprising of the '60s—perhaps still do, for all I know. When I walk the two-and-a-half blocks to H St. NE, to stop in at the bank, to leave my boots off at the shoe-repair-and-lock shop, I am most usually the only white person in sight. I've seen two other whites, women, in the year I've lived here. (This does not count white folks in cars, passing through. In official language, H St., NE, is known as "The H Street Corridor," as in something to be passed through quickly, going from your place, on the way to elsewhere.)

When I walk three blocks in a slightly different direction, down Maryland Avenue, to go to my lover's house, I pass the yards of Black folks: the yard of the lady who keeps children, with its blue-and-red windmill, its roses-of-sharon; the yard of the man who delivers vegetables with its stacked slatted crates; the yard of the people next to the Righteous Branch Commandment Church-of-God (Seventh Day) with its tomatoes in the summer, its collards in the fall. In the summer, folks sit out on their porches or steps or sidewalks; when I walk by, if I lift my head and look toward them and speak, "Hey," they may speak, say, "Hey" or "How you doing?" or perhaps just nod. In the spring, I was afraid to smile when I spoke, because that might be too familiar, but by the end of summer I had walked back and forth so often, I was familiar, so sometimes we shared comments about the mean weather.

I am comforted by any of these speakings for, to tell you the truth, they make me feel at home. I am living far from where I was born; it has been twenty years since I have lived in that place where folks, Black and white, spoke to each other when they met on the street or in the road. So when two Black men dispute country matters, calling across the corners of 8th St— "Hey, Roland, did you ever see a hog catch a rat?"—"I seen a hog catch a *snake.*"—"How about a rat? Ever see one catch a *rat*?"—I am grateful to be living within sound of their voices, to hear a joking that reminds me, with a startled pain, of my father, putting on his tales for his friends, the white men gathered at the drug store.

The pain, of course, is the other side of this speaking, and the sorrow: when I have only to turn two corners to go back in the basement door of my building, to meet Mr. Boone, the janitor, who doesn't raise his eyes to mine, or his head, when we speak. He is a dark red-brown man from the Yemassee in South Carolina—that swampy land of Indian resistance and armed communities of fugitive slaves, that marshy land at the headwaters of the Combahee, once site of enormous rice plantations and location of Harriet Tubman's successful military action that freed many slaves. When we meet in the hall or on the elevator, even though I may have just heard him speaking in his own voice to another man, he "yes ma'am's" me in a sing-song: I hear my voice replying in the horrid cheerful accents of a white lady: and I hate my white woman-hood that drags between us the long bitter history of our region.

I think how I just want to feel at home, where people know me; instead I remember, when I meet Mr. Boone, that home was a place of forced subservience, and I know that my wish is that of an adult wanting to stay a child: to be known by others, but to know nothing, to feel no responsibility.

Instead, when I walk out in my neighborhood, each speaking-to another person has become fraught, for me, with the history of race and sex and class; as I walk I have a constant interior discussion with myself, questioning how I acknowledge the presence of another, what I know or don't know about them, and what it means how they acknowledge me. It is an exhausting process, this moving from the experience of the "unknowing majority" (as Maya Angelou called it) into consciousness. It would be a lie to say this process is comforting.

I meet a white man on Maryland Avenue at ten at night, for instance: He doesn't *look* gay, and he's young and bigger than me. Just because he's wearing a three-piece suit, doesn't mean he won't try something. What's he doing walking here anyway? one of the new gentry, taking over? Maybe that's what the Black neighbors think about me. If I speak, he'll probably assume it's about sex, not about being neighborly. I don't feel neighborly toward him, anyway. If he speaks to me, is that about sex? Or does he still think skin means kin. Or maybe he was raised some-place where someone could say, "I know your mama," if he didn't behave. But he's probably not going to think about her, when he does whatever he does *here:* better be careful.

In the space of three blocks one evening, I can debate whether the young Black woman didn't speak because she was tired, urban-raised, or hates white women; and ask myself why I wouldn't speak to the young professional white woman on her way to work in the morning, but I do at night: and she doesn't speak at all: is it about who I think I may need for physical safety?

And I make myself speak to a young Black man: If I don't, it will be the old racial-sexual fear. Damn the past anyway. When I speak directly, I usually get a respectful answer: is that the response violently extorted by history, the taboo on white women? Last week the group of Black men on 10th Street started in on "Can I have some?" when Joan and I walked by: was that because they were three? we were white? we were lesbian? Or because we didn't speak? What about this man? He *is* a man. And I would speak to him in the *day* time.

After I speak and he speaks, I think how my small store of manners, how I was taught to be "respectful" of others, my middle-class, white-woman, rural Southern Christian manners, gave me no ideas on Sunday afternoon, in the northwestern part of the city, how to walk down the sidewalk by gatherings of Latinos and Latinas socializing there.

And I think of how I'm walking to visit my Jewish lover: When we walk around the neighborhood together, we just look like two white women: except the ladies in my building say we look like sisters, because we're close and they can see we love each other. But I'm blonde and blue-eyed, she dark-haired and brown-eyed: we don't look a bit like sisters. If the white people and the Black people we meet knew she was Jewish as well as white, how would their speaking alter?

By the amount of effort it takes me to walk these few blocks being conscious as I can of myself in relation to history, to race, to culture, to gender, I reckon the rigid boundaries set around my experience, how I have been "protected." In this city where I am no longer of the majority by color or culture, I tell myself every day: In this *world* you aren't the superior race or culture, and never were, whatever you were raised to think: and are you getting ready to be *in* this world?

And I answer myself back: I'm trying to learn how to live, to have the speaking-to extend beyond the moment's word, to act so as to change the unjust circumstances that keep us from being able to speak to each other; I'm trying to get a little closer to the longed-for but un-realized world, where we each are able to live, but not by trying to make someone less than us, not by someone else's blood or pain: yes, that's what I'm trying to do with my living now.

I take the moments when I speak and am spoken to, the exchange with dignity, respect, perhaps pleasure, as fragments of that world; but often the moment slips, the illusion of acceptance vanishes into the chasm of the world-as-it-is that opens up between me and another. Yesterday when I said "Hey," smiling to the white-headed white woman coming with difficulty down the walk, she spat at me, shout-singing, "How much is that doggy in the window?": her disdain for the uselessness and childishness of my manners in a world where she labored down the sidewalk. Why should she give me the approval of her smile?

The stark truth spoken in public, the terror of what is said about my place on the other side of the chasm between me and another, makes me want to pretend I didn't hear: cover the truth up. The reply, like the impulse, comes from home: where great-great-aunt Rannie stripped naked before company, against the remonstrance of her scandalized niece: "*Ran*-nie, you're nekkid as a jaybird!" "Yes," said Rannie, calmly, "and the jaybird is a pretty bird." Rannie reminds me to listen for the beauty in the stark truth that someone tells me, that which seems brutal and may terrify me. This listening is one way of finding out how to get to the new place where we all can live and speak-to each other for more than a fragile moment.

If you and I met today, reader, on Maryland Avenue, would we speak? I don't know what barriers of gender, color, culture, sexuality, might rise between us when we saw each other. Nor do I know what may come between us as I talk explicitly in these pages about the barriers that we struggle with every day, issues of morality like anti-Semitism and racism.

Here my friend Dorothy has protested: "Morality! I'd call it ethics." She hates the word, it having been used against her often. It's true: her Baptists, and my Presbyterians, not to mention others we could name, have turned the word on us too much. But, Dorothy, ethics sounds like classical Greece to me. What if I say, not morality but—

I'm trying to talk about struggling against racism and anti-Semitism as issues of how to live, the right-and-wrong of it, about how to respect others and myself. It is very hard for me to know *how* to speak of this struggle because the culture I was born and raised in has taught me certain ways of being that reduce the process of change to ought-to, that reduce the issue of how to live to ought-to.

I was taught to be a *judge*, of moral responsibility and of punishment only in relation to *my* ethical system; was taught to be a *martyr*, to take all the responsibility for change, *and* the glory, to expect others to do nothing; was taught to be a *peacemaker*, to mediate, negotiate between opposing sides because *I* knew the right way; was taught to be a *preacher*, to point out wrongs and tell others what to do. Nowadays, I struggle not to speak with the tones or gestures or notions of these roles when I raise, outloud, with other women, those interior questions that I have asked myself, about my understanding of anti-Semitism and racism.

Sometimes after I have spoken of these issues, women who are like me come up to me and say:

They feel so ashamed, I spoke and they didn't, they would never be able to act so bravely, I might be able to do it but not them, ever. Or they say how can I be so self-righteous, hurt and punish others, divide women, how can I think I am better than others. Sometimes they say they are glad I had pointed out the racism or anti-Semitism, they hadn't noticed, and didn't know how or what to do about these problems. Sometimes they say they are glad I spoke, since these problems are important, but they really don't see how any of this affects them personally.

Sometimes they say they are so tired of hearing about these issues, and they really don't see how any of this affects them personally. Or they say they are so tired of talk, why don't we just *do* something. Or maybe they say who do I think I am, to speak for them as white or gentile, their experience has been different. Sometimes they say, painfully, they couldn't speak as I had of these things to their best friends, who they felt as individuals and could not distance themselves from enough to challenge or comment.

I know that, sometimes, when women make these remarks to me it is because *I* was not clear about my own struggle, fears, mistakes, responsibility, complicity, plans for actions; or because I have failed in my struggle with the old ways of being, and am acting them out in my style, manner, tone, ideas. Sometimes, I believe, the remarks are made because women are handing their power and responsibility over to me, because of their own upbringing or assumptions that place me in a certain role in relation to them; and because they are not feeling their own various powers, bravery, creativity, knowledge, and ability to change.

I am struggling now to speak, but not out of any role of ought-to; I ask that you try not to place me in that role. I am trying to speak from my heart, out of need, as a woman who loves other women passionately, and wants us to be able to be together as friends in this unjust world; and as a woman who lives in relative security in the United States, and who is trying to figure out my responsibility and my need in struggles against injustice in a way that will lead to our friendship.

I am speaking my small piece of truth, as best I can. My friend Barbara Deming has reminded me: we each have only a piece of the truth. So here it is: I'm putting it down for you to see if our fragments match anywhere, if our pieces, together, make another larger piece of the truth that can be part of the map we are making together to show us the way to get to the longed-for world.

Where does the need come from, the inner push to walk into change, if by skin color, ethnicity, birth culture, we are women who are in a position of material advantage, where we gain at the expense of others, of other women? A place where *we* can have a degree of safety, comfort, familiarity, just by staying put. Where is our *need* to change what we were born into? What do we have to gain?

When I try to think of this, I think of my father: of how, when I was about eight years old, he took me up the front marble steps of the court-house in my town. He took me inside, up the worn wooden steps, stooped under the feet of folks who had gone up and down to be judged, or to gawk at others being judged, up past the courtroom where my grandfather had leaned back in his chair and judged for over forty years, up to the attic, to some narrow steps that went to the roof, to the clock tower with a walled ledge.

What I would have seen at the top: on the streets around the court-house square, the Methodist church, the limestone building with the county Health Department, Board of Education, Welfare Department (my mother worked there), the yellow brick Baptist church, the Gulf station, the pool hall (no women allowed), Cleveland's grocery, Ward's shoestore: then all in a line, connected, the bank, the post office, Dr. Nicholson's office, one door for whites, one for Blacks: then separate, the Presbyterian church, the newspaper office, the yellow brick jail, same brick as the Baptist church, and as the courthouse.

What I could not have seen from the top: the sawmill, or Four Points where the white mill folks lived, or the houses of Blacks in Veneer Mill quarters.

This is what I would and would not have seen, or so I think: for I never got to the top. When he told me to go up the steps in front of him, I tried to, crawling on hands and knees, but I was terribly afraid. I couldn't, or wouldn't, do it. He let me crawl down: he was disgusted with me, I thought. I think now that he wanted to show me a place he had climbed to as a boy, a view that had been his father's and his, and would be mine. But I was *not* him: I had not learned to take that height, that being set apart as my own: a white girl, not a boy.

Yet I was shaped by my relation to those buildings and to the people in the buildings, by ideas of who should be working in the Board of Education, of who should be in the bank handling money, of who should have the guns and the keys to the jail, of who should be *in* the jail; and I was shaped by what I didn't see, or didn't notice, on those streets.

Not the way your town was laid out, you say? True, perhaps, but each of us carries around those growing-up places, the institutions, a sort of back-drop, a stage-set. So often we act out the present against a back-drop of the past, within a frame of perception that is so familiar, so safe that it is terrifying to risk changing it even when we know our perceptions are distorted, limited, constricted by that old view.

So this is one gain for me as I change: I learn a way of looking at the world that is more accurate, complex, multi-layered, multi-dimensioned, more truthful: to see the world of overlapping circles, like movement on the millpond after a fish has jumped, instead of the courthouse square with me at the middle, even if I *am* on the ground. I feel the *need* to look differently because I've learned that what is presented to me as an accurate view of the world is frequently a lie: so that to look through an anthology of women's studies that has little or no work by women of color is to be up on that ledge about the town and be thinking that I see the town, without realizing how many lives have been pushed out of sight, beside unpaved roads. I'm learning that what I think that I *know* is an accurate view of the world is frequently a lie: as when I was in a discussion about the Women's Pentagon Action with several women, four of us Christian-raised, one Jewish. In describing the march through Arlington Cemetery, one of the four mentioned the rows of crosses. I had marched for a long time through that cemetery; I nodded to myself, visualized rows of crosses. No, said the Jewish woman, they were head-stones with crosses or stars-of-David engraved above the names. We four objected; we all had seen crosses. The Jewish woman had some photographs of the march through the cemetery, laid them on the table. We saw rows and rows and rows of rectangular gravestones, and in the fore-ground, clearly visible, one inscribed with a name and a star-of-David.

So I gain truth when I expand my constricted eye, an eye that has only let in what I have been taught to see. But there have been other constrictions: the clutch of fear around my heart when I must deal with the *fact* of folks who exist, with their own lives, in other places besides the narrow circle I was raised in. I have learned that my fear is kin to a terror that has been in my birth culture for years, for centuries: the terror of a people who have set themselves apart and *above*, who have wronged others, and feel they are about to be found out and punished.

It is the terror that in my culture has been expressed in lies about dirty Jews who kill for blood, sly Arab hordes who murder, brutal Indians who massacre, animal Blacks who rise in rebellion in the middle of the night and slaughter. It is the terror that has *caused* the slaughter of all those peoples. It is the terror that was my father, with his stack of John Birch newspapers, his belief in a Communist-Jewish-Black conspiracy. It is the desperate terror, the knowledge that something is *wrong*, and tries to end fear by attack.

When I am trying to understand myself in relation to folks different from me, when there are discussions, conflicts about anti-Semitism and racism among women, criticisms, criticism of me, and I get afraid: when, for instance, in a group discussion about race and class, I say I feel we have talked too much about race, not enough about class, and a woman of color asks me in anger and pain if I don't think her skin has something to do with class, and I get afraid; when, for instance, I say carelessly to my Jewish lover that there were no Jews where I grew up, and she begins to ask me: how do I know? do I hear what I'm saying? and I get afraid; when I feel my racing heart, breath, the tightening of my skin around me, literally defenses to protect my narrow circle, I try to say to myself:

Yes, that fear is there, but I will try to be at the edge between my fear and outside, on the edge at my skin, listening, asking what new thing will I hear, will I see, will I let myself feel, beyond the fear. I try to say to myself: To acknowledge the complexity of another's existence is not to deny my own. I try to say: When I acknowledge what my people, what those who are like me, have done to people with less power and less safety in the world, I can make a place for things to be different, a place where I can feel grief, sorrow, not to be sorry *for* the others, but to mourn, to expand my circle of self, follow my need to loosen the constrictions of fear, be a break in the cycle of fear and attack. When I can do this, that is a second gain.

To be caught within the narrow circle of the self is not just a fearful thing, it is a *lonely* thing. When I could not climb the steps that day with my father, it marked the last time I can remember us doing something together, just the two of us; thereafter, I knew on some level that my place was with women, not with him, not with men; later I knew more clearly that I did not want his view of the world. I have felt this more and more strongly since my coming out as a lesbian. Yet so much has separated me from other women, ways in which my culture set me apart by race, by ethnicity, by class. I understood abruptly one day how lonely this made me when a friend, a Black woman, spoke to me casually in our shared office: and I heard how she said my name, the drawn-out accent: so much like how my name is said at home.

Yet I knew enough of her history and mine to know how much separated us: the chasm of murders, rapes, lynchings, the years of daily humiliations done by my people to hers. I went and stood in the hallway and cried, thinking of how she said my name like home, and how divided our lives were. It is a pain I come to over and over again, the more I understand the ways in which I have been kept from other women, and how I keep myself from them. The pain, when, for instance, I realize how *habitually* I think of my culture, my ethics, my morality, as the culmination of history, as the logical extension of what has gone before; the kind of thinking represented by my use, in the past, of the word *Judeo-Christian*, as if Jewish history and lives have existed only to culminate in Christian culture, the kind of thinking that the U.S. government is using now to promote Armageddon in the Middle East; the kind of thinking that I did until recently about Indian lives and culture in my region, as if Indian peoples have existed only in museums since white folks came to this continent in the 1500's; the kind of thinking that separates me from women in cultures different from mine, makes their experience less central, less important than mine. It is painful to keep understanding this separation within myself and in the world. Sometimes this pain feels only like despair: yet I have felt it also to be another kind of pain, where the need to be with other women can be the breaking through the shell around me, painful, but a coming through into a new place, where with understanding and change, the loneliness won't be necessary. And when this happens, then I feel a third gain.

How do we begin to change, and then keep going, and act on this in the world? How do we *want* to be different from what we have been? Sometimes folks ask how I got started, and I must admit that I did not begin by reasoning out the gains: this came later and helped me keep going.

But I began when I jumped from my edge and outside myself, into radical change, for love: simply love: for myself and for other women. I acted on that love by becoming a lesbian, falling in love with and becoming sexual with a particular woman; and this love led me directly, but by a complicated way, to work against racism and anti-Semitism.

It is another kind of breaking through to even write this, to put these words before you. I anticipate the critical voices that say, "Your sexuality is irrelevant to the serious issues of racism and anti-Semitism"; that say, "You are being psychologizing, individualistic"; the voices that say, "You should want to work on these issues because they are right, for justice, for general principles." I anticipate the other, perhaps sub-vocal, words: "Disgusting." "Perverted." "Unnatural." "Not fit to live."

I think these voices may be sounding now because I have heard them before: from folks on the street, from political co-workers, from women at my job, from the man I was married to, from my mother. They are the judging, condemning voices that despise me, that see me as dangerous, that put me in danger, because of *how I love*: because of my intimate, necessary, hopeful love: for which I have been punished and been made to suffer bitterly: *when I have disclosed it.*

I could conceal it from you. I could hide this part of myself as other light-skinned, European-looking folks in this country have hidden parts of themselves that kept them from fitting in, assimilating, being safe in white Christian culture: hidden their religion, or the poverty or working class of their people; or their ethnicity, any connection to "undesirable" people, to Jews, or Mediterranean or Middle Eastern peoples, or Native Indians, or Asian peoples, or to any people of color.

I could pass in this way, by hiding part of myself. I fit neatly into the narrow limits of what is "normal" in this country. Like most lesbians, I don't fit the stereotype of what a lesbian looks like; unless my hair is cut quite short and unless I am wearing the comfortable, sturdy clothes and shoes that are called "masculine," I look quite stereotypically "American," like the girl in the toothpaste ad.

But in this writing, I can not hide myself, because it is how I love that has brought me to change. I have learned what it is to lose a posi-tion of safety, to be despised for *who I am*. For being a lesbian, I have lost those I loved almost as myself, my children, and I have had my pride, as Barbara Deming says, "assaulted in its depth . . . since one's sexuality is so at the heart . . . at the heart of one."[1] It was my joy at loving another woman, the risks I took by doing so, the changes this brought me to, and the losses, that broke through the bubble of skin and class privilege around me. Barbara Deming has called "liberation by analogy"[2] the fighting someone else's fight because you can't for whatever reason acknowledge and fight your own oppression. So I speak here of how I came to my own fight, and to an understanding of how I am con-nected to the struggle of other women and other people different from myself.

In the fall of 1974, I moved with my husband and children to an eastern North Carolina town whose center was not a courthouse, but a market house, with a first story of four arched brick walls, a closed brick second story, a circle of streets around it. I heard the story of the market house at a dinner that welcomed my husband to his new job. In a private club overlooking the central circle, the well-to-do folks at the table, all white, chatted about history, the things sold in the past at the market house, the fruits and vegetables, the auctioned tobacco. "But not slaves," they said.

The Black man who was serving set down the dish, and broke through the anonymity of his red jacket. No, he said, there *were* slaves there: men, women, children sold away from their mothers. Going to the window, he looked down on the streets and gave two minutes of facts and dates; then he finished serving and left. The white folks smiled indulgently, and changed the subject. I recognized their look, from home. I was shocked that he had dared speak to them, yet somehow felt he had done so many times before, and knew, without letting myself know, that as he spoke, there stood behind him the house slaves who had risked whipping or worse when they whittled with their words at the white folks' killing ignorance.

What he told me was plain enough: This town was a place where some people had been used as livestock, chattle, slaves, cattle, capital, by other people; and this use had been justified by the physical fact of a different skin color and by the cultural fact of different ways of living. The white men and their families who had considered Black people to be animals with no right to their own children or to a home of their own still did not admit that they had done any wrong, nor that there had *been* any wrong, in *their* town. What he told me was plain enough: Be warned: they have not changed.

By the end of dinner, I had forgotten his words. They were about the past, seemed to have nothing to do with me returning, after almost ten years in university towns, to the landscape of my childhood, to a military town that was enlarged, urban, with buying and selling at its heart, the country club its social center rather than the church (but Blacks and Jews still not welcome), a town with a more conspicuous police presence, the U.S. Army's second largest home base, with combat veterans who had trained to the chant, "Here is my prick, here is my gun, one is for killing, the other for fun."

Every day I drove around the market house, carrying my two boys between home and grammar school and day care. To me it was an impediment to the flow of traffic, awkward, anachronistic. Sometimes in early spring light it seemed quaint. I had no knowledge and no feeling of the sweat and blood of people's lives that had been mortared into its bricks: nor of their independent joy apart from that place.

What I was feeling was that I would spend the rest of my life going round and round in a pattern that I knew by heart: being a wife, a mother of two boys, a teacher of the writings of white men, dead men. I drove around the market house four times a day, travelling on the surface of my own life: circular, repetitive, like one of the games at the county fair, the one with yellow plastic ducks clacking one after the other on a track, until they fall abruptly off the edge, into inevitable meaningless disappearance: unless, with a smack, one or two or three vanish from the middle, shot down by a smiling man with a gun.

For the first time in my life, I was living in a place where I was afraid because I was a *woman.* No one knew me by my family: there were no kindnesses because someone knew my mama or my pa, and no one was going to be nice to me because of my grandfather. I was only another woman, someone's wife, unless I was alone; then, walking down Hay Street to the library, I could be propositioned as a prostitute, or, driving at night on the Boulevard, threatened as a cunt. At home when I complained about the smiling innuendo of a gas-station attendant, my husband said I should be complimented; this in a town where "R & R" stood for "Rape and Recreation."

Not such a surprising realization: to understand that women are used as sexual pets, or are violently misused, are considered prey. But, there it was: for the first time I felt myself to be, not theoretically, but physically and permanently, in the class of people labeled *woman*: and felt that group to be relatively powerless and at the mercy of another class, *men.*

I was not at all accustomed to thinking of myself as belonging to an *oppressed* group. The last time I had conceptualized myself as belonging to a specific class of people was when I was a teenager. At the height of Black civil rights demonstrations in Alabama, and of the brutality of white police and citizens, I received a request from a German penpal for my views on what was going on: and wrote what my mother remembers as an eloquent justification of white superiority and supremacy. Though I'd read *The Diary of Anne Frank* I did not reflect on what repetition of history, what cries of Nazi/Aryan superiority and Jewish inferiority were in my words. Sliding aside the polite lie that "Here we just treat everyone as individuals," I justified how we were treating folks: us the superior class, me in the group *white.*

By the time I was mid-way through college, I had slipped into being unselfconscious of myself as white; this happened as I became liberal. This meant that I looked on with my Philosophy class as a few students demonstrated while Gov. Lurleen Wallace, in a jeep, reviewed the ROTC troops, the students getting trained to defend Alabama from "outsiders": all the white boys saluted under the white dogwoods flowering on the quad, while we debated the usefulness of protest. A year later, the night of Dr. King's death, I drove with my husband and a friend into Birmingham, curfewed after a day of violence, drove in to look around the empty downtown streets in the spring rain, looking for I don't know what, and not finding it, went to the Tutwiler for drinks, not thinking of ourselves as white, of course, nor in any way out of place on the streets that night, because we were intellectuals, not at all like James Earl Ray or any white person who did violence.

I slipped from thinking of myself as white, to thinking of myself as *married*, without much regard for other categories in the meantime, except for a few startling moments. I felt *gentile* (though I didn't know the word) when the Jewish man I was dating called it off because I was "too much like a girl he might marry." I was baffled by this: I thought of Jewishness as a state of being defined by Christianity, a category changeable by conversion or association with Christians: I couldn't understand why this was something he didn't seem to want to do.

Going through the negotiations to marry a Catholic-raised man, I had some longer moments of feeling *Protestant*: as debates went on between my husband-to-be and the priest who was counseling us under the new guidelines of Vatican II, I puzzled over the need for an intricate resolution between *them* about what kind of birth control I would, or would not, use.

After the wedding, I was relieved to be myself: a non-religious, thinking person. I tried not to think of myself as *woman*, a reality that bulged outside the safe bounds of *wife*, a reality that had shaken and terrified me with my two unplanned pregnancies. Walking to my classes at graduate school, I put the width of the sidewalk between me and the woman sitting at the literature table in front of the library. The pamphlets and the 2¢ newsletters—*Research Triangle Women's Liberation Newsletter*, August 11, 1969—were loose on the cardboard table and were not *in* the library.[3] At the other edge of the sidewalk, I tried to separate myself from the new ideas about what it meant to be a woman. I rushed away slowly through the humid air, weighted by my unborn second child, who sat like a four-month-old rock in my stomach.

During the last months of my pregnancy, I shared a class with Elizabeth, the woman from the lit table. The class was "Shakespeare's History Plays." Elizabeth analyzed men and power, fathers and sons in *Henry IV*; the other students thought she was crazy; I was afraid she was. One evening, as I carried my enormous heavy belly from the seminar table to my car, she told me that she thought I was brave to stay in school, unlike so many other married women with children, and she wished me well. The men in my department had begun to joke that they would get stuck with me in the elevator, and I'd go into labor. That evening I cried the ten miles home: she had spoken to me as *a woman*, and I'd been so lonely, without knowing it: her speaking to me changed how I thought of myself and my life.

The ideas of women's liberation came rushing toward me, arrived at the town through the writings of feminist and lesbian-feminist groups, like the Furies of Washington, D.C., and through individual women, like Sara Evans Boyte at the university, who had heard them from New Haven, by way of Chicago, by way of white women who had worked in the civil rights movement in the South, who had learned the principles of liberation in the homes and at the sides of Black women, young and old, who were the political organizers in their commuities.[4]

When I found myself in the market town, where the circle of my life was becoming more and more narrow: I felt like I was being brick-walled in: the ideas that I'd learned from Elizabeth and the other women became personal to me. I began to feel the restrictions around me as woman, through the pressure of neighbors and country-club social friends about how I should act as a wife, through the extremity of the violence reported daily in the news: "Fourteen-year-old girl taken from car at county fair, raped at gun-point." I still moved unthinkingly through the town as a white born to the culture, unaware of how much this fact pushed away from me the daily limits placed on other women by men.

For being a woman was the constriction that I felt. There I was in a place so much like home: grown-up and I didn't want to be there: curfewed by night, watched by day, by some of the twenty-five thousand more men than women in the town. I felt surrounded. I wanted to go some place where I could just be; I was homesick with nowhere to go.

The place that I missed sometimes seemed like a memory of childhood, though it was not a childish place. It was a place of mutuality, companionship, creativity, sensuousness, easiness in the body, curiosity in what new things might be making in the world, hope from that curiosity, safety, and love.

It was like a memory of July: the slash of morning sun on my face as I walked with my cousin Annie down to the gravelpit, through the maze of small canyons with clay walls: the place where I put my face against the clay, the sweat of cool water in the heat, the flesh of the earth. We would stay all day there, get cleanly dirty, dig clay, shape pots, retreat to the cool, then out in the heat again in a place we knew was ancient because of the fossil rocks we found, ancient and serenely a home.

It was a place I had been to with my father, who took me to the woods, not to hunt (for he was not a hunter) but to walk, he with a double-bladed ax that he raised to trim dead branches, with his silence except to name the trees (black-jack oak, sweet bay) and to say how to step (high over logs where copperheads liked to rest cool): his silence that may have been his prayer to the trees that he counted on weekdays at the sawmill as dead board feet (but he is dead now, and I will never know what went on in his mind: his silence that taught me to listen to the life rushing through the veins of the animal world).

It was a place I had been in recently, just before my move to the market town, when with a few other women I had begun the talking about the forbidden that was called consciousness-raising: making a place where I had said the word *masturbation* outloud for the first time. In the startled silence of the other women, I felt that I had abruptly created a new world out of the stuffy plastic apartment where we were meeting.

In the market town I began to try, steadily, to make a place like the memory, yet that would last longer than a morning or an evening: it was to be a place where I could live without the painful and deadly violence, without the domination: a place where I could live free, *liberated*, with other women. I began doing some political work, organized another consciouness-raising group. Then I fell in love with another woman, after she told a secret to the group. I thought I had come again to the place of intense curiosity, powerful creativity. It was March, it was April, wisteria, dogwood, pink tulip magnolia. I began to dream my husband was trying to kill me, that I was running away with my children on Greyhound buses through Mississippi. I began to dream that I was crossing a river with my children; women on the other side, but no welcome for me with my boys.

The place I wanted to reach was not a childish place, but my understanding of it was childish. I had not admitted that the safety of much of my childhood was because Laura Cates, Black and a servant, was responsible for me; that I had the walks with my father because the woods were "ours" by systematic economic exploitation, instigated, at that time, by his White Citizens' Council; that I was allowed one evening a month with woman friends because I was a wife who would come home at night. Raised to believe that I could be where I wanted and have what I wanted, as a grown woman I thought I could simply claim what I wanted, even the making of a new place to live with other women. I had no understanding of the limits that I lived within, nor of how much my memory and my experience of a safe space to be was based on places secured by omission, exclusion or violence, and on my submitting to the limits of that place.

I should have remembered, from my childhood, Viola Liuzzo, who was trying to reach the place by another way, shot down in Lowndes County, Alabama, while driving demonstrators during the Selma-to-Montgomery march. Her death was justified by Klan leader Robert Shelton on the grounds that she "had five children by four different husbands," "her husband hadn't seen her in two, three months," "she was living with two nigger men in Selma," "she was a *fat* slob with crud . . . all over her body," "she was bra-less."[5] Liuzzo, Italian, white-but-not-white, gone over to the other side, damned, dead.

I didn't die, trying to make a new life for myself out of an old life, trying to be a lover of myself and other women in a place where we were despised. I didn't die, but by spring of the next year, by May, watching the redbud tree drop flowers like blood on the ground, I felt like I had died. I had learned that children were still taken from their mothers in that town, even from someone like me, if by my wildness, by sexual wildness, I placed myself in the wilderness with those feared by white Southern men: with "every wolf, panther, catamount and bear in the mountains of America, every crocodile in the swamps of Florida, every negro in the South, every devil in Hell."[6] I had learned that I could be either a lesbian or a mother of my children, either in the wilderness or on holy ground, but not both.

I should not have been surprised at the horror of my sophisticated liberal husband; he was also an admirer of the apologists for the Old South, like the poet who named woman and the land as the same: beautiful, white, pure: "the Proud Lady, of the heart of fire,/The look of snow . . . The sons of the fathers shall keep her, worthy of/What these have done in love." But I was no longer pure; I had declined to be kept. I no longer qualified as sacred, eligible for the protection promised by a KKK founder, protection for "the [white] women of the South, who were the loveliest, most noble and best women in the world . . . ."[7] (I asked my father, in his extreme age, to tell me about his mother, the woman I'm named for; he could only say, "She was the best woman in the world.")

Why was I surprised when my husband threatened and did violence, threatened ugly court proceedings, my mother as a character witness for him, restricted my time and presence with the children, took them finally and moved hundreds of miles away? I was no longer "the best of women": what did I expect? But I *had* expected to have that protected circle marked off for me by the men of my kind as my "home": I had expected to have that place with my children. I expected it as my *right*. I did not understand I had been exchanging the use of my body for that place.

I learned, finally: I stepped outside the circle of protection. I said, "My body, my womb, and the children of my womb are not yours to use." And I was judged with finality. Without my climbing the steps to the stale rectangular courtrooms of Cumberland County, I was given a judgment: without facing the judge, since my lawyer feared that "calling the attention of the court" to my lesbian identity would mean that I would never see my children again. I was dirty, polluted, unholy. I was not to have a home with my children again. I did not die, but the agony was as bitter as death: we were physically separated: they were seven and six, hundreds of miles away: I had held them before they were born and almost every day of their lives, and now I could not touch them. During this time I discovered that expressions I had thought to be exaggerations were true: if you are helpless with grief, you do, unthinkingly, wring your hands; you can have a need to touch someone that is like hunger, like thirst. The inner surface of my arms, my breasts, the muscles of my stomach were raw with my need to touch my children.

I could have stolen them and run away to a place where no one knew them, no one knew me, hidden them, and tried to find work, under some other name than my own. I could not justify taking them from all their kin, or their father, in this way. Instead, from this marriage I carried away my clothes, my books, some kitchen utensils, two cats. I also carried away the conviction that I had been thrust out into a place of terrible loss by laws laid down by men. In my grief, and in my ignorance of the past of others, I felt that no one had sustained such a loss before. And I did not yet understand that to come to a place of greater liberation, I had to risk old safeties. Instead I felt that I had no place, that, as I moved through my days, I was falling through space.

I became obsessed with justice: the shell of my privilege was broken, the shell that had given me a shape in the world, held me apart from the world, protected me from the world. I was astonished at the pain; the extent of my surprise revealed to me the degree of my protection.

I became determined to break the powers of the world: they *would* change, the powers that would keep me from touching my children because I touched another woman in love. Beyond five or six books on women's liberation, and the process of consciousness-raising, I had few skills and little knowledge of how to act for justice and liberation. I had no knowledge of any woman like me who had resisted and attempted to transform our home in preceding generations; I had no knowledge of other instances of struggle, whose example might have strengthened and inspired me in mine.

For instance:

I knew nothing of the near-by Lumbee Indians, descendants of the folk who came into first contact with Raleigh's English in the 1500's, who four hundred years later had been part of a three-way segregated school system: white, Black, Indian: who succeeded in the 1950's in breaking up Klan rallies and cross-burnings that had warned them to "keep their place."[8]

Even though I was teaching at a historically Black college, I had no understanding of the long tradition of Black culture and resistance in the town, which reached back before the Civil War, and had produced Charles W. Chesnutt, president in the 1870's of the school where I was then teaching, author of novels that described the town of the market house, political organizing by Blacks, their massacre by whites during the 1898 Wilmington elections, even the story of a white man returning to his home town who dreamed of, and worked toward, a racially just society.[9]

I knew nothing of the nourishing of Jewish culture in that hostile Bible belt town, nor of Jewish traditions of resistance. I learned only much later that one of the few townspeople who I knew to be politically progressive, Monroe Evans, was Jewish: that his family had emigrated from Lithuania to escape the 1881 May Laws against Jews, the confiscation of property, limitations on travel and on the right to have homes, the conscription of Jewish children into the tsar's army, the violent pogroms: that they had struggled to make a place in the town, one of two or three Jewish families, trying to maintain their identity among folk who alternately asked them how big was Noah's ark or called them Christ-killer: how they learned Yiddish in the home, took weekend trips to Holt's Lake to gather with other Jews from small North Carolina towns, to break their isolation.[10]

Nor did I know of the huge rallies against the Viet Nam war in the 1970's, masses of people around the market house, chanting in the streets, traffic stopped; nor that Carson McCullers, a woman very like me, living there in the '30's, had written of the maddening, rigid effects of military life and thinking, and of the small resistances of an Army wife.[11]

I knew nothing, then, of the lesbians stationed at Ft. Bragg or Pope

AFB, who might spend all day scrubbing out jet fuel tanks, light-headed, isolated, inside a metal cavern, and come out at night to the Other Side, to dance with lovers, play pool no matter that the CID cruised by on Russell St. writing down license plate numbers, no matter the risk of being thrown out; and later I discovered Bertha Harris' novel of being a lesbian lover, with extravagant stories that might have been told in that bar, being a passing woman in the Wilmington shipyards, being lovers with a movie star, with "hair like gold electricity," hair like my lover's hair, a book that was published the year I moved to the town that out-rageous Bertha had long since grown up in and left.[12]

I knew nothing of these or other histories of struggle for equality and justice and one's own identity in the town I was living in: not a particularly big town, not liberal at all, not famous for anything: an almost rural eastern North Carolina town, in a region that you, perhaps, are used to thinking of as backward. Yet it was a place with so many resistances, so much creative challenge to the powers of the world: which is true of every county, town, or city in this country, each with its own buried history of struggle, of how people try to maintain their dignity within the restrictions placed around them, and how they struggle to break those restrictions.

But as yet I knew nothing of this. I entered the struggle, adding my bit to it, as if I were the first to struggle, joining with five or six other women like me, in the local NOW chapter. For the next few years, I worked on education programs (women working in the home, out of the home, women and health, power, education, the media, the military, women and rape, women in religion, minority women, women and North Carolina law); I worked on self-defense classes for women, on establish-ing a rape crisis line and a shelter for women who were being beaten, on editing a local newsletter, on producing women's cultural events, on nights and nights of phone calls for the ERA, on a fight with the local clerk of court to make him admit women's independent name changes, on day care, on Black women's studies courses and a daily women's news program at the college where I taught; on a county advisory group for women's issues where we struggled with the local Democratic machine to try to get a Black woman appointed as our coordinator, where we pressed for implementation of our recommendations with county money, and were perceived as so radical that the courthouse rumor was "Lesbi-ans have taken over."

We wanted to change the world; we thought we knew how it needed changing. We knew we were outnumbered: in a town where the Berean

Baptist Church owned its own fleet of buses and shuttled hundreds of its members to every legislative meeting to oppose the ERA, the handful of us in NOW were the only folks using the word "women's liberation." We tried everything we could think of to "reach more women."

We were doing "outreach," that disastrous method of organizing; *we* had gone forward to a new place, women together, and now were throwing back safety lines to other women, to pull them in as if they were drowning, to save them. I understood then how important it was for me to have this new place; it was going to be my home, to replace the one I had lost. I needed desperately to have a place that was mine with other women, where I felt hopeful. But because of my need, I did not push myself to look at what might separate me from other women. I relied on the hopefulness of all women together: what I felt, deep down, was hope that they would join me in my place, which would be the way I wanted it. I didn't want to have to *limit* myself.

I didn't understand what a limited, narrow space, and how short lasting, it would be, if only *my* imagination and knowledge and abilities were to go into the making and extending of it. I didn't understand how much I was still inside the restrictions of my culture, in my vision of how the world could be. I, and the other women I worked with, limited the effectiveness of our struggle for that place by our own racism and anti-Semitism.

With a minimal understanding of history, we knew that, because of civil rights work, Black women in town were probably organized, might be potential allies: so our first community forum had one panel out of six designated with the topic "minority women," and five of the twenty speakers for the day were Black women. This was in a day's activities which were planned, the speakers chosen, the location selected, and the publicity arranged, by three middle-class white women, me included, who had not *personally* contacted a single Black women's organization, much less considered trying to co-plan or co-sponsor with such a group: and who had no notion of the doubts or risks that Black women in that town might have about our endeavor. Neither did we consult our commonsense to discover that "minority women" in Fayetteville included substantial numbers of Thai, Vietnamese, Cambodian, Laotian, Korean, and Japanese women, as well as Lumbee women and Latinas. Attendance at the forum was overwhelmingly white; we questioned our publicity, instead of our perspective on power.

Similarly, our thinking about allies out of the civil rights movement of the '60s did not include the possibility that there might be Jewish women in town who had worked in that struggle, who might be interested in our work. Well-schooled by my past in how Jews (and Communists) were the source of "outsider trouble," the old theory that if Jews are present and visible, they must be in control, I did not turn this teaching around to question if the significant participation of Jews in civil rights work might not have had something to do with their own history of oppression. In fact, I didn't think of Jews as being *in* the town, even though I drove past a large and modern synagogue on Morganton Road every time I went to grocery shop. Blacks were definitely Southern, and American even though they'd come from Africa, (the continent a blur to me), even though I'd heard men at home mouthing off about "Send them back." But a Black woman had raised me, Black women and men came in and out of my kinfolks' houses, cooking, cleaning; Black people worked *for* white people; I knew (I thought) what their place was. I had no place for Jews in the map of my thoughts, except that they had lived before Christ in an almost mythical Israel, and afterwards in Germany until they were killed, and that those in this country were foreign, even if they were here: they were always foreign, their place was always somewhere else.

So I drove past the synagogue, and when we scheduled a discussion on religion, the two women who spoke were a professor of religion and a Methodist minister; no representation was requested from the women of the local Jewish congregation, since "religion" meant denominations of Christianity. We held the session on a Saturday because, after all, Sunday was when folks went to church, or just took it easy; we had no grasp that there might be some Jewish women who would want to come, but not be able, since their Sabbath was sundown Friday to sundown Saturday night.

My sense of the history of the town was distorted as my perspective on its demographics, or its geography, or its theology. When we were organizing a day's program on rape, I was concerned that Black women know and come, so I drove up and down Murchison Road to post flyers, ignoring my uneasiness, the training of years of warnings about which parts of a town were "safe" for me and which were not. I could have paused to trace that uneasiness to a fear of Black men: but I did not, nor did I wonder about the history of white women in relation to Black men, or white men to Black women, or *then* question what the feelings, not to mention the experience of Black women in relation to rape might be, compared to mine. I stapled posters to telephone poles, I politely asked permission to place them in the windows of Black-owned businesses, without ever thinking the word "lynching," or wondering about how sexual violence was used racially by white men to keep Blacks and white women from joining forces.

Nor when we were struggling so hard with ERA ratification, during miserable nights in a borrowed doctor's office, calling strangers' names listed on file cards, during the crisis when one of our key local representatives had a religious renewal and became a born-again Christian just before the vote, during none of the three votes, over six years, did I examine the long complicated relation between the struggle for women's suffrage and Black suffrage through constitutional amendments. I did not learn that white women's suffrage leaders, including Elizabeth Cady Stanton, had failed to take the long view required of coalition work in their disappointment over the Fifteenth Amendment being passed for manhood, rather than universal, suffrage. They had refused to make the reciprocal actions that would have pushed for post-Civil War voting rights enforcement for Black men in the South, so necessary for the success of revolutionary Reconstruction governments, and therefore, ultimately, for the establishment of legislatures favorable to Black and white women's suffrage.[13] I did not learn of the deliberate segregationist tactics, used by Susan B. Anthony, of refusing to organize Black women in the South for fear of alienating Southern white women from the suffrage movement.[14] Nor did I speculate over what could have happened had there been more support by Southern white women of voting rights for Blacks in the '60's and '70's: would Black legislators have been elected, more favorable to the ratification of the ERA? I puzzled over why Black women were not more active in the ERA campaign without figuring out how "women's rights" had been a code for "white women's rights."

When we worked to establish a battered women's shelter, even a temporary place where a woman could come be safe from male violence, I didn't wonder if it would be experienced as a "white woman's home" or if a Thai woman with perhaps her own language needs, a Jewish woman with perhaps her own food needs, a Black woman with perhaps a need not to experience white ignorance of her life, if any of these women or others might feel so dubious of their "safety" that they would choose not to come.

And even as we worked in all these ways to try to change the world, to make it safer (we thought) for all women, I did not reflect on how hesitant I was to mention my lesbian identity except to a trusted few women. I did not feel safe with many of my political co-workers; I had lost my children; I could still lose my job; and I could lose my place in this fragile new world-space for women I thought we were making. After all, our answer to attacks on the ERA "because it would legalize homosexual marriages" was to say that this just wouldn't happen. *I* didn't answer that there was nothing wrong with lesbians or gay men wanting public recognition of our relationships.

I was, in fact, not seeking liberation as my particular, complex self. I was working desperately to make the new place where I could live safely with other women, while denying publicly a basic part of myself, while not seeing the subtle and overt pressures on other women to also deny their different aspects, in order to exist in the outside world, and in order to come to our place. In newspaper interviews I spoke obliquely of conscious choices, alternatives, possibilities: but I did not yet understand with my heart Lillian Smith's statement that "our right to be different is, in a deep sense, the most precious right we human beings have."[15]

By 1979 I was watching the second wave of the women's movement, which had swept through this Southern town about ten years later than the rest of the country, be increasingly directed into electoral politics and social services, and less and less into grassroots women's work. I knew that I felt painfully isolated as a lesbian, but I did not analyze this in the context of our tiny movement's failure to deal with issues of difference, nor did it occur to me, as Bettina Aptheker has said of women in the first wave of feminism, that ". . . in the context of American politics, the neglect of or acquiescence in racism would inevitably force . . . women into a more and more conservative and politically ineffectual mold."[16]

Instead I withdrew from our struggling projects, in the evenings didn't go to meetings but wrote poetry or read, stayed at home; it was so peaceful in my three-room apartment; at night I would burn candles on the mantelpiece, no sounds but the blapping of my typewriter, or maybe the rain on the porch roof outside, fresh smells coming through the screen front door. I did not have my children, but I had these rooms, a job, a lover, work I was making. I thought I had the beginnings of a place for myself.

But that year in November my idea of what kind of work it would take to keep my bit of safe space, my very idea of that space, my narrow conception, was shattered. In writing of the change in her own culture-bound perceptions, Joanna Russ speaks of "that soundless blow, which changes forever one's map of the world."[17] For me the blow was literal, the sound was rifle-fire. In broad daylight, in Greensboro, North Carolina, about 50 miles from where I lived, Klansmen and Nazis drove into an anti-Klan demonstration, shouting "Nigger! Kike! Commie bastard!" They opened fire, killed five people: four white men, two of them Jews, one Black woman; labor union organizers, affiliated with the Communist

Workers Party. The next day I saw in the newspaper an interview with Nancy Matthews, wife of one of the Klansmen. She said, "I knew he was a Klan member, but I don't know what he did when he left home. I was surprised and shocked . . . ."[18] But the Klansmen defended their getting out of their cars at the rally, rifles in hand, by saying they saw the car holding some Klanswomen being attacked and were "rushing to their rescue."[19]

And I thought: I identify with the demonstrators; I am on *their* side: I've felt that danger. Yet in what way am I any different from this woman? Am I not surprised and shocked that this could happen? Yet it did, and there must be a history behind it. Do I have any notion, *any*, of what white men have been doing outside home, outside the circle of my limited white experience? I have my theory of how I lost my home because I was a woman, a lesbian, and that I am at risk because of who I am: then how do I explain the killing of Jews, communists, a Black woman, the killing justified in the name of "protecting white women"?

I set out to find out what had been or was being done in my name. I took Nancy Matthews' words seriously, and began by asking what had happened outside my home, outside the circle of what I knew of me and my people where I grew up. I asked my mother: she recounted Klan activity in my Alabama home town, in the 1920's, marches, cross-burnings, a white woman beaten for "immorality," but she didn't know what they did to Blacks; our family not implicated, but the contrary, she was proud to say: my grandfather the judge stood up to them, political death in that era, by refusing to prosecute Black men who acted in self-defense.

I read Black history: Ida B. Wells' records show that Black men were lynched in my home county, and one in my home town, for allegedly raping white women, in 1893, shortly after my grandfather opened his law practice there.[20] I wondered what he did then: anything? And my grandmother, for whom I was named: what did she do? what did she think? I gathered family letters and documents. They told me explicitly what had never been said by my kin: that on both the maternal and paternal sides of my family, we had owned slaves: twelve to fifteen, on small "family-sized" farms: that what place and money my family had got by the mid-nineteenth century, we had stolen from the work and lives of others; and that the very ground the crops grew in was stolen: I saw the government form that bountied 160 acres to my great-grandfather Williams for fighting the Seminoles in the Creek Wars, driving them from their homes in South Georgia, bounty, a bonus for "good work." I read transcripts of legal proceedings from after the Civil War, from testimony about the counties my folks had lived in, and where I had grown up: the voices of Black men and women came to me out of the grave, to tell of homes broken into or burned, the beatings, rapes, murders, during their attempts to secure Black suffrage and a redistribution of land, telling of the attacks by men determined to keep control in the name of white, Christian civilization.

These voices came to me: and I thought of my children and the grief and anger, the shame and failure, I felt because I had not been able to fight for them and have a home for me and them, against the man my husband, and other legal men, and the history of this town, with its market house point-of-interest where within some people's memory families *had* been sold apart from one another. The voices came: and I thought of my small but comfortable apartment, my modestly well-paying job at a Black college, gotten with my segregated-university education, gotten with the confidence and financial help of men and women who had occupied and held the security of a certain place, despite the upheaval of Reconstruction, for three and four generations.

During the time that I was first feeling all this information, again I lived in a kind of vertigo: a sensation of my body having no fixed place to be: the earth having opened, I was falling through space. I had had my home and my children taken away from me. I had set out to make a new home with other women, only to find that the very ground I was building on was the grave of the people my kin had killed, and that my foundation, my birth culture, was mortared with blood.

Until this time, I had felt my expanding consciousness of oppression as painful but ultimately positive: I was breaking through to an understanding of my life as a woman, as a way to my *own* liberation: the cracking and heaving and buckling in my life was the process of freeing myself. I had felt keenly the pain of being punished for who I was, and had felt passionately the need for justice, for things to be set right. When, after Greensboro, I groped toward an understanding of injustice done to others, injustice done outside my narrow circle of being, and to folks *not* like me, I began to grasp, through my own experience, something of what that injustice might be, began to feel the extent of pain, anger, desire for change.

But I did not feel that my new understanding simply moved me into a place where I joined others to struggle *with* them against common injustices. Because *I* was implicated in the doing of some of these injustices, and I held myself, and my people, responsible, what my expanded understanding meant was that I felt in a struggle with myself, *against* myself. This breaking through did not feel like liberation but like destruction.

As in a story from my childhood, one of Poe's stories that I read late at night, I was scared but fascinated by the catastrophic ending: when the walls of a house split, zigzag, along a once barely noticeable crack, and the house of Usher crumbled with "a long tumultuous shouting sound like the voice of a thousand waters." A woman is the reason for the fall of that house, a place of "feudal antiquity"; she is the owner's twin-sister who dies and is confined in a chamber deep under the house. The brother, who suffers from a continual and inexplicable terror, "the grim phantasm FEAR," becomes more terrified; his friend reads a romance to soothe him, a crude tale of a knight who conquers by slaying a dragon; the sounds in the story of ripping wood, grating clanging brass, piercing shrieks, begin to be heard in the very room where the two men are seated. In horror the brother reveals that he knew he had buried the sister alive, but he *had dared not speak*: the sounds are "the rending of her coffin and the grating of the iron hinges of her prison . . . ." At that moment, the doors rush open; the lady stands before them, bloody in white robes, and then falls upon her brother in violent death-agonies, bearing him to the ground a corpse, shattering the house over them.

Read by me a hundred years after it was written in the 1840's, a time of intensifying Southern justification of slavery, Poe's description of the dread, nervousness, fear of the brother, pacing through the house from "whence for many years, he had not ventured forth" could have been a description of my father, trapped inside his beliefs in white supremacy, the purity of (white) women, the conspiracy of Jews and Blacks to take over the world.

And the entombment of the lady was my "protection": the physical, spiritual, sexual containment which men of my culture have used to keep "their women" pure, our wombs to be kept sacred ground, not polluted by the dirty sex of another race, our minds, spirits and actions to be Christian, not "common," but gentlewomanly, genteel, gentile; thereby ensuring that children born of us are theirs, are "well-born," of "good" blood, skin, family; and that children raised by us will be "well-rasied," not veering into wild actions, wayward behavior.

It was this protection that I felt one evening during the height of the civil rights demonstrations in Alabama, as the walls that had contained so many were cracking, when my father called me to his chair in the living room. He showed me a newspaper clipping, from some right-wing paper, about Martin Luther King, Jr.; and told me that the article was about how King had sexually abused, used, young Black teen-aged girls. I believe he asked me what I thought of this; I can only guess that he wanted me to feel that my danger, my physical, sexual danger, would be the result of the release of others from containment. I felt frightened and profoundly endangered, by King, by my father: I could not answer him. It was the first, the only time, he spoke of sex, in any way, to me.

This was the "protection" that I had romanticized in the hot thunderstormy summers of my adolescence as I read Tennyson's poetry, kings and queens, knights and ladies: and the "protection" that during the actual Crusades of 1095 to 1270 C.E.* meant metal chastity belts locked around the genitals of their wives by Christian European knights, who travelled to Jerusalem to free the holy places from "the pollution and filth of the unclean," the Islamic Persians, who, when Jerusalem was taken in 1099, were beheaded, tortured, burned in flames, while the Jews of the city were herded into a synagogue and burned alive.[21]

It was the "safety" offered by the Knights of the Ku Klux Klan in 1867 "as an institution of Chivalry" for the purpose of "protecting the homes and women of the South"[22]; and in 1923 as "swift avenger of Innocence despoiled" and preservers of the "sanctity of the home"[23]; and in 1964 as working with "sincere Christian devotion" to stop mongrelization of the white race by Blacks and Jews"[24]; and in 1980 as defenders of the family and white civilization who, in Klan rituals "advance to the next step of knightly honor," are baptized, and vow that they are white American citizens, not Jews.[25] Within this "protection," the role of women, as described by California Klan Corps member Dorraine Metzger is to have "lots of babies to help the white race along . . . at least two or three babies because the minorities are just going crazy . . . babies, babies everywhere."[26] What this "chivalric" behavior has meant historically is the systematic rape of Black women[27]; the torture, mutilation, and killing of Black men (over 1000 lynched between 1900 and 1915, many on the pretext of having raped a white woman)[28]; the death of Leo Frank, a Jew (accused of being the "perverted" murderer of a young white girl; falsely convicted) lynched by the Knights of Mary Phagan, who became the core of a modern national Klan 15 million strong at its height in the 1920's.[29] This "knightly honor" also meant the harassment and attempted intimidation of any of "their women" who rejected the "protection": the women who came South to teach Blacks during Reconstruction,[30] women who asserted their sexual autonomy during the '20's,[31] women who spoke out against segregation,

---

*C.E. or Common Era, is an alternate to A.D., or Anno Domini, "in the year of the Lord."

racism, anti-Semitism from the '40's to the '60's,[32] women who asserted economic autonomy by fighting to work in the mines in the '70's,[33] women who were openly lesbians at the International Women's Year Conference[34] and women who are now doing anti-Klan organizing as open lesbians.[35]

It is this threatening "protection" that white Christian men in the U.S. are now offering. In his 1984 State of the Union address President Reagan linked his election to a "crusade for renewal," "a spiritual revival" in America, denounced the "tragedy of abortion," stated that "families stand at the center of our society," and announced that this country has "brought peace where there was only bloodshed."[36] All this was in language that paralleled the words of Jerry Falwell's 1984 State of the Union address in which the Moral Majority leader preached a "moral awakening" for the country and condemned the "decadence" of abortion and gay rights.[37] All this in a year when abortion clinics are being bombed by a group called the Army of God[38]; when the Klansmen and Nazis indicted in the Greensboro massacre have been acquitted by an all-white jury because U.S. Justice Department prosecution allowed them to plead that they were "patriotic citizens just like the Germans," who were also fighting against communists[39]; when each U.S. citizen under the Reagan budget will pay $555 more to the military and $88 less to poor children and their mothers[44]; when a group of white farm wives visiting D. C. from the Midwest had U.S. policy in the Caribbean and Central America (including the invasion of Grenada) officially explained to them as a way to prevent "a Brown Horde," "a massive wave of immigration," if "communist takeovers" occur in the region.[41]

If I have come to the point of consciousness where I have begun to understand that I am entrapped *as* a woman, not just by the sexual fear of the men of my group, but also by their racial and religious terrors; if I have begun to understand that when they condemn me as a lesbian and a free woman for being "dirty," "unholy," "perverted," "immoral," it is a judgment that has been called down on people of color and Jews throughout history by the men of my culture, as they have shifted their justification for hatred according to their desires of the moment; if I have begun to understand something of the deep connection between my oppression and that of other folks, what is it that keeps me from acting, sometimes even from speaking out, against anti-Semitism and racism? What is it that keeps me from declaring against and rejecting this "protection" at every level?

The image from my childhood, from Poe's story, returns to me: the woman who escapes with superhuman effort, from a coffin whose lid is fastened down by screws, from a vault with iron doors of immense weight: she may free herself, but then she dies violently, carrying with her the home and her kin: catastrophe. Melodramatic: yet twenty years after I first read the story, when I began to admit to myself how I had been buried by my culture, coffined heart and body, and how this was connected to my sex, my race, my class, my religion, my "morality"; when I began to push through all this, I felt like my life was cracking around me.

I think this is what happens, to a more or less extreme degree, every time we expand our limited being: it is upheaval, not catastrophe: more like a snake shedding its skin than like death: the old constriction is sloughed off with difficulty, but there is an expansion: not a change in basic shape or color, but an expansion, some growth, and some reward for struggle and curiosity. Yet, if we are women who have gained privilege by our white skin *or* our Christian culture, but who are trying to free ourselves *as* women in a more complex way, we can experience this change as loss. Because it is: the old lies and ways of living, habitual, familiar, comfortable, fitting us like our skin, were *ours*.

Our fear of the losses can keep us from changing. What is it, exactly, that we are afraid to lose?

As I try to strip away the layers of deceit that I have been taught, it is hard not to be afraid that these are like wrappings of a shroud and that what I will ultimately come to in myself is a disintegrating, rotting *nothing*: that the values that I have at my core, from my culture, will only be those of negativity, exclusion, fear, death. And my feeling *is* based in the reality that the group identity of my culture has been defined, often, not by positive qualities, but by negative characteristics: by the *absence of*: "no dogs, Negroes, or Jews"; we have gotten our jobs, bought our houses, borne and educated our children by the negatives: no niggers, no kikes, no wops, no dagos, no spics, no A-rabs, no gooks, no queers.

We have learned this early, and so well. Every spring, almost, when I was in grammar school, our field trip would be an expedition to Moundville State Park, where part of our education was to file into a building erected over a "prehistoric" Indian burial ground; and stand overlooking the excavated clay, dug out so that small canyons ran between each body, the bundles of people's bones, separating each from each, as if water had eroded, except it was the hands of a probably white, probably

Christian archaeologist from the university, meticulously breaking into the sacred ground. Floodlights exposed people curled or stretched in the final vulnerability of death, while we stood in the safe darkness of the balconies, looking down.

It has taken a long time for me to understand that this place was sacred not because it had been set aside for death, but because it was a place where spiritual and physical life returned to life, bones and bodies as seeds in the fertile darkness of the earth. It took me so long because so much in my culture is based on the principle that we are *not* all connected to each other, that folk who seem different should be excluded, or killed, and their living culture treated as dead objects.

No wonder, then, that if we have been raised up this way, when we begin to struggle with the reality of our anti-Semitism and racism, we may simply want to leave our culture behind, disassociate ourselves from it. In order to feel positively about ourselves, we may end up wanting not to *be* ourselves, and may start pretending to be someone else. Especially this may happen when we start learning about the strong traditions of resistance and affirmation sustained for centuries by the very folks *our* folks were trying to kill.

Without a knowledge of this struggle for social justice in our own culture, we may end up clothing our naked, negative selves with something from the positive traditions of identity which have served in part to help folks survive our people. We may justify this "cultural impersonation"[42] by our admiration and our need for heroines, as did one woman at an evening of shared spirituality which I attended: a Euro-American woman, very fair-haired and fair-complexioned, renamed herself in a ritual during which she took three women's names, each from a different tribe of native American people; she explicitly stated that the names represented powers and gifts she desired, those of healing, leadership, love, qualities she felt she was lacking in. We may justify taking the identity of another as our own by stating a shared victimization, as I have heard from some Christian-raised women when they have mentioned that they have "always felt like a Jew" because of how they have felt exclusion and pain in their lives: sometimes they have then used this feeling to assert that they were Jews and to justify a conversion to Judaism.

Sometimes the impersonation comes because we are afraid we'll be divided from someone we love if we are ourselves. This can take very subtle forms: as when I wrote a poem for my lover, whom I'd been dealing with about issues of Jewish-gentile differences; anxious, without admitting it to myself, about the separation that opened at times between us, I blurred our difference in the poem by using images and phrases from a Jewish women's spiritual tradition as if they were from my *own*, using them to imply that she and I were in the same affirming tradition.

Sometimes we don't pretend to *be* the other, but we take something made by the other and use it for our own: as I did for years when I listened to Black folk singing church songs, hymns, gospels, and spirituals, the songs of suffering, enduring, and triumph. Always I would cry, baffled as to why I was so moved; I understood myself only after I read a passage in Mary Boykin Chesnutt's diary in which she described weeping bitterly at a slave prayer meeting where the Black driver shouted "like a trumpet": she said, "I would very much have liked to shout too."[43] Then I understood that I was using Black people to weep for me, to express *my* sorrow at my responsibility, and that of my people, for their oppression: and I was mourning because I felt they had something I didn't, a closeness, a hope, that I and my folks had lost because we had tried to shut other people out of our hearts and lives.

Finally I understood that I could feel sorrow during their music, and yet not confuse their sorrow with mine, or use their resistance for mine. *I needed to do my own work*: express my sorrow and my responsibility myself, in my own words, by my own actions. I could hear their songs like a trumpet to me: a startling, an awakening, a reminder, a challenge: as were the struggles and resistance of other folk: but not take them as replacement for my own work.

In groups of white women I sometimes hear a statement like this: "We have to work on our own racism; after all, white people are responsible, so we shouldn't expect women of color to help us, or to show us where we are wrong, or tell us what to do." And I believe a similar generalization may be beginning to be made about anti-Semitism: "Christian-raised women should take responsibility, and not expect Jewish women to explain our mistakes." I agree with both of these statements: but I think we will act on them only when we know and *feel* them as part of a positive process of recreating ourselves, of making a self that is not the negative, the oppressor.

I believe that we don't want to be like the U.S. government stealing Native American land for national parks and bomb test sites: nor like Boy Scouts who group by ancient tribal placenames to practice dimly understood dances to perform at shopping malls. If we don't want to perpetuate the Euro-American tradition of theft, of *taking* from others, in large and small ways, I believe we must remember our relation to other women in the context of a national history in which we can tour the U.S. Capitol, with its elaborate murals about freedom and its statues to liberty, but if we ask about the builders, we will *not* be told: "The building was the work of hired-out slaves."[44] We must think about our relation to other women and their work if we can attend a celebration of International Women's Day, as I did this year, hear accounts of the brave women organizing in New York's garment district, how their work was the foundation for our work, but we are *not* told: "Sixty-five percent of the women in the striking shirtwaist makers, of the 'Uprising of the 20,000,' were Jewish women, and six of the women on the board of Local 25 who led them were Jews."[45]

When we begin to understand that we have benefitted, for no good reason, from the lives and work of others, when we begin to understand how false much of our sense of self-importance has been, we do experience a loss: our self-respect. To regain it, we need to find new ways to be *in* the world, those very actions a way of creating a positive self.

Part of this process, for me, has been to acknowledge to myself that there are things that I *do not know*: an admission hard on my pride, and harder to do than it sounds: and to try to fill up the emptiness of my ignorance about the lives of Jewish women and women of color. It has also been important for me to acknowledge to myself that most of my learning has been based on the work of these women: that I would never have grasped the limits on my understanding and action if I had not read the work of North American Indian women: Leslie Silko, Joy Harjo, the anthology *A Gathering of Spirit*, edited by Beth Brant; the work of Black women: Toni Morrison, Alice Walker, Audre Lorde, *Home Girls: a Black Feminist Anthology*, edited by Barbara Smith; the work of Jewish women: Muriel Rukeyser, Ruth Seid, Anzia Yezierska, the lesbian anthology *Nice Jewish Girls*, edited by Evelyn Torton Beck; and the work of Asian-American women, Latinas, and other women of color in such collections as *The Third Woman*, edited by Dexter Fisher, *Cuentos: Stories by Latinas*, edited by Alma Gomez, Cherríe Moraga and Mariana Romo-Carmona, and *This Bridge Called My Back: Writings by Radical Women of Color*, edited by Gloria Anzaldúa and Cherríe Moraga.[46]

And part of my regaining my self-respect has been to struggle to reject a false self-importance by acknowledging the foundation of liberation effort in this country *in* the work of women, and men, who my folks have tried to hold down. For me this has meant not just reading the poetry, fiction, essays, but learning about the long history of political organizing in the U.S. by men and women trying to break the economic and cultural grip a Euro-American system has on their lives. But my hardest struggle has been to admit and honor their daily, constant work when this means correction of *my* ignorance, resistance to *my* prejudice. Then

I have to struggle to remember that I don't rule the world with my thoughts and actions like some judge in a tilt-back chair; and that by listening to criticisms, not talking back but listening, I may learn how I might have been acting or thinking like one of the old powers-that-be.

For me, to be quite exact, honoring this work means saying that I began to re-examine my relation as a white woman to safety, white men, and Black people, after I told as a joke, a ludicrous event, the story of the Klan marching in my hometown: and a Black woman who was a fellow-teacher said abruptly to me, "Why are you laughing? It isn't funny." And I began to re-examine my relation to the first people who lived in this country because a Shawnee woman, with family origins in the South, criticized my *use* of the Choctaw people's experience as a parallel to the experience of the white women of my family: she asked, "Who of your relatives did what to who of mine?" I started to examine my grasp of the complexities of my anti-Semitism when I spoke angrily about the disrespect of Arab male students, from Saudi Arabia and Kuwait, toward me as a female teacher, while also saying I resented their loudness, their groupiness, the money that enabled them to take over our financially shaky Black college, while my Black students, men and women, were working night jobs to survive: and the Jewish woman, my lover, who was listening to all this said quietly, "You are just being anti-Arab."

And when a month ago, I walked into my corner grocery, DC Supermarket, 8th and F Streets, NE, with a branch of budding forsythia in my hand, and the owners, men and women I had termed vaguely to myself as "Oriental," became excited, made me spell *forsythia*, wrote it in Korean characters on a piece of scratch paper so they would remember the name in English: and said it was a flower from their country, *their* country, pronouncing the name in Korean carefully for my untrained ears: and then I had to think again about what I understood about what was "mine" and what "somebody else's," what I didn't understand about immigration and capitalism and how I had taken without thinking, like picking a flower, the work and culture of Asian folk, without even being able to distinguish between the many different peoples.

As I've worked at stripping away layer after layer of my false identity, notions of skin, blood, heart based in racism and anti-Semitism, another way I've tried to regain my self-respect, to keep from feeling completely naked and ashamed of who it is I am, is to look at what I have carried with me from my culture that could help me in the process. As I have learned about the actual history and present of my culture, I didn't stop loving my family or my home, but it was hard to figure out what from there I could be proud and grateful to have: since much of what I *had* learned had been based on false pride. Yet buried under the layers, I discovered some strengths:

I found a sense of connection to history, people, and place, through my family's rootedness in the South; and a comparative and skeptical way of thinking, through my Presbyterian variety of Protestantism, which emphasized doubt and analysis: I saw that I had been using these skills all along as I tried to figure out my personal responsibility in a racist and anti-Semitic culture.

I found that my mother had given me hope, through the constancy of her regard for her mother and sisters and women friends, and through her stubbornness in the undertaking and completing of work. I found that my father had given me his manners, the "Pratts' beautiful manners," which could demonstrate respectfulness to others, if I paid attention; and he had given me the memory of his sorrow and pain, disclosing to me his heart that still felt the wrong: that, somehow, my heart had learned from his.

In my looking I also discovered a tradition of white Christian-raised women in the South, who had worked actively for social justice since at least 1849, the year a white woman in Bucktown, Maryland, hid Harriet Tubman during her escape from slavery, in her house on the Underground Railroad.[47] From the 1840's to the 1860's, Sarah and Angelina Grimké of South Carolina, living in the North, had organized both for the abolition of slavery and for women's rights, linking the two struggles. Angelina wrote:

> True, we have not felt the slaveholder's lash; true, we have not had our hands manacled, but our *hearts* have been crushed . . . . I want to be identified with the negro; until he gets his rights, we shall never have ours.[48]

In 1836 in her *Appeal to the Christian Women of the Southern States*, she said:

> I know you do not make the laws, but . . . if you really suppose you can do nothing to overthrow slavery, you are greatly mistaken . . . 1st. You can read on this subject. 2d. You can pray over this subject. 3d. You can speak on this subject. 4th. You can act on this subject . . . .[49]

When copies of the *Appeal* reached Charleston, the sisters' home town, the papers were publicly burned, like other abolitionist literature, by the postmaster; the police notified the Grimkés' mother that they would prevent Angelina from ever entering the city again. In a letter to her family to explain her and her sister's writings, Angelina said:

> It cost us more agony of soul to write these testimonies than any thing we ever did . . . . We wrote them to show the awful havock which arbitrary power makes in human hearts and to incite a holy indignation against an institution which degrades the *oppressor* as well as the oppressed.[50]

From the 1920's to the 1940's, Jessie Daniel Ames of Texas led an anti-lynching campaign, gathering women like herself into the Association of Southern Women for the Prevention of Lynching. By the early 1940's, the ASWPL included over 109 women's organizations, auxiliaries of major Protestant denominations and national and regional federations of Jewish women, with a total membership of over 4 million. The women used a variety of methods to stop the violence done by the men who were of their kin or their social group, including: investigative reporting for the collection and publication of facts about lynching locally; attempts to change white news reporting of lynchings toward a less sensational and inflammatory treatment; signature campaigns to get written pledges from white sheriffs and other law enforcement officers to prevent lynchings; publication in their communities of the names of white "peace officers" who gave up prisoners to lynch mobs; mobilization of local peer pressure in the white community with face-to-face or over-the-phone confrontations with white men by the women; and direct intervention by the women to persuade a mob to stop its violence, including one ASWPL woman in Alabama who stopped the lynching of the Black man accused of raping her seven-year-old daughter.[51] The Association repudiated the "myth of mob chivalry"; its statement of purpose said " . . . the claim of the lynchers [is] that they were acting solely in the defense of womanhood . . . . we dare not longer permit this claim to pass unchallenged nor allow those bent upon personal revenge and savagery to commit acts of violence and lawlessness in the name of women."[52]

Lillian Smith of Georgia, who traced her political roots to the ASWPL, was an eloquent novelist, essayist, and speaker against the forces of segregation from the 1940's to the 1960's; in addition, she edited with Paula Snelling, the magazine *South Today*, and ran a summer camp for girls where she raised social issues like racism and nuclear war by having her campers create dramatic enactments of the struggle between justice and injustice as they saw it in their daily lives. She is the woman who wrote in "Putting Away Childish Things":

> Men who kill, riot, use foul words in the name of race will kill, riot, use foul words in the name of anything that safely provides

outlet for their hate and frustrations . . . . They are the 'bad' people. And we? We are the people who dream the good dreams and let the 'bad' people turn them into nightmares . . . . we need ourselves to become *human* . . . . when we reserve this humanity of ours, this precious quality of love, of tenderness, of imaginative identification, for people only of our skin color (or our family, our class), we have split our lives . . . .[53]

In the 1940's Nelle Morton of Tennessee was also actively organizing interracial college chapters of the Fellowship of Southern Churchmen in the South specifically to protest anti-Semitic and Klan activity, and Southern interracial summer camps for Black, white, Arab and Asian students.[54] During the same time Anne Braden from Alabama was moving from being a reporter on the 1945 trial of Willie McGee into a lifetime of activist work; she is the woman who has said:

I believe that no white woman reared in the South—or perhaps anywhere in this racist country—can find freedom as a woman until she deals in her own consciousness with the question of race. We grow up little girls—absorbing a hundred stereotypes about ourselves and our role in life, our secondary position, our destiny to be a helpmate to a man or men. But we also grow up white—absorbing the stereotypes of race, the picture of ourselves as somehow privileged because of the color of our skin. The two mythologies become intertwined, and there is no way to free ourselves from one without dealing with the other.[55]

And in the late 1950's and early 1960's young Southern women came out of their church experience to work in the civil rights movement, and later in the women's liberation movement: Sandra "Casey" Cason and Dorothy Dawson from Texas, Sue Thrasher and Cathy Cade from Tennessee.[56] In my looking I found all these women who had come before me, whose presence proved to me that change is possible: and whose lives urged me toward action.

I have learned that as the process of shaping a negative self identity is long, so the process of change is long, and since the unjust world is duplicated again every day, in large and small, so I must try to recreate, every day, a new self striving for a new just world. What do we *do* to create this new self? Lillian Smith said: do *something*, to overcome our "basic ambivalence of feelings," by which we move through our way of life "like some half-dead thing, doing as little harm (and as little good) as possible, playing around the edges of great life issues."[57]

There *are* lists of "Things To Do"; Smith published one herself in 1943.[58] We can learn something from such a list, but most of it is commonsense: we already know that work against anti-Semitism and racism can range from stopping offensive jokes, to letters to the editor, to educational workshops, to changing the law, to writing poetry, to demonstrations in the street, to a restructuring of the economy. But because knowing what to do in a situation that you suspect may be racist or anti-Semitic, even knowing that the situation *is*, involves judgment and ethics and feelings in the heart of a new kind than we were raised with, then we will only be able to act effectively if we gather up, not just information, but the threads of life that connect us to others.

Even though we may have begun to feel the pull of the ties that connect us to women different from ourselves, we may not have the confidence to follow that connection toward a new world. For, as Bernice Johnson Reagon says: "We aren't from our base acculturated to be women people, capable of crossing our first people boundaries—Black, White, Indian . . . ."[59] When we discover truths about our home culture, we may fear we are losing our self: our self-respect, our self-importance. But when we begin to act on our new knowledge, when we begin to cross our "first people boundaries," and ally ourselves publicly with "the others," then we may fear that we will lose the people who are our family, our kin, be rejected by "our own kind."

If we come from backgrounds where anti-Semitism and racism were overt and acceptable, then our deep fear may be that action against these hatreds will be, as Lillian Smith says, "a betrayal of childhood love for our parents—for most of us have never learned to separate this love from the 'right' and the 'wrong' which our parents taught us."[60] If we betray them, then they will repudiate us. But even if we are from "liberal" backgrounds, I believe we know, also on a deep level, that we can go "too far."

If we ally ourselves with the "other" group, in a direct, personal, or public way, even if it is an issue of justice, if we threaten our folks' or self-interest, or definition of self, then there is the risk of being thrown out. It is a real fear: we know the stories: the white Southern woman whose family rejected her when she began civil rights work; and the woman whose mother didn't speak to her for seven years after she married a Black man; and a woman whose parents disowned her, after she became a lesbian, and wouldn't see her for twenty years.

This is a fear that can cause us to be hesitant in making fundamental changes or taking drastic actions that differ from how we were raised.

We don't want to lose the love of the first people who knew us; we don't want to be standing outside the circle of home, with nowhere to go.

Sometimes it is possible to make a fundamental change and still re-enter the familiar circle: when this happens it can seem like the future, not the present, like a new world happening. I have been there for a day, in that place, as a grown woman with my mother when she welcomed me at home with the woman who, as a lesbian, as a Jew, as my lover, I feared she might treat as an enemy; but she made a place for us, fed us in the kitchen, family not company, noon dinner, as she cooked butterbeans, and told us stories: how she'd talked to the tortoise she'd found while weeding in the daylilies: "I spoke to him, I said 'Mr. Tortoise, now where are you going to?' but he still didn't answer me." We talked of none of our differences that day.

But when we act on our beliefs close to home, there is also the pos-sibility of upheaval in that familiar place. Then we may again dread destruction: as when I told my mother, last August, that I had gone on the March on Washington for Jobs, Peace, and Freedom, the 20th anni-versary marking the march led by Dr. King. I hadn't gone to Selma in the '60's, thirty miles from my home, where white police had driven marchers who were heading toward Montgomery, back up the bridge arched like a hill, high over the cold water of the Alabama, driven them like cattle back into town. I had not marched in Selma, so I made a beginning at the anniversary march.

Walking as a lesbian, with a group of Third World and white lesbians, with the thousands, with the half million people streaming slowly be-tween the monumental government buildings, past the hot marble walls, I affirmed to myself that I finally was grasping the interconnectedness of me and "the others."

My act seemed more symbolic than challenging; nevertheless what I had done quite safely in D.C. was "wrong" to my mother: "Some day you will understand that what you all are doing is wrong." From her conversation, and later letters, I learned that the "you" doing wrong included not just the marchers, mostly Blacks: but myself, Joan, lesbians, feminists, and Jews who named themselves Zionists because such Jews "control the world." She loved me and felt much pain, and shame: I was going the wrong way; I had walked away, and seemed to have turned my back on home.

The profound differences in our beliefs opened like a chasm between us: and I couldn't help but fear a separation more sharp than the old love between us was strong. (And yes, Mama, even here I risk it again, in this writing, which I have hesitated over so long, out of that fear: I say I do love you, and I am compelled *by my own life* to strive for a different place than the one we have lived in.)

I believe that as we begin to act, to try to do some one thing about anti-Semitism or racism, it is not just kin we fear losing, but friends who are our family now. If we define ourselves as "feminist," we may have worked hard to gather together women friends who will be a replacement for our blood-kin, from whom we are separated by our disruptively mobile, economically displacing culture. Over the last ten years we have been building a "women's community": festivals, yearly conferences, political organizations, land groups, businesses, magazines and news-papers. But if we are from families and a culture that enforced, either overtly or subtly, separation by skin and blood, I believe we need to look seriously at what limitations we have placed in this "new world" on who we feel "close to," who we feel "comfortable with," who we feel "safe" with. We can ask ourselves what we are doing *actively* to make our lives and work different from that of women who say they joined the Klan because it gives them a family closeness, a "white family," like "sisters," some of them women who support the Equal Rights Amendment, and express sympathy with aspects of the women's movement that have helped them gain confidence to work outside the home, start their own businesses, be more independent.[61]

I believe we can question what pressures we may put on women in our communities to be *like* us, to assimilate to our culture, be like our family, so we can feel comfortable, "at home." In what ways do we press women to talk like us, think like us, fight like us: the Arab woman who is told by Anglo friends that she fights "too angrily," the Black woman who is thought to be "too loud" by white women at a party. How does what we do differ from the obliteration practiced by the rest of the dominant culture?

When women differ from us by ethnicity, by "blood," but are white-skinned, how much does our desire to have them be like us have to do with our thinking racially in either-or categories: either you are white, or you are not: and how much does that have to do with our desire to ignore the history of rape by white men, the forced assimilation caused by rape? How much does avoiding the complexities of women's existences have to do with our not wanting to ask: Who, actually, is *in* our family? What are the possible connections by blood? And what have been the intimate daily connections, like mine to the Black woman who raised me, that we have been taught not to honor with the responsibility of family?

When we begin to ask ourselves in what ways we have recreated in our "new" world, our "women's world," a replica of our segregated culture-bound homes, then we also raise other questions. What will happen if we challenge the racism or anti-Semitism there? Will this mean destruction of our work?

We ask ourselves because we hear all the objections made by women like ourselves, in many different kinds of women's gatherings, when issues of diversity have been raised: from academic feminists at the 1981 National Women's Studies Conference who feared a "loss of unity," "a disintegration," because the focus for all workshops was "Women Respond to Racism"; from women activists at an organizing conference who asked why we had to talk about homophobia and racism, couldn't we "just be women together"; from lesbians at a cultural conference who didn't want "divisive issues" raised during one of the few times they had "to be together as lesbians"; from women who felt that bringing up anti-Semitism was just adding another troublesome item on a list of political correctness, next to the item of racism.

We hear these objections: and we know how much they echo our own; we ask: What if I say, I need this to change? Will I next be unwelcome *here*? Then comes the fear of nowhere to go: no old home with family: no new one with women like ourselves: and no place to be expected with folks who have been systematically excluded by ours. And with our fear comes the doubt: Can I maintain my principles against my need for the love and presence of others like me? It is lonely to be separated from others because of injustice, but it is also lonely to break with our own in opposition to that injustice.

But the fear of loss of community because issues of diversity are raised is like the fear of loss of self when we discover the connections between racism and anti-Semitism and our life as women: if we can go to the other side of this fear, we can see that there are gains. Every time we speak or act there is the likely chance that we'll find out more about how we need to go on changing, and that we'll meet other women who also want their lives to be the creation of a more just, more loving world.

Every year for the past five years I have gone South to a lesbian writers' conference, driving between red clay banks, past walls of kudzu; it is a small gathering, maybe sixty to eighty women, sometimes two or three Black women, a few Jewish women, the rest of us white, Christian-raised, of different classes. Every year we struggle over the same ground: over when and how, and even whether, issues of racism and anti-Semitism and other matters of diversity will be faced in that brief, four-day community: which *is*, objectors point out, about *writing*; which *is*, those of us on the other side say, about *life*. I have learned from the going back and back to the same place, and to the same people often, since many of us return every year, what a struggle it is, to change the habits of a life-time, and the beliefs of centuries. I have learned from trying to explain how, exactly, I feel issues which seem to be about "other" people are connected to my life as a white gentile lesbian. I get tired of trying to do this, and I get scared doing this, but every year it is a place also of great hope for me because of what I learn there.

I learned to think more clearly about the context of "safe" women's space, when I researched the land where our gathering was located as a way of trying to make specific the connection between our "women's world" and the surrounding countryside. When I discovered it was land taken from the Creeks by the State of Georgia with the collu-sion of a man who was also a slave trader, and had been, in the 1960's, a regional Klan organizing site, I could comment that as lesbians we shared these enemies, men who even today wished us dead because of who we were. What I learned was that these facts alone merely dis-couraged and depressed women who were already struggling with daily small-town repression as women and as lesbians, and that I needed to figure out positive reasons for our dealing with racial and cultural difference.

I learned how *structural* racism and anti-Semitism are, not just in the county or national government, but in a women's organization, when it gets started by a non-diverse group; if the diversity is not in the planning sessions, a shift later, in how and what decisions are made, is exceedingly difficult; I learned that this didn't stop us from struggling there with the issues of diversity, anyway. I learned that there are ways of creating songs, rituals, stories, poems, not to escape but to carry us forward with some hope in the struggle, so that we do not become suicidal with self-criticism.

I learned something of how the process of criticism has been shaped, for women like me, by Christianity: when I objected, strongly, to some writing that a woman read which I felt to be racist, another woman told me later that she didn't listen to my explanation, because I had simply reminded her of her self-righteous grandmother, who used to be sweet to her in private, and then, when they got to church, would expose all her sins publicly before the congregation.

I learned from this that I had to be more clear about why *I* was personally hurt by something that was anti-Semitic or racist, so that I wasn't criticizing another woman like me in a way that just seemed to be I'm-good-and-you're-bad. In this particular case, I realized that my fumbling comments had been that the description of the Black woman (from a historical novel) was stereotypical, based on "jungle animal" metaphors: I had criticized the *words.* But my actual distress came because the Black woman was graphically portrayed in the act of being an erotic slave to a white woman; I realized that the reading of the passage aloud had aroused me sexually, and that then I had felt angry and ashamed because I was being drawn into participating in the degradation of a Black woman. And though I didn't understand this at all at the moment, I was able to figure it out in the process of trying to explain my objection to other women, who were upset that I had objected.

From this experience and others, I also learned that, unless a method or a time for criticism is structured into a gathering, I am on my own responsibility to comment or interrupt something that I feel is insulting; when and how to do so is usually confusing, and I've learned speaking-up is often seen as "inappropriate" or "disruptive" or threatening to the unity of the group, even when I have felt that the insulting comment or act is what has been disruptive; and that criticism of style, timing and "appropriateness" can be an avoidance of the questionable act or comment.

But when I passively witness the repetition of the old ways of doing things, and do nothing, I feel my rigid circle close around me, tightening, painful: I feel myself closing into a narrow world, away from the friendships and the creative possibilities of a place where diverse women live. In my inertia and ignorance, I do not always speak or act: when I do, there is fear, but also the exhilaration of going forward toward that place.

If we push our work against racism and anti-Semitism beyond our "home," beyond our women's groups, what fears make us hesitate to act, what gains come from acting? Last fall I went home to speak publicly, outside my women's community, about my struggles to free myself as a woman, as a lesbian, and about the connection of this to my struggle to reject what I had been taught as a white and a Christian. As I prepared for the trip, I began to have nightmares; and what I feared was this:

On the night before my birthday, I slept and thought I heard someone walking through my apartment; I wanted it to be my lover, but it was my father, walking unsteadily, old, carrying something heavy, a box, a heavy box, which he put down by my desk: he came through the darkness, smoking a cigarette, glints of red sparks, and sat down on my bed, wanting to rest: he was so tired; I flung my hands out angrily, told him to go, back to my mother; but crying, because my heart ached; he was my father and so tired; he left, and when I looked the floor was a field of sandy dirt, with a diagonal track dragged through it, and rows of tiny green seed just sprouting.

The box was still there, with what I feared: my responsibility for what the men of my culture have done, in my name, my responsibility to try to change what my father had done, without even knowing what his secrets were. I was angry: why should I be left with this: I didn't want it; I'd done my best for years to reject it: I wanted no part of what was in it: the benefits of my privilege, the restrictions, the injustice, the pain, the broken urgings of the heart, the unknown horrors.

And yet it is mine: I am my father's daughter in the present, living in a world he and my folks helped to create. A month after I dreamed this, he died; I honor the grief of his life by striving to change much of what he believed in: and my own grief by acknowledging that I saw him caught in the grip of racial, sexual, cultural fears that I still am trying to understand in myself.

The second fear came in a dream on the same night: I was in a car parked near a barn in the country, at night, at home, near a field that could have been the green seeds grown to corn; a young white man drove his tractor past me, then came toward me; he could have been any of the boys I went to high school with; he had a shotgun in his hands and he *looked at me*: he knew *who I was*, not just by my family, but by what kind of person I was, and he knew I was no longer on his side; he aimed the gun and fired; I felt a hot shock in my head: death.

It was the first tme I'd had this dream, but it seems not uncommon, since other women like me, dealing with similar issues in their lives, have told me of such nightmares. It is, in its most extreme form, the fear that can make us hesitate to act: the fear that if we challenge the men of our culture, if we break with them by saying publicly: *Do not do your violent work in our names:* then *we* will be punished.

But this is a dream of their inventing, where all the power lies in *their* hands; it is based in their fear, and if we let ourselves be ruled by that fear, we are acquiescing in the lies taught us about who we are as women: that say we are isolated, helpless, can not work with women like ourselves and other women to widen the place of change.

Instead of this nightmare, I prefer to think of this possibility: in the early 1960's, as men in White Citizen Councils in the South planned severe economic reprisals against political Blacks, they counted on "their women" to agree to fire the Black maids and cooks working for their families. What if the white women had refused? Had understood their place at the edge between the force of containment and the power of liberation: and had chosen to stand with the other women?

Instead, I prefer to remember that when I went South last fall I *was* with such women who were making that choice: a gathering of workers from battered women's shelters, the Southern Coalition Against Domestic Violence, who were working intensely to find the connections between racial and cultural hatreds and woman-hating, as part of their work of making shelters into places where women could be safe from male violence, and also safe in their own complex identities, not subjected to the violence of racial or ethnic slurs.

We are offered some false gains to keep us from making that choice to stand with women different from ourselves. One is that of a material security equal to the men of our culture, if we side with *them* as we move outside the home, into the larger world. We are offered, not the nightmare image of the slaughtered woman, but the image that, as a girl, I saw flashed on the screen in a darkened theatre: a beautiful young white woman is weeping because her past affluence is gone, her plantations and her slaves; her family is without food, the garden trampled, but she digs her hands into the red clay and vows: "I'm never going to be hungry again. No, nor any of my folks. If I have to steal or kill—as God is my witness, I'm never going to be hungry again." She goes on to become financially secure, using white men for protection when necessary, using her "connections" to make sure she lets nothing go to others during the social revolution of Emancipation and Reconstruction.

When I was a child, Scarlett was a heroine, in her strength as a woman within the myth of my land as I had learned it; today she is to me a person ready to take what is offered to her as a woman who is white, a lady of the culture, with no caring about where the land came from and who has worked it, willing to leave all others except her immediate family behind, in order to secure a narrow place of safety, that she foolishly thinks is secure: the place of equality with white men.

That this is foolish security is evidenced by the number of women in poverty in this country, white as well as women of color, a number increasing every year.[62] Anne Braden points out that historically the struggle for economic and social justice for the most disadvantaged group, Blacks in slavery, substantially benefited all other folk who were not in control of land and money; she likens this to a shift in the foundation stone of a house that causes all else to move.[63]

Today the economic foundation of this country is resting on the backs of women of color here, and in Third World countries: they are harvesting the eggplants and lettuce for Safeway, they are typing secretarial work sent by New York firms to the West Indies by satellite.[64] The real gain in our material security as white women would come most surely if we did not limit our economic struggle to salaries of equal or comparable worth to white men in the U.S., but if we expanded this struggle to a restructuring of this country's economy so that we do not live off the lives and work of Third World women.

A second false gain that we, if we are privileged women, are being offered now is more "protection": this time not just in our "sacred homes," but protection of us living in the U.S. from the "powers of evil" in the rest of the world. The foreign policy of the Reagan administration is being shaped by evangelical Christian beliefs that hold the U.S. has a divine calling to "protect the free world" from godless, evil, "perverted" communism.[65] This apocalyptic thinking interprets all world events as enacting Biblical prophecies, especially those in *Ezekiel, Daniel,* and *Revelations,* which predict, evangelicals think, a struggle between the "forces of good and evil," the U.S. and Russia, culminating in the battle of Armageddon on the Hill of Megiddo, near Haifa, Israel.

Christian evangelical theology believes that the forces of good *must* win such a battle in order to bring the second coming of Christ, the destruction of the present world, and the creation of a new heaven and earth.[66] Thus, theology-shaped U.S. foreign policy has supported Israel, but *not* because of the recognition that Jews who have been expelled from or exterminated in other countries for thousands of years need a place to be, as Jews; instead Reagan has said, as have Christian evangelicals, that Israel is important to the U.S. as the only "base for democracy" in the Middle East, as a place that the Christian forces of good can *use* in their battle with the "evil empire."[67]

In fact, in evangelical theology, the establishment of the state of Israel, the growth of an "Arab-Moslem confederacy," the rise of "red" Russia and China, are seen as important only as preparation for the second coming of Christ; the Christian messiah will come again only when Arabs and Jews in the Middle East "fight a battle into which all of the world's nations will be drawn," Armageddon.[68] All non-Christians will suffer horribly in these "end-days," which are described as specifically a time of "purification" for Jews. *Christian* believers will escape this holocaust, which some of them think might be a "limited" nuclear war, because they will be caught up into heaven in "the Rapture," and return to earth only after Christ's coming has prevented the destruction of the planet. Such Christian believers, in their Arab-hating and their Jew-hating (disguised as Jew-loving, the right-wing "Friends of Israel") have no motivation to work for peace in the Middle East, no interest in mutual recognition and respect between Arab countries and Israel, no interest in the needs of *both* Palestinians and Israelis for safe homelands. Reagan has said, to Jerry Falwell, that he believes "We're heading very fast for Armageddon."[69]

The U.S. economy is being mobilized to enact a Christian morality play, with U.S. soldiers, or forces in the pay of the U.S., acting as an Army of God, fighting "anti-communist" interventions throughout the world, especially now in the Caribbean and in Central America, as well as in the Middle East. In the statements of the men running this country, I hear echoes of the condemnation by my folk of the civil rights movement of Black people; Third World people fighting for economic and political freedom are condemned as "communists" and "godless"; under these comments are the old racist beliefs: that people of color are "uncivilized," "immoral," "dirty," "naturally evil," "need to be controlled." Meanwhile, Third World countries, like Nicaragua, that need to use limited resources for literacy and health campaigns, for building a self-sufficient economy, instead must spend enormous sums of money for arms to defend against a U.S. that is re-enacting the Crusades, trying to "save" the Western hemisphere.

And the people at home supposedly "protected" by these actions are suffering also. To fund the military build-up, cuts have been made in health programs, educational programs, job training programs, with disproportionately severe effects on all women and children, and on people of color, while about 9,500 jobs for all women are lost for every $1 billion shifted from civilian to military spending; 63% of the current U.S. budget goes to pay for preparation for war and the debt for past wars.[70] And the Children's Defense Fund has said, "One third of President Reagan's proposed military increase could lift every single American child out of poverty."[71] Again, it seems that if we are women who want a place for ourselves and other women in a just, peaceful, free world, we should be saying, *as* white and Christian-raised women, *Not in my name.*

From where I live I can walk down Maryland Avenue to the Capitol; it's just a few blocks; nowadays the oak trees are blooming and there is a green pool of fallen pollen under each tree. There are concrete barricades all around the Capitol building now; around the White House, too. The barricades went up after we invaded Grenada last fall; they are supposed to prevent "terrorist attacks." Sometimes, when I'm down near the White House, I veer around the barricades and stand at the fence, just to speak to Reagan through the railings, toward wherever he is behind the guards and the ground-to-air missiles buried in the lawn: to tell him I think he should be ashamed of himself.

From the White House, along the Mall, up to the Capitol, all the buildings are on a monumental scale, but the Capitol dome could be the courthouse, just larger and better lit at night: the same men running things. It is hard not to feel discouraged, hard to hold on to the powers of change. Nevertheless, as I walk around my neighborhood, I hang on to these bits of possibility:

I got hopeful, after the invasion of Grenada and the bombing of U.S. Marines who were occupying Lebanon, when I talked to my oldest son on the phone; he asked me urgently what I thought of these events. He said that he, himself, was "ashamed" of the U.S., that we "were acting like a bully"; he dreaded war in Central America, his generation being called up to fight. We ended up talking about the draft, the possibilities of resistance.

Going down to the Air & Space Museum, at the Mall, to leaflet against U.S. invasions with my small action group gave me hope, and that we are planning a gay and lesbian protest of the North Carolina Klan/Nazi acquittals, down in front of the Justice Department. And I get hope from being in a c-r group of white women, Christian-raised and Jewish, who meet regularly to try to grasp the impact of racism on our lives, in this town that is now our hometown, and within the communities of women here; we try to help each other think of ways to change, actions to take.

And I get hopeful when I think that with this kind of work there is the possibility of friendship, and love, between me and the many other women from whom I have been separated by my culture, and by my own beliefs and actions, for so long. For years, I have had a recurring dream: sleeping, I dream I am reconciled to a woman from whom I have been parted: my mother, the Black woman who raised me, my first woman lover, a Jewish woman friend; in the dream we embrace, with the sweetness that can come in a dream when all is made right. I catch a glimpse of this possibility in my dream; it comes, in waking life, with my friends sometimes, with my lover: not an easy reconciliation, but one that may come when I continue the struggle with myself and the world I was born in.

NOTES

[1] Barbara Deming, *We Are All Part of One Another,* ed. Jane Meyer-ding (Philadelphia: New Society Publishers, 1984), p. 326. Other works by Barbara Deming that have helped me include *Prison Notes* (New York: Grossman, 1966); *Revolution and Equilibrium* (New York, Grossman, 1971); *We Cannot Live Without Our Lives* (New York: Grossman/Viking, 1974); and *Remembering Who We Are* (Pagoda Publications, 1981).

[2] Deming, "Confronting One's Own Oppression," in *We Are All Part of One Another,* p. 237.

[3] Continuously published since 1969, except for a one-year lapse, this newsletter went through many transformations and is now *Feminary* magazine, which moved from its North Carolina collective in 1984 to a California collective of women; its new address is: *Feminary,* 1945 20th St., San Francisco, California 94107.

[4] Sara Evans, "Southern White Women in a Southern Black Move-ment," in *Personal Politics: the Roots of Women's Liberation in the Civil Rights Movement and the New Left* (New York: Vintage, 1979), pp. 23-59.

[5] Patsy Sims, *The Klan* (New York: Stein and Day, 1978); pp. 108-109.

[6] Susan Laurence Davis, *Authentic History of the Ku Klux Klan, 1865-1877* (New York: S. L. Davis, 1924), p. 121.

[7] Mrs. S. E. F. (Laura Martin) Rose, *The Ku Klux Klan or Invisible Empire* (n.p.: 1913), p. 22.

[8] John Stewart, *KKK Menace: The Cross Against People* (Durham, N.C.: John Stewart, 1980), p. 30.

[9] Works by Charles Waddell Chesnutt include *The House Behind the Cedars* (1900), set in Fayetteville; *The Marrow of Tradition* (1901) set in Wilmington; and *The Colonel's Dream* (1905).

[10] Eli Evans, *The Provincials: A Personal History of Jews in the South* (New York: Atheneum, 1980), pp. 73, 79-84.

[11] Carson McCullers published *Reflections in a Golden Eye* in 1941.

[12] Bertha Harris' *Lover* was published in 1976 (Plainfield, Vermont: Daughters, Inc.). More information and creative discussion of Southern lesbian writers can be found in Mab Segrest's articles, "Southern Women Writing: Toward a Literature of Wholeness," in *Feminary* (Volume X,

no. 1 1979), pp. 28-42; and "Lines I Dare to Write: Lesbian Writing in the South," in *Southern Exposure* (Volume IX, no. 2, 1981).

13 Bettina Aptheker, "Abolitionism, Woman's Rights and the Battle Over the Fifteenth Amendment," in *Woman's Legacy: Essays on Race, Sex, and Class in American History* (Amherst: University of Massachusetts Press, 1982), p. 32.

14 Ida B. Wells-Barnett, *Crusade for Justice*, ed. Alfreda M. Duster (Chicago: University of Chicago Press, 1970), p. 230.

15 Lillian Smith, *The Winner Names the Age*, ed. Michelle Cliff (New York: W. W. Norton, 1978), p. 154.

16 Aptheker, p. 50.

17 Joanna Russ, *How to Suppress Women's Writing* (Austin: University of Texas Press, 1983), p. 137.

18 "Death Suspects 16 to 60," Fayetteville (N.C.) *Observer* (November 6, 1979), p. A1.

19 "Klan/Nazi Defendants Claim Self-Defense," (Durham) *North Carolina Anvil* (October 31, 1980), p. 10.

20 Ida B. Wells-Barnett, *On Lynchings: A Red Record* (New York: Arno Press, 1969 reprint).

21 Will Durant, *The Age of Faith: A History of Medieval Civilization* (New York: Simon and Schuster, 1950), pp. 591-593.

22 Rose, p. 1.

23 *Papers Read at the Meeting of Grand Dragons, Knights of the Ku Klux Klan* (Asheville, N.C.: July, 1923), p. 136.

24 Sims, p. 243.

25 Jerry Thompson, "My Life with the Klan," special report from the (Nashville) *Tennessean* (December 11, 1980), pp. 1 and 14.

26 "The 'New' Klan: White Racism in the 1980's," special report from the *Tennessean* (n.d.), p. 31.

27 Gerda Lerner, "The Rape of Black Women as a Weapon of Terror," in *Black Women in White America* (New York: Vintage, 1972), pp. 173-193.

28 *The Chronological History of the Negro in America*, comp. Peter M. and Mort N. Bergman (New York: New American Library, 1969), p. 376.

[29] Leonard Dinnerstein, *The Leo Frank Case* (New York: Columbia University Press, 1968), pp. 19, 51, 71, 119, 132, 150.

[30] *Testimony Taken By the Joint Select Committee to Inquire Into the Conditions of Affairs in the Late Insurrectionary States* (Washington, D.C., 1972), vols. 8-10.

[31] Henry P. Fry, *The Modern Ku Klux Klan* (Boston: Small and Maynard, 1922) pp. 189, 191.

[32] Anthony P. Dunbar, *Against the Grain: Southern Radicals and Prophets, 1929-1959* (Charlottesville: University Press o Virginia, 1981), pp. 230, 241.

[33] Letter from Mary Weidler, American Civil Liberties Union of Alabama, Birmingham, September 26, 1979.

[34] "Klan at IWY," *Do It Now: Newspaper of the National Organization for Women* (September/October 1977), p. 5.

[35] Conversation about National Anti-Klan Network organizing in North Carolina, with E. Holland, Washington, D.C., April 30, 1984.

[36] "U.S. 'Is Too Great for Small Dreams,'" *Washington Post* (January 26, 1984), pp. A 16-17.

[37] Letter from the Moral Majority, Inc., February 9, 1984.

[38] "More Abortion Clinics Firebombed," *off our backs* (May 1984), p. 3.

[39] "Green Light to Get Reds," *The Guardian* (April 25, 1984), p. 18.

[40] "Less for Kids," *off our backs* (April 1984), p. 6.

[41] "Chief Sees Migration, Not Mining, as Public Worry," *New York Times* (April 16, 1984), p. A7.

[42] Cynthia Ozick, "Cultural Impersonation," in *Art and Ardor: Essays* (New York: Knopf, 1983).

[43] Mary Boykin Chesnutt, *A Diary from Dixie* (Boston: Houghton Mifflin, 1949), pp. 148-149.

[44] Constance McLaughlin Green, *The Secret City: a History of Race Relations in the Nation's Capital* (Princeton, New Jersey: Princeton University Press, 1967), p. 15.

[45] Charlotte Baum, Paula Hyman, and Sonya Michel, *The Jewish Woman in America* (New York: New American Library, 1975), pp. 140-141.

46*This Bridge Called My Back* has an extensive bibliography of writing by and about women of color; it is now reprinted and available from Kitchen Table: Women of Color Press, PO Box 2753, Rockefeller Center Station, NY, NY 10185. *Cuentos* and *Home Girls* are also published by and available from Kitchen Table Press. *A Gathering of Spirit* can be ordered from *Sinister Wisdom*, PO Box 1023, Rockland, ME 04841. *Third Woman* was published in 1980 by Houghton-Mifflin; *Nice Jewish Girls* has been reprinted by The Crossing Press, Trumansburg, NY. Specific books by the authors I named which have helped me are: Leslie Marmon Silko's novel, *Ceremony* (New York: New American Library, 1977); Joy Harjo's poems, *She Had Some Horses* (New York: Thunder's Mouth Press, 1983); Toni Morrison's *The Bluest Eye* (New York: Holt, Rinehart, 1970) and *Song of Solomon* (New York: Knopf, 1977); Alice Walker's novel, *The Third Life of Grange Copeland* (New York: Harcourt Brace Jovanovich, 1970), stories, *You Can't Keep A Good Woman Down* (New York: Harcourt Brace Jovanovich, 1982), and essays, *In Search of Our Mothers' Gardens* (New York: Harcourt Brace Jovanovich, 1984); Audre Lorde's essays, *Sister Outsider* (Trumansburg, New York: The Crossing Press, 1984); Muriel Rukeyser's poems, a collected edition by McGraw-Hill in 1982; Ruth Seid's (Jo Sinclair) novel *Wasteland* (New York: Harper, 1946); Anzia Yezierska's autobiography, *Red Ribbon on a White Horse* (New York: Persea, 1950).

47Aptheker, p. 35.

48Gerda Lerner, *The Grimké Sisters from South Carolina* (New York: Schocken, 1971), p. 353.

49Lerner, *The Grimké Sisters,* p. 139.

50Lerner, *The Grimké Sisters,* p. 267.

51Jacquelyn Dowd Hall, *Revolt Against Chivalry: Jessie Daniel Ames and the Women's Campaign Against Lynching* (New York: Columbia University Press, 1979), pp. 175, 223-253.

52Jessie Daniel Ames, *The Changing Character of Lynching, 1931-1941* (Atlanta: Commission on Interracial Cooperation, 1942), p. 64.

53Lillian Smith, in *From the Mountain: Selections from . . . South Today,* ed. Helen White and Redding S. Suggs Jr. (Memphis: Memphis State University Press, 1972), pp. 131, 136-137.

54Dunbar, p. 230.

55Anne Braden, *Free Thomas Wanley: a Letter to White Southern Women* (Louisville: Southern Conference Educational Fund, 1972).

56Evans, pp. 33-36.

[57] Smith, "Addressed to Intelligent White Southerners," in *From the Mountain*, pp. 116-117.

[58] Smith, pp. 116-131.

[59] Bernice Johnson Reagon, "Coalition Politics: Turning the Century," in *Home Girls*, p. 361.

[60] Smith, "Putting Away Childish Things," in *From the Mountain*, p. 135.

[61] Bonnie Wolf, unpublished paper, Cambridge, Massachusetts, 1981, p. 17. For other discussions about femaleness and white Christian culture see: Maureen 'Brady, "An Exploration of Class and Race Dynamics in the Writing of *Folly*," in *13th Moon* (Vol. XVII, nos. 1 & 2), pp. 145-151; Pamela Culbreth, "A Personal Reading of *This Bridge Called My Back*," in *Sinister Wisdom 21* (Fall 1982), pp. 15-28; Andrea Dworkin, *Right-Wing Women* (New York: Perigee, 1983); Nadine Gordimer, "Living in the Interregnum," *New York Review of Books* (January 20, 1983), pp. 21-29; Marilyn Frye, "On Being White: Toward a Feminist Understanding of Race and Race Supremacy," in *The Politics of Reality: Essays in Feminist Theory* (Trumansburg, New York: The Crossing Press, 1983); Adrienne Rich, "Disloyal to Civilization: Feminism, Racism, Gynephobia," in *On Lies, Secrets, and Silence* (New York: W. W. Norton, 1979), pp. 275-310; Lillian Smith, *Killers of the Dream* (New York: Anchor, 1963).

[62] "The International Feminization of Poverty," *off our backs* (August/ September 1983), p. 5.

[63] Anne Braden, "Lessons from a History of Struggle," *Southern Exposure* (Vol VIII, no. 2), p. 61.

[64] "International Feminization," p. 5.

[65] Robert Zwier, *Born Again Politics: the New Christian Right in America* (Downers Grove, Illinois: InterVarsity Press, 1982), pp. 42, 45.

[66] Hal Lindsey, *The 1980's: Countdown to Armageddon* (New York: Bantam, 1981), pp. 9-16.

[67] "Does Reagan Expect A Nuclear Apocalypse?" *Washington Post* (April 8, 1984), C4.

[68] Lindsey, p. 53.

[69] "Does Reagan Expect . . .?", C4.

[70] "Your Income Tax at Work," *The Washington Peace Center Newsletter* (March 1984), pp. 1 and 5. In this article, figures are from *The*

Budget of the U.S. Government-FY 1985; percentages were computed *after* amounts for Social Security were removed.

71 "Less for Kids," p. 6.

BETWEEN A ROCK AND A HARD PLACE:

RELATIONSHIPS BETWEEN BLACK AND JEWISH WOMEN

BY
BARBARA SMITH

from Yours In Struggle : Three Feminist Perspectives
on Anti-Semitism & Racism, Bulkin, Pratt,
Smith (Firebrand Books, 1984)

BETWEEN A ROCK AND A HARD PLACE:

RELATIONSHIPS BETWEEN BLACK AND JEWISH WOMEN

*Our strategy is how we cope—how we measure and weigh what is
to be said and when, what is to be done and how, and to whom
and to whom and to whom, daily deciding/risking who it is we
can call an ally, call a friend (whatever that person's skin, sex,
or sexuality). We are women without a line. We are women who
contradict each other.*[1]

Cherríe Moraga

I have spent the better part of a week simply trying to figure out
how to begin. Every day, I've asked myself, as I sifted through files and
pages of notes that were not getting me one bit closer to a start, "Why in
hell am I doing this?" and when most despairing, "Why me?" Despair
aside, I knew that if I could remember not just the reasons, but the feelings that first made me want to speak about the complicated connections
and disconnections between Black and Jewish women, racism and
anti-Semitism, I might find my way into this piece.

The emergence in the last few years of a Jewish feminist movement
has of course created the context for this discussion. Jewish women have
challenged non-Jewish women, including non-Jewish women of color, to
recognize our anti-Semitism and in the process of building their movement Jewish women have also looked to Third World feminists for political inspiration and support. Not surprisingly, as these issues have been
raised, tensions that have characterized relationships between Black and
Jewish people in this country have also surfaced within the women's
movement. Jewish women's perception of Black and other women of
color's indifference to or active participation in anti-Semitism and Third
World women's sense that major segments of the Jewish feminist move-

ment have failed to acknowledge the weight of their white-skin privilege and capacity for racism, have inevitably escalated suspicion and anger between us.

To be a Black woman writing about racism and anti-Semitism feels like a no-win situation. It's certainly not about pleasing anybody, and I don't think it should be. I worry, however, that addressing anti-Semitism sets me up to look like a woman of color overly concerned about "white" issues. What I most fear losing, of course, is the political support and understanding of other women of color, without which I cannot survive.

This morning, for guidance, I turned to Bernice Johnson Reagon's "Coalition Politics: Turning the Century," because besides all the pain that has led me to examine these issues, there is also the positive motivation of my belief in coalitions as the only means we have to accomplish the revolution we so passionately want and need. She writes:

> I feel as if I'm gonna keel over any minute and die. That is often what it feels like if you're *really* doing coalition work. Most of the time you feel threatened to the core and if you don't you're not really doing no coalescing. . . . You don't go into coalition because you just *like* it. The only reason you would consider trying to team up with somebody who could possibly kill you, is because that's the only way you can figure you can stay alive.[2]

It helps to be reminded that the very misery that I and all of us feel when we explore the volatile links between our identities and the substance of our oppressions is only to be expected. If we weren't upset about the gulfs between us, if we weren't scared of the inherent challenge to act and change that the recognition of these gulfs requires, then we wouldn't "really [be] doing no coalescing."

What follows is one Black woman's perspective, necessarily affected by the generally complicated character of Black and Jewish relations in this country. This is not pure analysis. Far from it. I am focusing on relationships between Black and Jewish women, because in my own life these relationships have both terrorized me and also shown me that people who are not the same not only can get along, but at times can work together to make effective political change. Although this discussion may be applicable to dynamics between other women of color and Jewish women, I am looking specifically at Black-Jewish relationships because of the particular history between the two groups in the U.S. and because as an Afro-American woman this is the set of dynamics I've experienced first hand. Although the subject of Black and Jewish relationships cannot help but make reference to systematically enforced racism and anti-Semitism, I am emphasizing interactions between us because that feels more graspable to me, closer to the gut and heart of the matter.

Because of the inherent complexities of this subject, one of the things I found most overwhelming was the sense that I had to be writing for two distinct audiences at the same time. I was very aware that what I want to say to other Black women is properly part of an "in-house" discussion and it undoubtedly would be a lot more comfortable for us if somehow the act of writing did not require it to go public. With Jewish women, on the other hand, although we may have a shared bond of feminism, what I say comes from a position outside the group. It is impossible for me to forget that in speaking to Jewish women I am speaking to white women, a role complicated by a racist tradition of Black people repeatedly having to teach white people about the meaning of oppression. I decided then to write sections that would cover what I need to say to Black women and what I need to say to Jewish women, fully understanding that this essay would be read in its entirety by both Black and Jewish women, as well as by individuals from a variety of other backgrounds.

EMBEDDED IN THE VERY SOIL

I am anti-Semitic. I am not writing this from a position of moral exemption. My hands are not clean, because like other non-Jews in this society I have swallowed anti-Semitism simply by living here, whether I wanted to or not. At times I've said, fully believing it, that I was not taught anti-Semitism at home growing up in Cleveland in the 1950's. In comparison to the rabid anti-Semitism as well as racism that many white people convey to their children as matter-of-factly as they teach them the alphabet and how to tie their shoes, my perception of what was going on in my house is relatively accurate. But only relatively.

On rare occasions things were said about Jews by members of my family, just as comments were made about white people in general, and about Cleveland's numerous European immigrant groups in particular. My family had "emigrated" too from the rural South during the 1920's, 30's, and 40's and their major observation about Jewish and other white people was that they could come to this country with nothing and in a relatively short period "make it." Our people, on the other hand, had been here for centuries and continued to occupy a permanent position on society's bottom. When I was growing up there were Jewish people living in Shaker Heights, one of the richest suburbs in the U.S., where Blacks were not allowed to purchase property even if they had the money, which most, of course, did not. The fact that Jews were completely barred from other suburbs and perhaps restricted to certain sections of Shaker Heights was not of great import to us. I remember vividly when my aunt and uncle (my mother's sister and brother) were each trying to buy houses in the 1950's. They searched for months on end because so many neighborhoods in the inner city including working-class ones were also racially segregated.[3] I was six or seven, but I remember their exhausted night-time conversations about the problem of where they might be able to move, I felt their anger, frustration, and shame that they could not provide for their families on such a basic level. The problem was white people, segregation, and racism. Some Jews were, of course, a part of that, but I don't remember them being especially singled out. I did not hear anti-Semitic epithets or a litany of stereotypes. I do remember my uncle saying more than once that when they didn't let "the Jew" in somewhere, he went and built his own. His words were edged with both envy and admiration. I got the message that these people knew how to take care of themselves, that we could learn a lesson from them and stop begging the white man for acceptance or even legal integration.

Despite how I was raised, what I've come to realize is that even if I didn't learn anti-Semitism at home, I learned it. I know all the stereotypes and ugly words not only for Jews, but for every outcast group including my own. Such knowledge goes with the territory. Classism, racism, homophobia, anti-Semitism, and sexism float in the air, are embedded in the very soil. No matter how cool things are at home, you catch them simply by walking out of the house and by turning on the t.v. or opening up a newspaper inside the house. In the introduction to *Home Girls,* I wrote about this unsettling reality in relationship to how I sometimes view other women of color:

> Like many Black women, I know very little about the lives of other Third World women. I want to know more and I also want to put myself in situations where I have to learn. It isn't easy because, for one thing, I keep discovering how deep my own prejudice goes. I feel so very American when I realize that simply by being Black I have not escaped the typical American ways of perceiving people who are different from myself.[4]

I never believe white people when they tell me they aren't racist. I have no reason to. Depending on the person's actions I might possibly believe that they are actively engaged in opposing racism, are anti-racist, at the very same time they continue to be racially ignorant and cannot help but be influenced as white people by this system's hatred of people of color. Unwittingly, anti-racist whites may collude at times in the very system they are trying to fight. In her article "Racism and Writing: Some Implications for White Lesbian Critics," Elly Bulkin incisively makes the distinction between the reality of being *actively* anti-racist and the illusion of being non-racist—that is, totally innocent.[5] She applies to racism, as I do here to anti-Semitism, the understanding that it is neither possible nor necessary to be morally exempt in order to stand in opposition to oppression. I stress this point because I want everybody reading this, and particularly Black women, to know that I am not writing from the position of having solved anything and because I have also heard other Black women, white non-Jewish women, and at times myself say, "But I'm not anti-Semitic." This kind of denial effectively stops discussion, places the burden of "proof" upon the person(s) experiencing the oppression, and makes it nearly impossible ever to get to the stage of saying: "This is an intolerable situation. What are we going to do about it?"

A LOVE-HATE RELATIONSHIP

If somebody asked me to describe how Black and Jewish feminists, or Blacks and Jews in general, deal with each other I would say what we have going is a love-hate relationship. The dynamic between us is often characterized by contradictory and ambivalent feelings, both negative and positive, distrust simultaneously mixed with a desire for acceptance; and deep resentment and heavy expectations about the other group's behavior. This dynamic is reflected in the current dialogue about Jewish identity and anti-Semitism in the feminist movement, when Jewish women seem to have different expectations for Black and other women of color than they do for white non-Jewish women. Often more weight is placed upon the anti-Jewish statements of women of color than upon the anti-Semitism of white non-Jewish feminists, although they are the majority group in the women's movement and in the society as a whole, and have more direct links to privilege and power.

I think that both Black and Jewish people expect more from each other than they do from white people generally or from gentiles generally. Alice Walker begins a response to Letty Cottin Pogrebin's article "Anti-Semitism in the Women's Movement" by writing:

> There is a close, often unspoken bond between Jewish and black women that grows out of their awareness of oppression and injustice, an awareness many Gentile women simply do not have.[6]

Our respective "awareness of oppression" leads us to believe that each other's communities should "know better" than to be racist or anti-Semitic because we have first-hand knowledge of bigotry and discrimination. This partially explains the disproportionate anger and blame we may feel when the other group displays attitudes much like those of the larger society.

It's true that each of our groups has had a history of politically imposed suffering. These histories are by no means identical, but at times the impact of the oppression has been brutally similar—segregation, ghettoization, physical violence, and death on such a massive scale that it is genocidal. Our experiences of racism and anti-Semitism, suffered at the hands of the white Christian majority, have sometimes made us practical and ideological allies. Yet white Jewish people's racism and Black gentile people's anti-Semitism have just as surely made us view each other as enemies. Another point of divergence is the fact that the majority of Jewish people immigrated to the United States to escape oppression in Europe and found a society by no means free from anti-Semitism, but one where it was possible in most cases to breathe again. For Black people, on the other hand, brought here forcibly as slaves, this country did not provide an escape. Instead, it has been the very locus of our oppression. The mere common experience of oppression does not guarantee our being able to get along, especially when the variables of time, place, and circumstance combine with race and class privilege, or lack of them, to make our situations objectively different.

The love-hate dynamic not only manifests itself politically, when our groups have functioned as both allies and adversaries, but also characterizes the more daily realm of face-to-face interactions. I think that women of color and Jewish women sometimes find each other more "familiar" than either of our groups find Christian majority W.A.S.P.s. A Black friend tells me, when I ask her about this sense of connectedness, "We don't come from quiet cultures." There are subliminal nuances of communication, shared fixes on reality, modes of expressing oneself, and ways of moving through the world that people from different groups sometimes recognize in each other. In his collection of interviews, *Working*, Studs Terkel uses the term the "feeling tone."[7] I think that Black and Jewish people sometimes share a similar "feeling tone." Melanie Kaye/Kantrowitz corroborates this perception in her instructive article, "Some Notes on Jewish Lesbian Identity." She describes the difficulties a group of non-Jewish women had with her "style" during the process of interviewing her for a job:

Most of the women troubled by me had been sent to expensive colleges by their fathers, they spoke with well-modulated voices, and they quaked when I raised mine. They didn't understand that to me anger is common, expressible, and not murderous. They found me "loud" (of course) and "emotional." Interestingly, I got along fine with all the women of color in the group . . . . [8]

In a different situation a woman of color might very well feel antangonism toward a Jewish woman's "style," especially if she associates that "style" with a negative interaction—for example, if she experiences racist treatment from a Jewish woman or if she has to go through a rigorously unpleasant job interview with someone Jewish.

Nevertheless, Black and Jewish women grow up knowing that in relationship to the dominant culture, we just don't fit in. And though the chances of a Jewish woman being accepted by the status quo far exceed my own, when I'm up against the status quo I may turn to her as a potential ally. For example, on my way to an all white writer's retreat in New England, I'm relieved to find out that the female director of the retreat is Jewish. I think she might understand the isolation and alienation I inevitably face as the only one. Feelings of outsiderness cover everything from self-hatred about features and bodies that don't match a white, blue-eyed ideal, to shame about where your father works, or how your mother talks on the telephone. These feelings of shame and self-hatred affect not just Black and Jewish women, but other women of color and white ethnic and poor women. Class can be as essential a bond as ethnicity between women of color and white women, both Jewish and non-Jewish. Chicana poet Cherríe Moraga describes her differing levels of awareness about Jewish and Black genocide in "Winter of Oppression, 1982," and also remarks on the positive link that she has felt to Jewish people:

> . . . I already understood
> that these people were killed
> for the spirit-blood
> that runs through them.
>
> They were like us in this.
> Ethnic people with long last names
> with vowels at the end or the wrong
> type of consonants
> combined   a colored kind of white people[9]

There are ways that we recognize each other, things that draw us together. But feelings of affinity in themselves are not sufficient to bridge the culture, history, and political conditions that separate us. Only a conscious, usually politically motivated desire to work out differences, at the same time acknowledging commonalities, makes for more than superficial connection.

TO JEWISH WOMEN

I was concerned about anti-Semitism long before I called myself a feminist, indeed long before there was a feminist movement in which to work. Perhaps because I was born a year after World War II ended, that whole era seems quite vivid to me, its essence conveyed by members of my family. I got a basic sense about the war years and about what had happened to Jewish people because people around me, who had been greatly affected by those events, were still talking about them. Books, films, and history courses provided facts about Jewish oppression. Being friends with Jewish kids in school provided me with another kind of insight, the perception that comes from emotional connection.

My problems with recent explorations of Jewish identity and anti-Semitism in the women's movement do not result from doubting whether anti-Semitism exists or whether it is something that all people, including people of color, should oppose. What concerns me are the ways in which some Jewish women have raised these issues that have contributed to an atmosphere of polarization between themselves and women of color. My criticisms are not of Jewish feminism in general, but of specific political and ideological pitfalls that have led to the escalation of hostility between us, and that cannot be explained away as solely Black and other women of color's lack of sensitivity to anti-Semitism.

These polarizations have directly and painfully affected me and people close to me. One major problem (which I hope this essay does not contribute to) is that far too often these battles have been fought on paper, in published and unpublished writing. Besides the indirectness of this kind of confrontation, I want to say how sick I am of paper wars, when we are living on a globe that is literally at war, where thousands of people are dying every day, and most of the rest of the world's people still grapple for the barest human necessities of food, clothing, and shelter. In *Home Girls* I wrote the following to Black women about negative dynamics between Black and Jewish women in the movement:

> . . . I question whom it serves when we permit internal hostility
> to tear the movement we have built apart. Who benefits most?
> Undoubtedly, those outside forces that will go to any length to
> see us fail.[10]

I ask the same question here of Jewish women.

One of the most detrimental occurrences during this period has been the characterizing of Black and/or other women of color as being more anti-Semitic and much less concerned about combatting anti-Semitism than white non-Jewish women. Letty Cottin Pogrebin's article "Anti-Semitism in the Women's Movement" which appeared in *Ms.* magazine in June, 1982, and which was widely read, exemplifies this kind of thinking. She cites "Black-Jewish Relations" as one of ". . . the five problems basic to Jews and sisterhood," and then uses a number of quotes from Black women who are unsupportive of Jewish issues, but who also are not apparently active in the women's movement.[11] I have already referred to the social and historical circumstances that have linked our two groups and that might lead to our higher expectations for commitment and understanding of each other's situations. The desire for recognition and alliances, however, does not justify the portrayal of Black women, in particular, as being a bigger "problem" than white non-Jewish women or, more significantly, than the white male ruling class that gets to enforce anti-Semitism via the system. Black women need to know that Jewish women can make distinctions between the differing impact, for example, of a woman of color's resentment against Jews, her very real anti-Semitism, and that of the corporate giant, the government policy maker, or even the Ku Klux Klan member. Jewish women need to acknowledge the potential for racism in singling out Black and other women of color and that racism has already occurred in the guise of countering anti-Semitism. I expect Jewish women to confront Black women's anti-Semitism, but I am more than a little suspect when such criticism escalates time and again into frontal attack and blame.

I think Jewish women's desire for support and recognition has also resulted at times in attempts to portray our circumstances and the oppressions of racism and anti-Semitism as parallel or even identical. The mentality is manifested at its extreme when white Jewish women of European origin claim Third World identity by saying they are not white but Jewish, refusing to acknowledge that being visibly white in a racist society has concrete benefits and social-political repercussions. How we are oppressed does not have to be the same in order to qualify as real. One of the gifts of the feminist movement has been to examine the subtleties of what comprises various oppressions without needing to pretend that they are all alike. As a Third World Lesbian I know, for example, that although her day-to-day circumstances may look nothing like my own, a white heterosexual middle-class woman experiences sexual oppression, that she can still be raped, and that class privilege does not save her from incest.

Trying to convince others that one is legitimately oppressed by making comparisons can either result from or lead to the ranking of oppressions, which is a dangerous pitfall in and of itself. In a letter responding to the Pogrebin article, a group of Jewish women write: "We sense a competition for victim status in Pogrebin's artcle and elsewhere . . . ."[12] I have sensed the same thing and I know it turns off women of color quicker than anything.

In a white dominated, capitalist economy, white skin, and if you have it, class privilege, definitely count for something, even if you belong at the very same time to a group or to groups that the society despises. Black women cannot help but resent it when people who have these privileges try to tell us that "everything is everything" and that their oppression is every bit as pervasive and dangerous as our own. From our frame of reference, given how brutally racism has functioned politically and historically against people of color in the U.S., such assertions are neither experientially accurate nor emotionally felt.

The fact that we have differing amounts of access to privilege and power can't help but influence how we respond to Jewish women's assertions of their cultural and political priorities. For example, in the last section of "Some Notes on Jewish Lesbian Identity," Melanie Kaye/Kantrowitz names Jewish women who resisted inside the concentration camps and in the Warsaw Ghetto, usually at the price of their lives. She concludes her article:

> Those were Jewish women. I come from women who fought like that.
>   I want a button that says *Pushy Jew Loud Pushy Jew Dyke.*[13]

Despite the fact that this is a proud affirmation, reading the last sentence makes me wince, not because I don't understand the desire to reshape the negative words and images the society uses against those of us it hates, but because my gut response is, "I don't want to be treated like that." The positive image of Jewish women, who, like many Black women, refuse to disappear, who are not afraid to speak up, and who fight like hell for freedom, comes up against my experience as a Black woman who has, at times, felt pushed around and condescended to by women who are not just Jewish, but, more significantly, white. Because I come from a people who have historically been "pushed" around by all kinds of white people, I get upset that a traditional way of behaving might in fact affect me differently than it does a white non-Jewish woman.

Black and other women of color are much more likely to take seriously any group which wants their political support when that group acknowledges its privilege, at the same time working to transform its powerlessness. Privilege and oppression can and do exist simultaneously. I know, because they function together in my own life. As a well educated, currently able-bodied individual from a working-class family, who is also Black, a woman, and a Lesbian, I am constantly aware of how complex and contradictory these intersections are. Being honest about our differences is painful and requires large doses of integrity. As I've said in discussions of racism with white women who are sometimes overwhelmed at the implications of their whiteness, no one on earth had any say whatsoever about who or what they were born to be. You can't run the tape backward and start from scratch, so the question is, what are you going to do with what you've got? How are you going to deal responsibly with the unalterable facts of who and what you are, of having or not having privilege and power? I don't think anyone's case is inherently hopeless. It depends on what you decide to *do* once you're here, where you decide to place yourself in relationship to the ongoing struggle for freedom.

Another extremely negative wedge that has been driven between women of color and Jewish women is the notion that white Jewish and non-Jewish women have been "forced" to confront racism while women of color have not been required to, or have been completely unwilling to confront anti-Semitism. This is, of course, untrue. There are Black and other women of color who have taken definite stands against anti-Semitism (and our commitment to this issue cannot be measured, as I suspect it probably has been, by what is available in print). On the other hand, obviously not all white feminists or white people have sufficiently challenged racism, because if they had, racism would be a thing of the past. The implied resentment at having been "forced" to confront racism, is racist in itself. This kind of statement belies a weighing mentality that has no legitimate place in progressive coalition politics. Our support for struggles that do not directly encompass our own situations cannot be motivated by an expectation of pay-back. Of course we're likely to choose ongoing political allies on the basis of those groups and individuals who recognize and respect our humanity and issues, but the bottom line has got to be a fundamental opposition to oppression, period, not a tit-for-tat of "I'll support 'your' issue if you'll support 'mine'." In political struggles there wouldn't be any "your" and "my" issues, if we saw each form of oppression as integrally linked to the others.

A final matter that I want to discuss that can be offensive to Black and other women of color is the idea put forth by some Jewish feminists that to be or to have been at any time a Christian is to be by definition anti-Semitic. Traditional, institutionalized Christianity has, of course, had as one of its primary missions the destruction and invalidation of other systems of religious belief, not only Judaism, but Islam, Buddhism, Hinduism, and all of the indigenous religions of people of color. Holy wars, crusades, and pogroms qualify, I suppose, as "Christian totalitarianism,"[14] but I have great problems when this term is applied to the mere practice of Christianity.

In the case of Black people, the Christian religion was imposed upon us by white colonizers in Africa and by white slaveowners in the Americas. We nevertheless reshaped it into an entirely unique expression of Black spirituality and faith, which has been and continues to be a major source of sustenance and survival for our people. Being Christian hardly translates into "privilege" for Black people, as exemplified by the fact that most white churches do not encourage Black membership and many actually maintain tacit or official policies of racial segregation. Christian privilege becomes a reality when it is backed up by race and class privilege. It is demoralizing and infuriating to have Black and other people of color's religious practices subsumed under the catch-all of white Christianity or Christian "totalitarianism." If anything has been traditionally encouraged in Afro-American churches, it is an inspirational identification with the bondage of "the Children of Israel" as recounted in the Old Testament. This emphasis did not, of course, prevent anti-Semitism (during slavery there was virtually no contact between Black and Jewish people in this country), but there needs to be some distinction made between being raised as a Christian, being anti-Semitic, and the historical role of the institutionalized Christian church in promoting anti-Semitism when its powers and goals have been directly tied to the power and interests of the state.

TO BLACK WOMEN

Why should anti-Semitism be of concern to Black women? If for no other reason, anti-Semitism is one aspect of an intricate system of oppression that we by definition oppose when we say we are feminist, progressive, political. The Ku Klux Klan, the Christian right wing, and the American Nazi Party all promote anti-Semitism as well as racism. Lack of opposition to anti-Semitism lines us up with our enemies. People of color need to think about who our cohorts are when we express attitudes and take stands similar to those of the most dangerous and reactionary elements in this society. I'm talking here out of political principles, which can be a useful guide for approaching complicated questions. But needless to say, principles are not what any of us operate out of one-hundred per cent of the time.

Certainly principles have only taken me so far in trying to deal with my gut responses to the ways that issues of anti-Semitism and Jewish identity have been raised in the women's movement. Like many Black feminists I could not help but notice how Jewish feminism arose just at the point that Third World feminist issues were getting minimal recognition from the movement as a whole. I saw how the feminism of women of color helped to lay the groundwork for Jewish feminists to name themselves, often without acknowledgment. I've seen how easy it has been for some Jewish women to make the shift from examining their role as racist oppressors, to focusing solely on their position as victims of oppression. I've also found the uncritical equating of the impact of anti-Semitism in the U.S. with the impact of racism absolutely galling.

If such "oversights" have made it difficult for us to get to the issue of anti-Semitism, continuing to experience racism from those women who seemingly want us to ignore their treatment of us and instead put energy into opposing an oppression which directly affects them has made commitment to the issue feel nearly impossible. The history of Black people in this country is a history of blood. It does not always dispose us to being altruistic and fair, because history has not been fair. Our blood is still being spilled. I know with what justification and fury we talk among ourselves about white people, Jews and non-Jews alike, and we will undoubtedly continue to talk about them as long as racism continues to undermine our lives.

In the case of racist Jewish people, we have something to throw back at them—anti-Semitism. Righteous as such comebacks might seem, it does not serve us, as feminists and political people, to ignore or excuse what is reactionary in ourselves. Our anti-Semitic attitudes are just that, both in the political sense and in the sense of reacting to another group's mistreatment of us. Although it isn't always possible or even logical for us to be "fair," being narrowminded and self-serving is not part of our Black ethical tradition either. Trying as it may seem, I think we are quite capable of working through our ambivalent or negative responses to arrive at a usable Black feminist stance in oppositon to anti-Semitism.

A major problem for Black women, and all people of color, when we are challenged to oppose anti-Semitism, is our profound skepticism that white people can actually be oppressed. If white people as a group are our oppressors, and history and our individual experiences only verify that in mass they are, how can we then perceive some of these same folks as being in trouble, sometimes as deep as our own? A white woman with whom I once taught a seminar on racism and sexism told me about a friend of hers, also a teacher, who used John Steinbeck's *The Grapes of Wrath* in a class that had a large number of Black students. She told me how these students were absolutely convinced that the characters in the novel were Black because their situation was so terrible. It had never occurred to them that white people could suffer like that and the instructor had quite a job to do to get them to believe otherwise. I think it was in many ways an understandable mistake on the Black students' part, given how segregated Black life still is from white life in this country; the extreme arrogance and romanticism with which white people usually portray themselves in the media; and also how lacking all North Americans are in a class analysis (economic exploitation was the major force oppressing Steinbeck's characters).

On the other hand, this incident points to a basic attitude among us that I think often operates when the issue of anti-Semitism is raised. Almost all Jews in the United States are white people of European backgrounds, and therefore benefit from white-skin privilege, which is often combined with class privilege. Our frequent attitude when this particular group of white people tells us they're oppressed is (in the words of Ma Rainey) "Prove it on me!"[15] Many Black women who I've either talked to directly or who I've heard talk about the subject of anti-Semitism simply do not believe that Jews are now or ever have been oppressed. From our perspective it doesn't add up, because in those cases where Jewish people have white skin, high levels of education, economic privilege, and political influence, they are certainly not oppressed like us. I have to admit that this is certainly the aspect of the position of Jewish people in this country that I have the most problems with and I think many other people of color do too. White skin and class privilege make assimilation possible and provide a cushion unavailable to the majority of people of color. Sometimes I actually get disgusted when I see how good other people can have it and still be oppressed. When white, economically privileged Jews admit to their privilege, as opposed to pretending that it either doesn't exist or that it has no significant impact upon the quality of their lives, then I don't feel so envious and angry.

Jewish oppression is not identical to Black oppression, but it is oppression brought to bear by the same white-male ruling class which oppresses us. An investigation of Jewish history, as well as of the current situation of Jews in countries such as Russia, reveals centuries of abuse by traditionally Christian dominated states. Anti-Semitism has taken many forms, including physical segregation, sanctions against the practice of the Jewish religion, exclusion from certain jobs and professions, violent attacks by individuals, state co-ordinated pogroms (massacres), and the Nazi-engineered Holocaust which killed one-third of the world's Jews between 1933 and 1945. Anti-Semitism has been both more violent and more widespread in Europe than in the U.S., but it is currently on the increase as the political climate grows ever more reactionary. Because it is not point-for-point identical to what we experience doesn't mean it is not happening or that it is invalid for people to whom it is happening to protest and organize against it.

Another instance of skepticism about whether white people can actually be oppressed sometimes occurs when Black people who do not identify with feminism are asked to consider that sexual politics affect all women. Their disbelief leads to at least two equally inaccurate responses. The first is that sexism is a white woman's thing and Black women are, of course, already liberated. The other is that it is not possible for a rich white woman, "Miss Ann type" to be oppressed in the first place. In neither response is sexual oppression taken seriously or seen as an independently operating system. White-skin privilege is assumed to compensate for lack of power and privilege in every other sphere. All white women are assumed to be exactly alike, a monolithic group who are wealthy, pampered, and self-indulgent. However, as Third World feminists we know that sexual oppression cuts across all racial, class, and nationality lines, at the same time we understand how race, class, ethnicity, culture and the political system under which one lives determine the specific content of that oppression. The ability to analyze complicated intersections of privilege and oppression can help us to grasp that having white skin does not negate the reality of anti-Semitism. As long as opposing anti-Semitism is narrowly viewed as defending white people's interests, we will undoubtedly be extremely reluctant to speak out about it,* We need to understand that we can oppose anti-Semitism at the very same time that we oppose white racism, including white Jewish people's racism.

In political dialogue and in private conversation, it is more than possible to attack and criticize racism and racist behavior without falling back on the stereotypes and ideology of another system of oppression. The bankruptcy of such tactics is exemplified by a front page headline in *The Black American* newspaper (notable for its reactionary stances on just about everything) which derisively referred to New York's mayor, Edward Koch, as a faggot.[16] Koch's general misrule and countless abuses against people of color in New York are a matter of public record. Homophobia aimed at him did not directly confront these abuses, however; his racism in no way justified a homophobic put-down; and finally such tactics were transparently the weapons of the weak and weakminded. The self-righteousness with which some individuals express homophobia parallels the self-righteousness with which some of these same individuals and others express anti-Semitism. In both instances, such

---

*It is also important to know that significant numbers of Jews outside the U.S. are people of color, including Jews from Ethiopia, China, India, Arab countries, and elsewhere.

attacks are not even perceived as wrong, because of the pervasive, socially sanctioned contempt for the group in question. I'm not suggesting that people merely talk nice to each other for the sake of talking nice, but that as progressive women of color it is our responsibility to figure out how to confront oppression directly. If we are not interested in being called out of our names, we can assume that other people don't want to be called out of theirs either, even when the larger white society thoroughly condones such behavior.

The disastrous situation in the Middle East is used as yet another justification for unbridled anti-Semitism, which crops up in political groupings ranging from the most reactionary to the most ostensibly radical. The fact that the left, including some Third World organizations, frequently couches its disagreements with Israel's politics in anti-Semitic terms further confuses us about how to state our criticisms effectively and ethically.[17] Too often when I've brought up the problem of anti-Semitism, a woman of color responds, "But what about the Middle East?" as if opposition to Israeli actions and support for the Palestinians' right to a homeland can only be expressed by making anti-Semitic remarks to reinforce valid political perspectives. This tactic "works" all too often because so many non-Jews do not perceive verbalized anti-Semitism as unacceptable or when confronted, they act as if it has not even occurred.

Without delving into the pros and cons of the convoluted Middle East situation, I think that it is essential to be able to separate what Israel does when it functions as a white male-run imperialist state from what individual Jewish people's responsibility in relation to that situation can be. What do Jewish people who are not the people who run that state, by and large, actually want and stand for? There is a peace movement in Israel of which Israeli feminists are a significant part. In this country progressive groups like the New Jewish Agenda are defining a more complex political stance of supporting the continued existence of the state of Israel, while voicing grave criticisms of current policies and recognizing the rights of Palestinians to a homeland. Black and other Third World women must express our opposition to Israeli actions in the Middle East, if in fact we are opposed, without assuming that every Jewish person both there and here uncritically agrees with Israeli actions and colludes with those policies. Can criticisms be expressed without throwing in the "obligatory" anti-Semitic remarks and attitudes? Can Jewish women hear criticisms of Israeli actions not only from women of color but also from white non-Jewish women without assuming that their rights as Jews and as human beings to continue to survive are being questioned?

Of course, there is an emotional layer to Black and Jewish women's attitudes about the Israeli-Palestinian conflict that is directly linked to who we are. Many Jewish women view Israel as a place of refuge. They support it as the only existing Jewish state, the one place where Jews were allowed to emigrate freely following the Holocaust, and where most Jews are still granted automatic citizenship.* Often Black and other women of color feel a visceral identification with the Palestinians, because like the Vietnamese, Nicaraguans, and Black South Africans, they are a colored people struggling for the liberation of their homeland. Our two groups very often have differing responses to the Middle East situation and I am not so naive as to expect total agreement between us about the best course for rectifying what has been up to now an intractable and violent situation. I am only asserting that our anti-Semitic or Jewish people's racist attacks do not comprise legitimate "criticisms" of the other group's point of view.

How we deal as Black women with anti-Semitism and with Jewish women ultimately boils down to how we define our politics which are admittedly diverse. What I've written here are some ways to think about these vastly complicated issues, growing out of my particular political perspective. As a Black feminist I believe in our need for autonomy in determining where we stand on every issue. I also believe in the necessity for short and long term coalitions when it is viable for various groups to get together to achieve specific goals. Finally, there is my personal belief that political interactions and all other human connections cannot work without some basic level of ethics and respect. We don't oppose anti-Semitism because we owe something to Jewish people, but because we owe something very basic to ourselves.

BETWEEN A ROCK AND A HARD PLACE

Some of the pitfalls that have characterized the growth of Jewish feminism can be traced to ideological tendencies in the women's movement as a whole. I want to outline several of these here, because of the effect they have had upon relationships between Black and Jewish women, as well as upon relationships between other women of different cultures, classes, and races. These tendencies have also led to numerous misunderstandings within feminism, generally, about the nature of oppression and how to fight it.

---

*Jewish Lesbians and gay men are excluded from the Law of Return.

The concept of identity politics has been extremely useful in the development of Third World feminism. It has undoubtedly been most clarifying and catalytic when individuals do in fact have a combination of non-mainstream identities as a result of their race, class, ethnicity, sex, and sexuality; when these identities make them direct targets of oppression; and when they use their experiences of oppression as a spur for activist political work. Identity politics has been much less effective when primary emphasis has been placed upon exploring and celebrating a suppressed identity within a women's movement context, rather than upon developing practical political solutions for confronting oppression in the society itself.

A limited version of identity politics often overlaps with two other currents within the movement: Lesbian separatism and cultural feminism (which emphasizes the development of a distinct women's culture through such vehicles as music, art, and spirituality). These approaches to dealing with being social-cultural outsiders only work when the more stringent realities of class and race are either not operative (because everybody involved is white and middle-class) or when these material realities are ignored or even forcibly denied. Lesbian separatism, which might be thought of as an extreme variety of identity politics, has seldom been very useful for poor and working-class white women or for the majority of women of color, because in attributing the whole of women's oppression to one cause, the existence of men (or of patriarchy), it has left out myriad other forces that oppress women who are not economically privileged and/or white. When Jewish feminism has subscribed to or been influenced by cultural feminism, separatism, or a narrow version of identity politics, it has been limited in both analysis and strategy, since, for example, anti-Semitism does not manifest itself solely as attacks upon individuals' identities, nor does it only affect Jewish women.

Another major misunderstanding within feminism as a whole that has affected the conception of Jewish feminism is the notion that it is politically viable to work on anti-Semitism, racism, or any other system of oppression solely *within* a women's movement context. Although all the systems of oppression cannot help but manifest themselves inside the women's movement, they do not start or end there. It is fallacious and irresponsible to think that working on them internally only with other feminists is ultimately going to have a substantial, permanent effect on the power structure from which they spring. I don't live in the women's movement, I live on the streets of North America. Internal women's movement solutions are just that. They have only fractional impact on the power of the state which determines the daily content of my life.

Although I've focused on relationships between Black and Jewish women, I do not think for a moment that the whole of our respective oppressions can be reduced to how we treat each other, which is yet another mistaken notion afloat in the movement. Yes, it helps for us as feminists to respect each other's differences and to attempt to act decently, but it is ultimately much more "helpful" to do organizing that confronts oppression at its roots in the political system as a whole.

There is a last point I want to make about the political work we do and the people we are able to do it with. My intention in addressing the issues of Black and Jewish relationships, racism and anti-Semitism has been to encourage better understanding between us and to support the possibility of coalition work. It is obvious, however, that there are substantial political differences and disagreements between us and that some of these, despite efforts to alleviate them, will no doubt remain. Ongoing coalitions are formed, in truth, not on the basis of political correctness or "shoulds," but on the pragmatic basis of shared commitments, politics, and beliefs. Some Jewish women and some women of color are not likely to work together because they are very much in opposition to each other *politically*. And that's all right, because there are other Jewish women and women of color who are already working together and who will continue to do so, because they have some basic political assumptions and goals in common.

Relationships between Black and Jewish women are the very opposite of simple. Our attempts to make personal/political connections virtually guarantee our being thrust between "the rock" of our own people's suspicion and disapproval and "the hard place" of the other group's antagonism and distrust. It is a lot easier to categorize people, to push them into little nastily-labelled boxes, than time and again to deal with them directly, to make distinctions between the stereotype and the substance of who and what they are. It's little wonder that so often both Black and Jewish women first label and then dismiss each other. All of us resort to this tactic when the impact of our different histories, cultures, classes, and skins backs us up against the wall and we do not have the courage or desire to examine what, if anything, of value lies between us. Cherríe Moraga writes, "Oppression does not make for hearts as big as all outdoors. Oppression makes us big and small. Expressive and silenced. Deep and dead."[18] We are certainly damaged people. The question is, finally, do we use that damage, that first-hand knowledge of oppression, to recognize each other, to do what work we can together? Or do we use it to destroy?

NOTES

Portions of this essay originally appeared in a shorter version, based upon my presentation at the plenary session on "Racism and Anti-Semitism in the Women's Movement" at the 1983 National Women's Studies Association Convention. See "A Rock and a Hard Place: Relationships Between Black and Jewish Women," *Women's Studies Quarterly,* Vol. XI, No. 3 (Fall, 1983), pp. 7-9.

[1] Cherríe Moraga, "Preface," *This Bridge Called My Back: Writings by Radical Women of Color,* eds. Moraga and Gloria Anzaldúa (New York: Kitchen Table: Women of Color Press, 1981, 1983), pp. xviii-xix.

[2] Bernice Johnson Reagon, "Coalition Politics: Turning the Century," *Home Girls: A Black Feminist Anthology,* ed. Barbara Smith (New York: Kitchen Table: Women of Color Press, 1983), pp. 356-357.

[3] Lorraine Hansberry's classic play *A Raisin in the Sun* written in 1958 revolves around this very dilemma of housing discrimination and a Black family's efforts to buy a house in an all-white neighborhood. Cleveland author Jo Sinclair's novel *The Changelings,* which I first read as a teenager, describes the summer when a working-class Jewish and Italian neighborhood begins to change from white to Black. The story is told from the perspective of a pre-teen-age Jewish girl, Vincent, and traces with more complexity and compassion than any work I know what it is that lies between us as Black and Jewish women. Despite my efforts to interest several women's presses in republishing *The Changelings,* it continues to be out of print, but is sometimes available in libraries. Jo Sinclair (Ruth Seid), *The Changelings,* (New York: McGraw-Hill, 1955).

[4] Barbara Smith, "Introduction," *Home Girls,* pp. xlii-xliii.

[5] Elly Bulkin, "Racism and Writing: Some Implications for White Lesbian Critics," *Sinister Wisdom* 13 (Spring, 1980), pp. 3-22.

[6] Alice Walker, "Letters Forum: Anti-Semitism," *Ms.* (February, 1983), p. 13.

[7] Studs Terkel, "Introduction," *Working* (New York: Pantheon Books, 1972, 1974), p. xviii.

[8] Melanie Kaye/Kantrowitz, "Some Notes on Jewish Lesbian Identity," *Nice Jewish Girls: A Lesbian Anthology,* ed. Evelyn Torton Beck (Trumansburg, New York: The Crossing Press, 1981, 1984), p. 37.

[9] Cherríe Moraga, "Winter of Oppression, 1982," *Loving in the War Years: Lo Que Nunca Pasó Por Sus Labios* (Boston: South End Press, 1983), pp. 73-74.

[10] Smith, p. xliv.

[11] Letty Cottin Pogrebin, "Anti-Semitism in the Women's Movement," *Ms.* (June, 1983), p. 46.

[12] Deborah Rosenfelt et al., "Letters Forum: Anti-Semitism," *Ms.* (February, 1983), p. 13.

[13] Kaye/Kantrowitz, p. 42.

[14] Gloria Greenfield, "Shedding," *Nice Jewish Girls*, p. 5.

[15] Gertrude "Ma" Rainey, "Prove it on Me Blues" (performed by Teresa Trull) *Lesbian Concentrate* (Oakland, California: Olivia Records, LF 915, 1977).

[16] "Diana Ross: The White Lady and the Faggot," *The Black American* (New York), Vol. 22, No. 29, July 14-July 20, 1983, pp. 23 ff.

[17] See for example the All African People's Revolutionary Party's Educational Brochure Number One, "Israel Commits Mass Murder of Palestinian & African Peoples: Zionism is Racism . . . . It Must Be Destroyed" (A-APRP, Box 3307, Washington, D.C. 20009).

[18] Moraga, *Loving in the War Years*, p. 135.

HARD GROUND:

JEWISH IDENTITY, RACISM, AND ANTI-SEMITISM

BY
ELLY BULKIN

*but when we are silent
we are still afraid.*

—Audre Lorde

I. ORIGINS

Origins are rarely simple. Take this article, for instance. It rests solidly in the Bronx, in the lower-middle- and working-class neighborhood where I grew up in the late Forties and early Fifties, where Jewishness and whiteness were the unquestioned norms; where Friday night meant dinner across the hall at the apartment of my grandmother, who would bless the candles before feeding us challah, chopped liver, and bland, overcooked chicken and vegetables; where in my six years of elementary school I had only a single non-Jewish (blonde and blue-eyed) classmate.

The messages I got in those days about being Jewish were mixed. My immigrant grandparents and father, my New York City-born mother, spoke a Yiddish that they did not pass on to my generation, using it in our presence only to keep us from understanding their words. My grandparents, who had emigrated from Austro-Hungary, said prayers which we were not taught and which had no apparent meaning in my parents' lives. We attended Seders designed more to satisfy the older generations than to pass on a culture, a tradition; for the children, they were primarily family get-togethers featuring large meals that could be served only after the rituals. The Ukrainian pogroms that my father had escaped in the century's first decade, the Holocaust that was in its deadly closing stages when I was born in late 1944—these were presented by my parents as something inextricably linked to me, and, at the same time, something past, historical, the product of an anti-Semitism that was no longer a "significant" problem.[1]

Yet my parents' friends were all Ashkenazi Jews, people who experienced the world as they did and had.[2] Each summer my parents vacationed in Jewish resort areas. Year after year, they sent my brother and me to Jewish camps where we learned the Hebrew songs and Friday night and Saturday morning services which were not a part of our home life. And they diligently noted the Jewish identity of every person who achieved something good. The accomplishment was not just of an individual, but of a group, a group that, depending on which silent message I could best hear at a given time, did or did not have something to fear. But definitely a group.

Much remained unspoken when I was young, but I am left with certain photo-sharp images: the absolutely vivid recollection of reading the front-page story about the June 19, 1953 execution of Jews Ethel and Julius Rosenberg, convicted in a display of anti-Communist hysteria; the image of my mother, who never watched television, stopping her afternoon work for the broadcast of the Army-McCarthy hearings during a witch-hunt that swept up a huge number of Jewish progressives.[3]

But if something was equivocal or unexplained about my earliest lessons, there was no doubt as I grew older about the evils of Bull Connor and George Wallace. I was taught that Jews played a positive role in the civil rights movement and that Jews, as oppressed people, had a "special understanding" of Black people. (Other people of color were beyond my parents' range of vision.) Only later did I come to recognize the extent of the paternalism of whites in the civil rights and anti-racist struggles, the oppression of people of color by white Jews.

I learned what I did in the unique crucible of New York City, with its increasing population of people of color—mostly Black, Latino, Asian-American—and the largest Jewish population of any city in the world, two million, about a quarter of the people in the city. Significant numbers of white Jews, second- or third-generation Americans, had achieved some measure of success and some measure of power—in education, in social services, in local government—over the city's Third World population. At times, the conflicts were to become particularly bitter. In 1968, a New York City school strike occurred over the issue of Black community control of the Ocean Hill-Brownsville school board and over the rights of long-term teachers, many Jewish, to continue to work in their assigned schools. In 1971, controversy broke out between the largely Jewish home-owners in Forest Hills and those supporting low-income housing in that Queens neighborhood. Over the years, persistent tension between Blacks and Hasidic Jews in Brooklyn has occasionally erupted into life-threatening violence.[4]

As I think about racism and Jewish oppression, geography is critical. I know the extent to which my perceptions of the issues I want to address are shaped by where I have lived for almost all of my life. I know as well how differently I might see things had I been raised—or later lived—in some other region of the country—a rural area or suburb, or a city with a different racial and ethnic composition. I know, too, how different my perspective might be had I been older and learned of the Holocaust through newsreels and daily newspapers, among Jews who were trying to comprehend the enormity of what had been done, what non-Jews had allowed to happen to European Jewry.

One of the strongest lessons about the intersection of Jewish oppression and racism grew out of my interactions with some Ashkenazi Jews who had lived through World War II in the United States. Unlike my parents, they saw their lives revolving around their Jewishness, as well as around their relationship to Israel. In the late Sixties, at the Queens home of my husband's parents, who had met at a Zionist youth camp in New Jersey in the late Thirties, raised four kids, and later would settle in Israel, I met some Ashkenazi Jews whose attitudes had a direct effect on my view of how Jews dealt with racism. My husband and I argued that we could condemn the anti-Jewish statements made by some Black community control advocates and still support decentralization in Ocean Hill-Brownsville. Sliding quickly into anti-Black racism, my in-laws' friends countered this Black anti-Semitism with remarks that dismissed any validity in the community control of education. On another day, we argued even more angrily as we insisted that the anti-Jewish statements made by some Black Panther leaders did not mean, as our adversaries contended, that the Panthers' free breakfast program for children was in itself a bad thing.[5] From this limited contact, I drew a false conclusion that would take me a long time to revise: the greater the concern among Jews about anti-Semitism, the less the concern about racism.

As a lesbian in the Seventies, I worked in some political organizations with Jewish-identified women whose strong opposition to anti-Semitism was not, it seemed to me, accompanied by much more than the acknowledgement that racism was a problem too. Compounded by my own ambivalence about being Jewish, exposure to their politics discouraged me from exploring further my Jewish identity or accepting it as an integral part of my feminist politics. I suspect that the gap in my politics, the fact that I put forward anti-racism as a priority while failing to make an analogous commitment to opposing Jewish oppression, similarly discouraged them from incorporating anti-racism fully into their own feminist analysis. We all bought the same general model, I think, though we subscribed to different versions of it. Inadvertently, we supported each other in perpetuating a false distinction which benefited none of us. The construct involved choice, in this case an either-or decision, the selection of racism *or* anti-Semitism as a center of political focus.

In other settings, most notably in the women's center where I worked for five years as assistant to the director, I found considerable support for the position I had chosen. The vast majority of the white women with whom I worked were Jewish and most, like me, had grown up in New York City. We saw our Jewish identities as a given, something that we spoke about at times, but which then formed no *focal* area of consciousness out of which to do our political work: providing battered women's services, legal information, lesbian support groups, welfare advocacy, abortion referrals, crisis counseling, a return-to-school project. We influenced administrative decisions to provide services for poor women, women without access to money, many of them women of color. The decisions themselves came, and I saw them coming, from white Jewish women, mainly lesbians, for whom Jewish identity and anti-Semitism were not major issues, but who would have quickly mentioned meeting the needs of women of color as one of the center's feminist priorities.

Among other things, our politics were shaped by our work in a center in which the majority of the thirty full- and part-time workers were women of color, almost all non-lesbians. They, no doubt, were affected, though in quite a different way, by the Jewish and lesbian identities of the two administrators and of other key white staff members. Initial overt conflicts arose over lesbianism, not over race or ethnicity.

Not until the late Seventies, after the women of color had made racism an open and critical issue and we began to address it more seriously, were anti-Semitism and Jewish identity tentatively explored. When all but one participant at an optional white women's anti-racism workshop for center staff were Jews, we began to talk about the influence our Jewish identities had had on our experiences with and perceptions of racism. Our focus remained on racism, as it did in a subsequent workshop series on Black-Jewish relations, but, at least for me, racism and anti-Semitism became linked in ways that supported my going beyond our discussions to attempt a further understanding and analysis of them.

As a result of my experiences in these groups and a rise in anti-Semitism in this country, I began to rethink my association of anti-racist activism with the lack of a strong Jewish identity. In 1980, I attended a discussion of "Jews and racism" scheduled as one of the New York City Jewish lesbian community meetings (1978-1980). Some of the speakers were very strongly rooted in both their Jewish identities *and* in a radical politics that included anti-Semitism and racism among its primary concerns. I worked on a committee with other white women, several Jewish, to set up a DARE (Dykes Against Racism Everywhere) forum on the rise of the Right that included a Jewish woman who spoke on the anti-Semitism of the U.S. Labor Party and a Black woman who spoke about the growth of the Klan. At the same time, I was working on an article, "Racism and Writing: Some Implications for White Lesbian Critics." Though I spoke there about how my grandmother's use of the pejorative Yiddish word *schvartze* (black) taught me something early and well about the otherness of Black people (and other people of color), my conscious perspective was that of a white lesbian, not a white Jewish lesbian.[6]

In addition to my individual lack of awareness, I was writing in a political climate that provided relatively little support for me—or other white Jewish women—to work out of both our ethnic and racial identities. While published criticism of "Racism and Writing" upset me at the time, I was far more deeply affected by women who contacted me personally or reported comments they had heard. When one woman said she had heard the article characterized as "very Christian," I did not understand how *anything* I did could possibly be described in that way. A non-Jewish Latina wrote me about her positive feelings about the role of Jewish women in anti-racist activities. An Ashkenazi woman wrote about her particular sense of connection to the article because it was written by a Jew. My Jewish identity was more important to these two women than, on a conscious level, it had been to me as I was writing.

The response, however limited, to a part of my identity which I had not emphasized provided me with an impetus to explore issues I had thought about while writing the article, but was not then ready to tackle. It made me trace some of my grown-up lessons back to those I had been taught as a child, and to look more avidly for the Jewish radical tradition and the Jewish anti-racist tradition that I had been told existed. I realized how deeply I needed models of Jewish women who combine a strong Jewish identity with a deep commitment to opposing both anti-Semitism and racism. I needed also to understand that, if I had been having some difficulty locating such models, it was partly because I had been looking in the wrong places. The question became not which political priority to choose, but how to choose both.

II. EXTENSIONS

My motivation for writing this article arises from my need to understand what "choosing both" actually means, not just for me but for other white-skinned Jewish women. Writing pushes me, not to *answers*, but to questions, criticisms, problems, and possible strategies. It intersects with my activism, makes me look even more closely at the political work I do and why and how I do it.

At the first meeting of the Jewish and Black women who were to publish in 1981 "'The Possibility of Life Between Us': A Dialogue Between Black and Jewish Women," Jewish lesbian Judith Stein said:

> *But none of the things I've read about Black and Jewish relations are by feminists. None of this is by women. So here we are, talk about groundbreaking, and that makes it real scary. Because in some ways I would like to do something that other women can build on, can use and build on.* [1]

I build on what these women have written, and I build on what women have done. I co-facilitated a workshop for Jewish women on "Jewish Identity, Racism and Anti-Semitism" at the 1981 National Women's Studies Association Conference; and, at a panel there on racism in the lesbian community, I spoke about the writers Muriel Rukeyser and Ruth Seid (pen name: Jo Sinclair), two strongly Jewish-identified, anti-racist white lesbians. [2]

These efforts paralleled the work of women in different parts of the country. The issues involved were relatively new for some of us; others had a long history of community activism relating to anti-Semitism *and* racism. Our work took place in various settings. The ad hoc caucus of Jewish women at the 1981 West Coast Women's Music Festival tried to cope with both the racism and anti-Semitism that were divisive at that gathering.[3] The 1982 Jewish feminist conference in San Francisco included workshops on Jewish oppression for women of color and on racism for Jewish women. And in New York City, long-time members of its Jewish lesbian community carried a banner reading "Jewish Lesbians Against Anti-Semitism and Racism" in demonstrations against United States policy in El Salvador and other Third World countries and against the 1982 Israeli invasion of Lebanon.

At these and other events, workshops on Jewish oppression and racism have sometimes been explosive. The difficulty in confronting these issues at all is evident in "'The Possibility of Life Between Us'." Although based on 11 hours of tape and solicited specifically to address them, the published dialogue did not, as Beverly Smith points out, *"deal directly, in detail with . . . Jewish racism and Black anti-Semitism in this country. Perhaps because the things we did talk about sometimes produced so much pain for us we were reluctant to take this on."*[4]

The conflicts begin, in fact, not outside the Jewish community, but within it. Although my focus here is primarily on relations between white-skinned Jews and non-Jewish people of color in this country, Jewishness is not, as many assume, equivalent to whiteness.[5] Racism is a significant problem among Jews, most critically at this time in Israel. Variations of culture and skin color among Jews, especially Sephardim —from Syria, Turkey, Ethiopia, Morocco, Spain, India, and elsewhere— prevent *categorizing* Sephardim as either "Jewish people of color" or "white Jews."[6]

With its tendency to dichotomize, the language available to describe Jews racially, which, lacking any other, I use here, is no more adequate than the common usage of "women of color" to describe an Arab or Latina or Native American whose skin color might be no darker than my own. Without being totally specific about each individual's national identity, country of origin, *and* skin color, I do not do justice to the ways Jews perceive ourselves as members of a particular racial or ethnic group. Similarly I do not sufficiently indicate how these characteristics influence the way Jews are seen—and thereby treated—by others, Jew and non-Jew alike.[7]

The problems of Jewish racism and Black anti-Semitism; of divisions and prejudices among Jews; of Jewish oppression generally, within and outside the women's movement, by whites and by people of color—are all issues which Jewish women are in the process of addressing seriously. The growth of Jewish feminist consciousness in the past few years is related in part to a significant upsurge in anti-Jewish acts in the United States and in other parts of the world. Prior to a slight drop in 1981-

1983, a threefold increase in reported anti-Jewish incidents from 1980 to 1981 in this country followed an earlier threefold increase from 1979 to 1980.[8] In the last few years, a rash of bombings and shootings has also occurred in European synagogues and neighborhoods; a woman who visited Amsterdam in the fall of 1982 told me how she had to "prove" she was Jewish before being allowed past the armed guards and into synagogue for Yom Kippur services.

The current Jewish feminist movement has been influenced too by much that is positive and has gone before: Jewish women's conscious-ness-raising groups going back at least to the very early Seventies; "the first group of articles on Jewish feminism . . . in a special issue of *Davka* magazine in 1971"; the 1971 creation of *Ezrat Nashim*, "perhaps the first group publicly committed to equality for women within Judaism," which appeared before the Rabbinical Assembly convention the follow-ing year; the 1972 special *off our backs* issue on Jewish women; the 1973 National Jewish Women's Conference in New York City and the first Midwest Jewish Women's Conference later in that year in Wisconsin; the 1973 publication of *The Jewish Woman: An Anthology*, a 192-page issue of the magazine *Response*, which contains over twenty essays; the 1974 establishment of the Jewish Feminist Organization, "divided into Eastern, Midwestern, Western, and Canadian regions," which led to the 1976 creation of *Lilith: The Jewish Women's Magazine;* the existence of such local pre-1975 groups as the Jewish Lesbian Gang in San Fran-cisco; the statement prepared by the Jewish Women's Caucus at the 1975 Socialist Feminist Conference at Yellow Springs, Ohio.[9]

Much as the women's movement of the late Sixties and early Seven-ties had its roots in the earlier civil rights struggle and the New Left,[10] both the increasing number of women who define ourselves as *Jewish* feminists and our growing activism against anti-Semitism within and outside the women's community owe a significant debt as well to the emergence in the last decade of a broad-based Third World feminist movement in this country. Women of color, especially lesbians, have been in the forefront of creating a theory and practice that insist on the importance of differences among women and on the positive aspects of cultures and identities. With "identity politics" as a basis, feminists of color have been able to link analysis with day-to-day political activism, as they lay out a range of ways in which individual and institutional oppression works.

The concept of identity politics has contributed greatly to the political thinking of other women who share both a positive identifica-tion and a specific oppression. The concept was first stated in a feminist context in the Combahee River Collective's "A Black Feminist Statement" (1977):

> We realize that the only people who care enough about us to
> work consistently for our liberation is us. Our politics evolve
> from a healthy love for ourselves, our sisters, and our communi-
> ty which allows us to continue our struggle and work.
>
>   This focusing upon our own oppression is embodied in the
> concept of identity politics. We believe that the most profound
> and potentially the most radical politics come directly out of
> our own identity, as opposed to working to end somebody else's
> oppression.[11]

For feminists as a whole, as well as for distinct groups of feminists—
Jewish, Third World women, lesbians, for instance—such self-affirmation
has been tremendously valuable in moving women to define and carry
out political strategies.

If narrowly conceived, however, "focusing on our own oppression"
can have drawbacks, hampering our attempts to understand issues that
are necessarily complex and often intertwined. It can, for example, result
in what one white woman, at the end of a positive review of *This Bridge
Called My Back: Writings by Radical Women of Color,* has called the
danger of "hunkering down in one's oppression," refusing to look beyond
one's identity as an oppressed person and, in some instances, wearing
that identity as a mantle of virtue.[12] How much easier it is for someone
to say simply that she is oppressed—as a woman, a Black, a lesbian, a low-
income woman, a Native American, a Jew, an older woman, an Arab-
American, a Latina—and not to examine the various forms of privilege
which so often co-exist with an individual's oppression. Essential as it is
for women to explore our particular oppression, I feel keenly the limitations of stopping there, of not filling in the less comfortable contours of
a more complete picture in which we might exist as oppressor, as well as
oppressed.

Seeing only the partial picture has ramifications for how—or even
whether—we can address central political issues. Some women remain
silent in response to what a friend has called "oppression privilege," what
she sees as the assumption that certain criticisms can be made only by
those who share a given identity: that it is unacceptable, for instance,
for a non-Jewish woman to criticize a Jewish woman, for a white woman
to take issue with a woman of color. In the present political climate
within the women's movement, those of us who are white have, for the
most part, done little direct questioning, little challenging of women of
color. It is therefore especially important for us to be as clear as we can
about our motivation, our mode of criticism, and our understanding of
both anti-Semitism and racism when we raise issues of Jewish oppression.

Obviously, that clarity will not necessarily protect us either from the charge that we are being racist or from the reality that, no matter how accurate we may be in discerning anti-Semitism, how justifiably ready we are to confront it, we might turn out to be racist in the manner in which we do so.

In writing this article, I am very much aware of the difficulty and potential risk of criticizing non-Jewish women of color for specific acts of anti-Semitism. But I assume that *all* non-Jews, even those without in-stitutional power, have internalized the norm of anti-Semitism in this culture and are thereby capable of being anti-Semitic, whether through hostility or ignorance. A detailed analysis of anti-Semitism among women of color needs to come from women of color themselves, Jewish and non-Jewish. But the analysis presented by myself and other white Jewish women should contribute to its development, as white women have gained in working out anti-racist strategies from the words and actions of women of color. Whatever our differences, efforts to address them directly should always be seen as attempts to break down divi-sions which are encouraged by—and which benefit—the rich white Christian men who run this country.

I hope that my writing will lead to further thought, discussion, *and* disagreement. I write as part of a dialogue among Jewish women about issues that have been insufficiently explored so far from a feminist, particularly a lesbian-feminist, perspective. The need to clarify relations among women of different racial, ethnic, and religious backgrounds seems critical to me in terms of individual understanding, personal relationships, political analysis, *and* consequent activism. I believe that within the women's movement, within and between the many communi-ties that comprise it, the goal of criticism and struggle is to engage in con-crete political actions against those who wield substantive power, and not to confuse those who are most accessible to us with "the real enemy."

Working from this perspective, I want to begin to explore connec-tions and similarities between racism and anti-Semitism; to distinguish among oppressions both without ranking them and without denying their historical parity, their dissimilar manifestations at given times and places; to touch on Jewish history in this country, its progressive and reaction-ary aspects, in connection to the history of people of color; to examine the effect on the analysis of anti-Semitism and racism of feminist theory which proposes woman-hating as the "primary oppression"; to consider how what happens—and has happened—"out there," beyond our various feminist or lesbian-feminist communities shapes feminist interactions and politics; to analyze the impact of racism and Jewish oppression on our understanding of the Israeli-Palestinian conflict; to look at the specific problem of anti-Arab racism; and to find ways both to raise anti-Semitism and racism in activist work and to perceive the links among people of different "minority" identifications. In addressing these issues in order to further dialogue and support coalitions, we may hear not just the other's pain and anger, but the other's history and most fundamental concerns.

III. THREADS

A traditional view of Jewish identity divides the world into "We" and "They." Seeing this as a lesson passed on from mother to child "in all cultures, classes, and societies," Holocaust historian Lucy Dawidowicz describes how "the Jewish mother enlarges the We to embrace all Jews, those living now and those of the past, those living here, there, and everywhere."[1] Certainly I was taught this by parents whose first question about a new friend was, "Is she Jewish?" I relearn it again in hard times: in July, 1982, on our way back from a New Jewish Agenda vigil against the Israeli invasion of Lebanon, another Jewish lesbian mentioned that she had simply stopped *talking* to non-Jewish friends about the Middle East; while she shares their objections to Israeli policies on the West Bank, Gaza Strip, and Lebanon, as well as their opposition to anti-Arab racism, she cannot cope with the anti-Jewish attitudes which her friends also express.

Although I value greatly the "We" assumed in such conversations, I balk at a framework that sets everything in a context of "We" and "They." As a woman, a lesbian, a Jew, I know that the division expresses both the joy and strength of who "We" are *and* the justified fear and mistrust of a dominant society which views us with hostility, a society which places us outside the boundaries of what it values, even when we are temporarily safe from its violence. At the same time, while I see sharply my link with the "We" in Dawidowicz' discussion, I also see other "We's" with whom I identify. In each instance, I feel bound by our shared identity and oppression, but also find that, where political views and actions diverge significantly, I experience little sense of commonality. I have learned a tremendous amount from Dawidowicz, for instance, and certainly identify with the "We" in her descriptions of Jew-hating.

But I lose that feeling of connection when, in a discussion of the book *Adolescent Prejudice,* she writes, "anti-Semitism and racial prejudice were more prevalent among the poor and *the stupid* (the study characterized them euphemistically as 'the economically and academically disadvantaged') than among *'the privileged'*"[2] (my emphasis), because in this statement her analysis of oppression does not extend beyond the lives of "We" Jews.

The complexities multiply when I consider that the Agenda vigil, held on Tisha B'Av, the anniversary of the Roman destruction of the Temple in Jerusalem in 70 A.D., was suddenly set upon by four members of the Jewish Defense League who called us traitors and chanted, "The Nazis had the Judenrat, the Arabs have Agenda."[3] In the long view of Jewish history—the Diaspora, pogroms, the Protocols of the Elders of Zion—Jews are all the same, simply "We."[4] On that evening, the "We" appeared a far fuzzier concept.

The problem as I—and, I think, a great many other Jewish feminists —see it is to embrace the "We" of our Jewish identities without seeing "They" as totally Other. We strive to acknowledge Jewish identity and Jewish oppression as fundamental components of our lives and histories, individually and collectively, and, at the same time, to use what we know of being Jewish—as of our other identities and oppressions—to understand generations of experience that have some parallels, yet are different from our own. This process is complicated, and the history between non-Jewish people of color and white Jews has not made it less so.

When I tell a friend, an Ashkenazi Jew, of my plan to write about some similarities between experiences of oppression and about their common roots in theories of "racial" inferiority, she tells me, "Be careful." She knows, as I do, how often such parallels have been used— and continue to be used—by some white Jewish people to discount the oppression of people of color or to imply that "we all have the same understanding, the same daily intimate experience of oppression," thereby suggesting that each oppression does not have its unique aspects. She knows too the frustration of pointing out Jewish oppression to some non-Jewish women of color who, in barely acknowledging its existence and in refusing to confront it, reflect society's prevalent anti-Semitism.

The problem is societal, not individual. As one Black lesbian-feminist has written:

> I don't feel it's just that we are anti-Semitic because we've had experiences of racism from individual Jews, but because we see these Jews as members of a group that is racist. When white Jews are racist toward people of color, I see them as advancing their privilege as white people. And when I am anti-Semitic in

response—i.e., if I can discern their Jewishness—I am advancing my privilege as a non-Jew. Each of us is exploiting the other's vulnerability in a racist, anti-Jewish system, and using our privilege in that system.[5]

Considering both the complexity and the sensitivity of such interactions, I move along rather gingerly. But I remain unwilling to ignore the connections that I do see. I think, for example, of how, since coming to the Americas, to Africa, to Asia, to Australia, to all of the continents where people of color had lived free of whites for thousands of years, white Europeans have attempted—often with success—to exterminate these indigenous peoples. I see similarities going way back to the earliest recorded attempts to enslave Jews, to ghettoize us, to destroy us.

Developed during centuries of Christian political domination, Jew-hating myths provided a basis for "racial" theories propounding Germanic and Anglo-Saxon supremacy which emerged in the mid-1800's and contributed to the Jewish history of the following hundred years. In Germany, virulent political anti-Semitism during the last century continued on into the Nazi era. In the United States, 1920's immigration laws lumped Arabs and Asians and Blacks and Jews and Latinos together as "undesirable races."[6] Anti-alien laws in the United States remained despite a 1939 attempt to admit 20,000 children from Germany, 2/3 of them Jewish; the American Legion, one of the groups opposed to the Child Refugee Bill, maintained that "it was traditional American policy that home life should be preserved and that the American Legion therefore strongly opposed the breaking up of families."[7] The politics of the Ku Klux Klan of the Twenties with its 3½ to 5 million members continue to be reflected in those of today's Klan, American Neo-Nazis, the Liberty Lobby, and other groups whose platforms violently oppose "mongrelizing" the white Christian "race." These groups clearly deny the rights—even the right to exist—of people of color, Jews, lesbians and gay men. The connections are brought into bold relief by the Invisible Empire of the Knights of the Ku Klux Klan, whose membership application requires one to "swear that I am a White Person of Non-Jewish ancestry."[8] It is only class which divides these groups from the "respectable" men in business suits who commit the far greater atrocities: the "scientific" advocates of Anglo-Saxon superiority in the Twenties, the Reagan administration in the Eighties.

If we are uncertain about who our enemies are, they have no doubt as to their prey. For them, hatred of Jews and hatred of people of color dovetail nicely. In writing about "the Boers' extermination of Hottentot tribes, the wild murdering by Carl Peters in German Southeast Africa, the decimation of the peaceful Congo population—from 20 to 40 million reduced to 8 million people" which occurred between 1890 and 1911, Hannah Arendt makes explicit such connections:

> African colonial possessions became the most fertile soil for the flowering of what later was to become the Nazi elite. Here they had seen with their own eyes how people could be converted into race and how, simply by taking the initiative in this process, one might push one's own people into the position of the master race.[9]

I think we can recognize the similarities without blurring the distinctions. The Middle Passage during which rows and rows of enslaved Africans lay chained in their excrement on their way to the "New World"; the cattle cars that crammed Jews standing up, befouled, on their way to Nazi death camps. The U.S. government decision to drop atomic bombs on the "non-white" enemies of the allies, while people of Japanese—but not German or Italian—ancestry in this country and Canada were "relocated," their property confiscated, as they were forcibly interned.[10] More recently, the Haitian refugees imprisoned for over a year, despite objections, despite multi-racial demonstrations led by Black people, despite the signs of members of Brooklyn New Jewish Agenda: "Our ancestors were held in camps too. Let these people go."

A Native American woman makes these connections from her own perspective. In a letter, she describes reading Helen Epstein's *Children of the Holocaust*, a book about children of survivors, and then passing it on to her mother and sister.[11] Like her, she writes, they have also survived a Holocaust and wonder at their luck, cope with their guilt. Among the 1.3 million surviving Native Americans in a land that once contained ten to twelve million of their people, they find a means to further understand and interpret their own history through a book about some of those who survived a genocide which killed a third of the world's 18 million Jews.

The issue is not only one of physical survival, but of survival as a group of people with a specific culture, language, history, tradition. Here too I can see parts of my own experiences and those of some other Jewish women mirrored in certain experiences of some non-Jewish women of color. One example: I am sitting in a coffee shop with Carmen, a Puerto Rican used to speaking Spanish daily, and Sylvia, a Chicana who is relearning the Spanish of her parents. Carmen, who works closely with a group of Salvadoran refugee women who have no knowledge of English, describes her frustration at a Chicana colleague who makes little personal contact with them. Her colleague, Carmen tells us, is "not a real Chicana." I start at the word "real," and sense Sylvia stiffen. Carmen explains that, by being unwilling to speak Spanish to the refugees, her co-worker has left them alone, acted inhospitably to other Latinas. Sylvia responds by talking about her own experience as a Chicana who has, to a certain extent, been assimilated, been severed from her roots because she was not raised to speak Spanish fluently.

Days later, I told Sylvia my response to the coffee shop interchange. It reminded me of some Ashkenazi women I know: our ambivalent relationship to Yiddish; the discussion in my Jewish lesbian group three years before about going to a Yom Kippur service—measuring our childhood experiences of religious rituals, our recollections of Hebrew prayers and songs, against the concept of being "a real Jew." It reminded me too of hearing about a Sephardic Jew who "as a child . . . had wanted to learn Yiddish to be part of what she then thought were the 'real Jews'," the Ashkenazim.[12] Sylvia and I do not understand all of the nuances of each other's reactions. But I find some comfort, as I work out the implications of my Jewish identity, in sharing some common ground with a woman of color who is not Jewish and who is also working out her relationship to her own culture and history.

Though our specific experiences differ, depending on class, age, region, and other variables, as well as on racial/ethnic identity, I know that I share with some women of color, non-Jewish and Jewish, as well as with other white Jewish women, a history of assimilation and reclamation. I think, for example, of the history of different Asian-American peoples, sorting out the meaning of both aspects of their self-description —Japanese-American, Korean-American, Chinese-American; the parts of their parents', their grandparents' languages and traditions they have held onto and those they have let go. And I think too of the decisions to celebrate one's identity: for those Native American women, Latinas, and Black women who could "pass" as white; for the Jewish woman whose father changed his name in the Thirties so he could "make it," and raised her, ignorant of her identity, as a Christian; for the Arab-American woman, who, after internalizing her racial oppression, came only in the last few years to identify as a woman of color; for the Jewish-Latina, the Arab-Jewish woman, for any Jewish woman of color who is too often, as one Jamaican-Jewish woman has said, "a token to everybody"; for any woman of color of mixed heritage—Chinese-Korean, Native American-Black, Asian-Black, Chicana; for the Arab-American dyke who is shunned because she is a lesbian by the only other Arab woman in town, the Jewish lesbian whose family sits *shivah** for her, the "bulldagger" whose Black community rejects her. All of the women who, told to choose between or among identities, insist on selecting all.

Shivah—seven-day mourning period after burial observed by the deceased's family.

IV. SEPARATIONS

If I am even to begin to make sense of all this, I need to be aware of these connections on a gut level, not just on an intellectual one. At the same time, I know the danger of leveling oppressions, of failing to recognize the specificity of each. In terms of anti-Semitism and racism, a central problem is how to acknowledge their differences without contributing to the argument that one is "important" and the other is not, one is worthy of serious political attention and the other is not.

Addressing this problem involves distinguishing between oppressions, not treating racism or Jewish oppression, in their various manifestations, as if they operated in exactly the same way within each geographical and historical setting. For example, since the arrival in 1654 of the first Jewish community—Sephardim escaping the spread of the Inquisition to Brazil who were allowed to stay in New Amsterdam despite the objections of Governor Peter Stuyvesant—the history of anti-Semitism in the United States has been significantly different from that in Europe.[1] In *The Holocaust and the Historian,* Lucy Dawidowicz refers to the United States as a country "where anti-Semitism has not been widely prevalent in social life or political thought. . . ."[2] In the introduction to *A Promise to Keep: A Narrative of the American Encounter with Anti-Semitism,* Nathan Belth says:

> Anti-Semitic behavior in America has often reflected European origins, but rarely, in over three centuries of history, have anti-Semitic incidents attained the intensity—and never have they extracted the fearful price—of European bigotry.
>
> Because it had few ideological roots, anti-Semitism in America rarely expressed itself in outbursts of violence.[3]

The critical point here is not that anti-Semitism in this country is not—

and has not been—present, serious, and essential to confront, but that the degree of it here must be seen in contrast to the greater intensity of its European forms. Understanding the history of Jews in Europe then is a *prerequisite* for understanding issues of Jewish identity and anti-Semitism in this country. A short fifty years after Hitler assumed power, the scars caused by the Holocaust remain. As Israeli author Amos Oz comments, "late on a hot summer night in Tel Aviv, when it is so insufferably hot and steamy that everyone leaves windows open to catch the slightest possible sea breeze, one can walk the streets of Tel Aviv and hear people having nightmares in twenty different languages."[4]

Among the U.S. population as a whole, stereotypes about Jews continue to prevail that one historian considers to be "strongly reminiscent of the forgeries known as the Protocols of the Elders of Zion . . . concocted by Tsarist officials in the early 1890's."[5] Finding fertile soil in the minds of Christians who had been taught that Jews were killers of Christ, devils, and ritual murderers of Christian children, the Protocols purported to describe a secret Jewish plan to control the world. Fuel for Russian pogroms at the turn of the century and after, they were first published in Germany in 1920 and were "at the very center of Hitler's thinking and of Nazi ideology."[6] They were first published in the United States in the Twenties by Henry Ford and remain a staple of anti-Jewish groups in this country. During the present deteriorating economic period, these continuing stereotypes are especially disturbing. One can readily see historical parallels to periods in Tsarist Russia, Nazi Germany, and other countries when anti-Semitism, particularly violence against those Jews deemed "responsible" for economic hardship or social unrest, markedly increased. According to the 1981 Yankelovitch poll, for instance, 43 percent of respondents think that "international banking is pretty much controlled by Jews"; 52 percent think that "Jews always like to be at the head of things"; 37 percent believe that "Jews have too much power in the business world"; 46 percent support the statement, "the movie and television industries are pretty much controlled by Jews"; and 48 percent agree that "Jews are more loyal to Israel than to America."[7]

All of these factors support the position taken by Irena Klepfisz in her article "Anti-Semitism in the Lesbian/Feminist Movement":

> If someone were to ask me did I think a Jewish Holocaust was possible in this country, I would answer immediately: "Of course." Has not America had other Holocausts? Has not America proven what it is capable of? Has not America exterminated others, those it deemed undesirable or those in its way? Are there not Holocausts going on right now in this

country? Why should I believe it will forever remain bene-
volent towards the non-Christian who is the source of all its
troubles, the thief of all its wealth, the commie betrayer of its
secrets, the hidden juggler of its power, the killer of its god?
Why should I believe that given the right circumstances America
will prove kind to the Jews? That given enough power to the
fascists, the Jew will remain untouched?[8]

In a country in which other Holocausts have taken place, other Holocausts are "going on right now," Jews can, in the long run, expect anything. That, after all, has been one of the prime lessons of Jewish history.
Along with the basic awareness that anti-Semitism is simply *wrong,* that
lesson should impel feminists, Jewish or not, to be vigilant in opposing
Jewish oppression, to make sure that the flashpoint is not again reached
where Jews face a newly conceived approach to our genocide.

The power of Jew-hating in the United States is illustrated by four
1983 rifle attacks on Jews affiliated with Yeshiva University in New
York City, resulting in several injuries and the death of one non-Jewish
woman; riding in a car in front of one containing Yeshiva students, she
was accidentally killed by a sniper. A further threat lies in the discovery
of "links among small groups of heavily armed right-wing extremists . . .
from the Nazi Party and the Ku Klux Klan to radical elements of the
farm protest movement"; these groups are joined by teachings like those
of the Ministry of Christ Church that "Jews are children of Satan and
should be exterminated."[9] The attack on a Jewish restaurant in Paris's
Jewish section, The Marais, in which six people, Jewish and non-Jewish,
were killed in a response to the Israeli invasion of Lebanon, stands as a
reminder—if one is needed—of the assumption that Jews—any Jews,
anywhere—are fair game, all being equally "culpable" for what is done by
any other Jew, all equally dispensable.

I find it easier to enumerate instances of anti-Semitism, current and
historical, than to distinguish among them or to distinguish how racism
and Jewish oppression operate at different times and places. I am well
aware of how the difficulty in making distinctions is compounded by
so much effort having to go into simply trying to get other women to
acknowledge anti-Semitism as more than historical aberration, something
past and done. The difficulty is particularly pronounced when one is
dealing not only with women who have not thought about, talked about,
worked against anti-Semitism, but also with women, Jewish and not,
who continue to take the position that the oppression of Jews today is
not "serious," perhaps arguing additionally that attendance at workshops
on internalized anti-Semitism merely reflects self-indulgence.[10] It is
further compounded when they argue that work against Jewish oppression necessarily drains energy from the fight against white supremacy,

that the presence of racism merits political opposition while the presence of anti-Semitism can be safely ignored. I think it vital to refute these arguments, as Jewish women have done in a range of personal and published responses.[11]

There needs also to be an acknowledgment that, while anti-Semitism has the potential for—and certainly the history of—unleashing violence against Jews, in the United States people of color face the probability of greater physical danger than do Jews. Although this assertion has been wrongly used by groups such as Women Against Imperialism and the Alliance Against Women's Oppression to dismiss Jewish oppression as a significant political issue, it can be used constructively to put anti-Semitism into an historical and contemporary context. At the beginning of an article on how Jews *are* oppressed in the United States, for example, Aviva Cantor wrote in 1970:

> . . . when we come to consider whether Jews in America are oppressed, we should not be side-tracked by the fact that they happen to be, by and large, economically well-off and not subject at the moment to the kind of physical oppression faced by blacks, Indians, and Chicanos. Oppression in America can be subtle and not easily recognized as such. . . .[12]

For women who *assume* the fundamental importance of anti-Semitism, who recognize its life-threatening aspects and history, and who want to look at what happens, what has happened, in this country, the distinctions made in Cantor's article bring some perspective to the relative situations of white Jews and of people of color, Jewish and non-Jewish.

As we develop an analysis of Jewish identity and anti-Semitism within a feminist context, it is essential for us to reject any approach which flattens oppressions, distorting their historical reality in an attempt to argue for their parity in the long run. An example of this "flattening" dynamic appears as a key paragraph in Evelyn Torton Beck's introduction to *Nice Jewish Girls: A Lesbian Anthology*. Its analysis of anti-Semitism has significant implications for approaches to both Jewish oppression and racism. Beck writes:

> Why is it often difficult to see parallels? Do we resist seeing them? Need one oppression cancel out another? Would the recognition that it is not *either/or* but *both/and* be too overwhelming? What would happen if we admitted that oppressed groups can themselves be oppressive? In the face of this complexity, a few facts remain clear: *oppression is never less oppressive simply because it takes a different form* [my emphasis]. Success has never protected the Jews from anti-Semitism. Even those Jews who considered themselves more German than Jewish were annihilated by the Nazis. Ironically, when Jews

have succeeded in integrating themselves into a society, it has been used against them: suddenly every Jew becomes "the rich Jew," the penny-pinching, exploiting miser. The great American dream, "from rags to riches," is simply not acceptable for Jews, whose success is somehow always tainted. Moreover, if at certain moments in history some Jews have entered into the mainstream, it is only because some powerful groups have "allowed" it: often this is done with the purpose of using Jews as a buffer and/or as an easy scapegoat when one is needed. It is an age-old pattern for Jews—*today*, allowed in, perhaps even encouraged; *tomorrow*, ignominiously thrown out. Many people fail to understand the implications of this recurrent fact of Jewish history, and even some Jews fall for the mirage, taking the surface for the whole, refusing to acknowledge the precariousness of Jewish existence. Is that why, even now, I feel I have to justify my concern? *To prove that any form of anti-Semitism is always a real danger?*[13]

"The precariousness of Jewish existence" throughout history, the ways in which certain limited economic privilege has been "allowed" Jews by white Christians who benefit from the Jewish role as "buffer" and "scapegoat," "*the real danger*" inherent in "*any form of anti-Semitism*" —all these points are incontrovertible. Each needs to be understood as central to Jewish responses to anti-Semitism.

Yet Beck distorts the nature of anti-Semitism—and, by extension, that of other oppressions—by arguing that "oppression is never less oppressive simply because it takes a different form." It seems far more accurate to me to acknowledge that the degree of oppressiveness *depends* on the form that a given oppression takes at different times, in different locations, and for different individuals. The "form" that anti-Semitism took in Nazi Germany or during the Spanish Inquisition is not the "form" that it has taken at different times in the United States. In turn, current forms of Jewish oppression in the United States differ from those in Ethiopia, where in the last decade, an estimated two thousand of its Jewish community, the Beta Yisroel (Falashas), have been killed and "seven thousand driven off the land," the study of Hebrew forbidden, and Jewish schools closed; in the Soviet Union, almost impossible for Jews to leave, where teaching or studying Jewish history or possessing Jewish books can bring fines, forced labor sentences, and incarceration in mental institutions; or in junta-run Argentina, where Jews were "a full 20% of the reported disappearances, while the Jewish population as a whole is under 1% of the Argentine population."[14]

To suggest that the degree of oppressiveness is equal regardless of its form fails to acknowledge, among other things, the virulence that anti-Semitism *can* attain. Being caught in a pogrom, losing a job because one is a Jew, having swastikas painted on one's house, being beaten by anti-Semites, or feeling invisible within a politcal movement—each reflects different degrees of Jewish oppression. As Cherríe Moraga has written about "lesbianism, . . . being brown, . . . being a woman, . . . being just plain poor," it is *"the specificity"* that matters.[15]

Within the Jewish community in this country, a tremendous range of oppression exists which is affected by the variables in the life of each individual. In the United States today, the poor Jew, the working-class Jew, the elderly Jew who subsists on decreasing government subsidy programs, the Jewish woman who is incarcerated in a state mental institution, and the disabled Jew who must rely on the rehabilitative services of a municipal clinic, are far more vulnerable to the anti-Semitism of the people with whom they come into contact than the Jews who are profes· sionals, entrepreneurs, or government officials.[16] While none is immune to Jewish oppression, its forms differ, as does the extent to which anti-Semitism undermines safety, controls lives, and threatens individual survival. Such distinctions have parallels among people in other groups. Under certain circumstances, for instance, an unemployed Black teenager and Reagan's lone Black Cabinet appointee, Secretary of Housing and Urban Development Samuel Pierce, can both be in equal danger of being lynched—as a Black transit worker was a few miles from my home in 1982—but on a day-to-day basis they experience quite different forms of racism.

The hatred motivating such violence is frequently multi-faceted— sometimes indisputably racial, sometimes inextricably linked with woman-hatred, queer-loathing, devaluation of the poor or aged, fear of political radicalism. As it might not be known whether an elderly Jew was beaten because the victim's Jewish identity made for even greater vulnerability, it can often remain unclear whether a lesbian of color raped by a white man was singled out because of her lesbian identity, as well as because of her race.

The issues of economic success, class privilege, and access to money further complicate the picture, but they are pivotal to any examination of Jewish oppression and racism. White Jews in this society are oppressed as Jews, yet privileged as people with white skin, potentially allowed by the white Christian ruling class to attain the level of "middlemen": a buffer between themselves and the poorer and darker, Jews are convenient scapegoats when needed. Yet we possess—and present—an inaccurate picture of Jewish life in the United States if we see financial success *only* as precarious and not also as a source of privilege and power. The tendency to present such a picture is, I think, partly due to the fact that "making it," as Beck says, has been used against Jews to buttress ancient stereotypes and to fuel anti-Jewish acts. At the same time, it reflects a women's movement that has, by and large, been notable for its failure to deal with class background and economic privilege.

Because it distorts the position of Jews in this country, the half-picture, the argument that "success has never protected Jews from anti-Semitism" without any explanation of what success has meant—and does mean—in *positive* terms, interferes with potentially fruitful dialogue with non-Jewish women of color. While the "precariousness of Jewish existence" argument must be made forcefully to explain how anti-Semitism functions, it is only one of several aspects of the relationship between class and white Jews that deserves attention. Among these, it is especially critical to counter vehemently the stereotypic assumption that poor and working-class Jews do not exist. A 1973 study, for instance, found:

1. 272,000 individuals, or 15.1 percent of the Jewish population of 1.8 million in New York [City], are poor or near poor. This figure includes 191,000 poor Jews and 81,000 who are near poor;
2. 190,300 families totaling 432,000 individuals are between the near poverty level and what the Bureau of Labor Statistics calls a moderate level of living. This is almost one quarter of New York City's Jewish population, and constitutes the Jewish working class.[17]

A 1983 study of Chicago Jews, which also found 15 percent to be "economically disadvantaged and vulnerable," suggests that the statistics of a decade ago have not changed markedly. Placed at a higher level than those used by the federal government to determine the poverty line, "the figures are approximately the same in St. Louis, and preliminary analysis of other cities reveals similar patterns."[18]

In addition to such statistical information, any discussion of the class position of Jews must consider that provided by Jewish women who speak out of their own experiences, their own histories: the lesbian whose father supported his family "on the income from a small tomato and banana stand at which he worked six days a week, twelve hours a day"[19]; the over-65 Jewish women who, like elderly women in all racial/ethnic groups, suffer the greatest economic poverty[20]; and the other Jewish women in our communities who live on SSI or food stamps, who work as waitresses or typists, who do not have college degrees, who have few marketable skills or whose skills are clearly "blue-collar," who work hard to survive and get ahead economically. In each instance, the problem is not simply invisibility, but assumptions about Jews and class (held as well by many middle-class Jews) which effectively block from public vision the poor or working-class Jew. As Renée Franco, a

Sephardic Jew whose family has lived in Atlanta for years, has written: "I have come to realize that people don't want to know they exist. What could they do with all their myths and stereotypes?"[21]

Emphasizing the existence of poor and working-class Jews can play a useful role in confronting stereotypes. While a large number of Jews are middle-class, the acknowledgment of this fact can be used to perpetuate myths, rather than to clarify what the real economic position of Jews is. Because stereotypes about Jewish success and Jewish privilege often translate into a belief in "Jewish control," it is essential to realize that, with a few token exceptions, Jews are intentionally excluded "from the central position of economic power," are absent from executive positions in large banks, the auto and oil industries, public utilities, and other conglomerates where national and international economic policy is shaped.[22] However, while white Christian men make up the economic and political elite in the United States, a high percentage of white Jewish men have nevertheless achieved a certain level of economic success: "seventy percent of Jews in the labor force are either professionals (29%) or managers and administrators (41%)."[23] In these fields, many factors—white skin undoubtedly being a highly significant one—have prevailed over both individual and institutional anti-Semitism.[24]

These statistics apply overwhelmingly to Jewish male workers: the 1972 National Jewish Population Study indicates that "only 16 per cent of the employed women were" managers or administrators, and "an estimated 42 per cent of Jewish working women were classified as 'clerical'."[25] Despite the disparity between female and male Jewish workers, statistics relating to Jewish men have direct implications both for Jewish women and for anyone examining the economic position of white Jews and people of color in this society. While it is true that the median income of white women is about half that of white men, the white woman with some ties to a middle-income white man—father, brother, ex-husband, uncle—finds in that connection the potential for some degree of financial access: college tuition, child support, a source of funds for medical or other emergencies, a possible inheritance. The white lesbian in this position, Jewish or not, who for personal or political reasons chooses to sever these ties, exercises a *choice* that is open to far fewer women of color; and, in any event, no such adult decision can undo a range of childhood "privileges"—adequate nutrition, satisfactory health care, safe housing. The disparity is evident from the 1980 Census, which places the following percentage of families in each group below the federal poverty line: Vietnamese, 35.1 percent; Puerto Rican, 34.9 percent; Black 26.5 percent; Native American 23.7 percent; Latino, 21.3 percent; white, 7.0 percent.[26] And for each of these groups, these statistics have daily implications that need to be considered in relation to racism and anti-Semitism.

My perception of the world around me and my place in it, for example, can easily be distorted as soon as I forget—or disregard—the fact that my freedom to write this article at all rests on assorted privileges I have gained as an Ashkenazi Jew from New York City whose family worked itself into the middle class. These advantages included public school and college teachers, all white and mostly Jewish, who regarded me as "smart"; the fellowship, the part-time teaching jobs, and the salary of my college professor husband, which contributed to putting me through graduate school with almost no debts incurred; the education and work credentials (and, in this economy, the good luck) to have a well-paying part-time job that allows me the flexibility to go to the library and do my own writing. My father came from the Ukraine, poor, with parents who knew no English, and worked in a candy factory while he got the schooling that would qualify him for the life-long civil service job he secured at a time when the newspapers were allowed to specify "Christian"—and "white"—in their employment ads. But he "made it," and I gained from that. My political arguments regarding anti-Semitism and racism have a flimsy foundation if I am not totally clear that neither his achievements nor my own just flowed "naturally" from our individual abilities and fortunes, if I am not prepared to recognize, analyze, and understand how race *has* affected my class prerogatives.

While for Jews, "the great American dream," as Beck writes, ". . . is somehow always tainted," a tremendous gulf separates those who can attain even the semblance of it and those for whom it is simply out of reach. In writing about the achievement of that "American dream" by white Jewish playwright Moss Hart, James Baldwin first quotes from Hart's response to instant success on Broadway as he takes a 3 a.m. taxi ride, and then adds his own comments:

> "It was possible [Hart writes] in this wonderful city for that nameless little boy—for any of its millions—to have a decent chance to scale the walls and achieve what they wished. Wealth, rank, or an imposing name counted for nothing. The only credential the city asked was the boldness to dream."
>
> But this is not true for the Negro [Baldwin says], and not even the most successful or fatuous Negro can really feel this way. His journey will have cost him too much, and the price will be revealed in his estrangement—unless he is very rare and very lucky—from other colored people, and in his continuing isolation from whites. Furthermore, for every Negro boy who achieves such a taxi ride, hundreds, at least, will have perished around him, and not because they lacked the boldness to dream, but because the Republic despises their dreams.[27]

And Beverly Smith has a similar response in "'The Possibility of Life Between Us'," when Judith Stein mentions positively the statement of a Jewish man "who was talking about 'this is how you stay alive in a culture that's totally hostile to you.' You have enough money that it's worth it for people to keep you going." Smith's reply is immediate and vehement: "I've got to say it! See, that sounds like a good idea. Black people don't have that. I feel anger when I hear about being rich as being a survival mechanism. *Running* for Black people was a survival mechanism."[28]

The history of white Jews in the United States needs to be looked at against the violence perpetrated since the late fifteenth century against people of color. At the most fundamental level, the issue comes down to physical survival, to the recognition that, while the pivotal racial ideology in Europe involved Jews and the other "inferior races" located in colonized countries and continents, the dominant racial ideology in the United States has consistently seen skin color as far more central than religion.

White-skinned Jews then need to look at the intersection of religion/ethnicity and skin color, the confluence of anti-Semitism and white skin privilege, and avoid the tunnel vision that perceives Jewish oppression but not racial prerogatives. During the Civil War, for instance, anti-Semitism emerged from the centuries-old stereotype of the Jew as "financial manipulator" and "shyster," as questionable in loyalty to the state. An 1862 order by Union General Ulysses S. Grant (canceled by President Lincoln) expelled "'Jews, as a class'" from the Department of Tennessee which was under his command because of Jewish peddlers' alleged trade with the enemy.[29] The 150,000 Jews, white Northerners and Southerners, had roughly the same attitude toward slavery as white Christians and were well represented in the armed forces of both sides. Judah P. Benjamin, Confederate Secretary of War and Secretary of State, who was essential to the war effort, was the victim of both Southern anti-Jewish attitudes blaming the economic ills of the area on Jewish "extortionists" whom he supposedly protected *and* Northern ones attacking him *as a Jew* for his role in the War.[30] This anti-Semitism manifested itself—and should be understood—in a society where, for Northern and Southern Blacks, the oppression and the stakes were of an entirely different magnitude.

The case of Leo Frank raises similarly complex issues. Lynched in 1915, Frank, president of the Atlanta Lodge of B'nai B'rith, was the New York-raised manager of his uncle's factory and therefore easy to pin with the stereotype of the "Jewish outsider," the "Jewish capitalist." Accused of the 1913 rape and murder of Mary Phagan, a 14-year-old white Christian employee, and convicted while a mob threatened, "Hang the Jew or we'll hang you," Frank was lynched as the culmination of an anti-Jewish campaign against him by Tom Watson, Populist leader, racist, anti-Catholic bigot, and later United States Senator, who observed after the murder, "Jew libertines take notice."[31] His killing led to threats against the Jewish citizens of Marietta, the site of the lynching; "in the aftermath of terror, about half of the 3,000 Jews in Georgia left the state."[32]

Several things are notable about the Frank case. It contributed to the formation in 1913 of the Anti-Defamation League of B'nai B'rith. The Knights of Mary Phagan reconstituted themselves in 1915 as the Knights of the Ku Klux Klan, giving new life to that moribund organization. While the Klan and other such groups have consistently expressed virulent anti-Semitism, Frank's was "only" the second known lynching of a Jew in the United States and the only one in which Jew-hating was *the* central motivation.[33] Although at least as much evidence implicated Black janitor Jim Conley, who was sentenced to one year as an accessory and admitted his own guilt for the murder to his lawyer, during and after Frank's trial anti-Semitism in many local white Christian people was roused to a level of blood lust that temporarily—and most uncharacteristically—outweighed their capacity for racist violence.

Commenting on the nature of anti-Semitism in the United States, a Jewish friend of Frank's observed that when Frank moved to Atlanta, "violence . . . probably never entered his head . . . in the South violence was reserved for Negroes."[34] No arrests had been made in the brutal deaths in Atlanta of eighteen Black women during the year-and-a-half preceding Phagan's murder.[35] During the month after Frank's lynching, "four Blacks had been lynched in Georgia; two days after the lynching of Frank, three Blacks were lynched in Alabama."[36] The violence feared by Jews in Georgia was a "normal" and constant threat for the region's Black citizens, 1,100 of whom were lynched between 1900 and 1917.[37] During approximately the same period, the Texas Rangers "executed, without due process of law, between one hundred and three hundred Mexican residents of the border counties" *alone.*[38]

The death toll among people of color in this country is limited by neither time nor place. Lakota lesbian Barbara Cameron explains her continuing political activism in terms of "the death of Anna Mae Aquash —Native American freedom fighter—'mysteriously' murdered by a bullet in the head; Raymond Yellow Thunder—forced to dance naked in front of a white VFW club in Nebraska—murdered; Rita Silk-Nauni—imprisoned for life for defending her child; my dear friend Mani Lucas-Papago— shot in the back of the head outside of a gay bar in Phoenix."[39] The list is interminable, differing from community to community. Twelve Black women are murdered in a five-month period in 1979 in Boston.[40] Black, Latino, Native American prisoners or suspects are shot in the back in New York, drowned while handcuffed in Texas, "inexplicably" strangled to death while the Los Angeles police "subdue" suspect after suspect with a chokehold (leading the Los Angeles police chief to suggest that "blacks might be more likely to die from chokeholds because their arteries do not open up as fast as they do on 'normal people'.").[41]

Several miles from my Brooklyn home, in June 1982 a group of fifteen to twenty white youths attacked three Black New York City transit workers who had stopped to pick up some food in a white neighborhood on their way home from work. Shouting racial epithets in the true spirit of a lynch mob, the youths kicked to death Willie Turks, the one Black man unable to escape.[42] Unlike nearly all murders of people of color, this one got a lot of attention from the white media in the city. I was shocked by it, both outraged and sickened. Turning on the radio, I picked up a program in the middle and heard Black lesbian activist Joan Gibbs from DARE expressing her anger that so many white people had responded to this particular killing when, as she said, *it happens all the time.* My reaction to the murder didn't change. But I did add to it, as I had many times before, a further sense of my privilege, as a white person, *not* to see that "it happens all the time." Some days later, at a protest rally at the Black housing project near where Turks had been killed, Reverend Herbert Daughtry, head of the Black United Front, observed, "If it's Blacks today, it'll be Jews the next day. . . ."

The central issue here is physical survival in the face of both overt violence and the shrouded kind, the kind which prevents people from getting enough food, enough heat, enough medical care, and so maims and kills too. Such violence is not the whole of any oppression. Nor does its relative absence negate the pain, the danger, the history, the fear of other aspects of racism and Jewish oppression. But it does help define how close each individual or each group is to oppression's sharpest edge. As I look at anti-Semitism and racism as they have been manifested in the past, and as they operate today, my attention is riveted again and again to the times and the places where that edge presses into the flesh and cuts through the bone.

V. LEFT LEANINGS

Communist Jews behind race riots
—placard in Birmingham, Alabama,
1955 (*I Heard It Through the Grapevine*)

I was raised to believe in the "inherent affinity" of Jewish people for society's most oppressed, those living at or near its margins, and to take pride in the role of American Jews, primarily Ashkenazi, in the labor movement of the turn of the century and after, in the various radical movements of the Twenties and Thirties, in the civil rights movement. In forging a Jewish identity that is positive, rather than a reactive one based largely on the persistence of anti-Semitism, I have found central the role of Jews in these various left/liberal movements, even as I know something of the limitations of that involvement.

An inveterate reader, I have taken special pleasure in the fiction of Ruth Seid, who learned her craft in the Works Progress Administration and who, looking back from the vantage point of the early Eighties, terms as "lifelong passions" of hers "Jews, racism, women, anti-Semitism, self-identity."[1] I have felt most connected to two of Seid's novels. *Wasteland* (1946) describes Debby, a white, strongly Jewish-identified lesbian writer who works in the Works Progress Administration and publishes stories about Black people and about the Spanish Civil War in the *New Masses,* a left periodical of the Thirties and Forties. *The Changelings* (1955) is the story of a Jewish neighborhood that is "changing," going from white to Black. Its focus is the relationship between two young adolescent girls, Vincent, who is Jewish, and Clara, who is Black, and the struggle Vincent encounters in opposing racism in her own family and community.[2]

I have cared especially about the poetry of Muriel Rukeyser, who wrote about the "Scottsboro Boys" being framed in Alabama for the rape of a white woman as protesters at their trial waved "hammers and sickles"; about poor people of all races during the Thirties. Writing later about breaking the "tabu" of loving another woman and about being jailed for civil disobedience against the Vietnam War, Rukeyser spoke consistently from the perspective of someone who felt that, as she wrote in 1944:

> To be a Jew in the twentieth century
> Is to be offered a gift. If you refuse,
> Wishing to be invisible, you choose
> Death of the spirit, the stone insanity.
> Accepting, take full life. Full agonies:
> Your evening deep in labyrinthine blood
> Of those who resist, fail, and resist . . . .[3]

And I have valued the work of Tillie Olsen who wrote in 1934 (under her maiden name, Tillie Lerner) from her then-Communist perspective about Chicanas sewing dresses for pennies a day, about the bloody San Francisco longshoremen's strike in which police killed two strikers. Twenty years later, Olsen published several stories, one in the voice of a white mother unable to help her daughter bridge the chasm between herself and her once-best friend, a Black girl, and another about an elderly Jewish woman who, dying, recalls vivid fragments of her turn-of-the-century imprisonment in Russia, of "the monstrous shapes of what has actually happened in the century."[4]

If the non-literary aspects of this Jewish tradition are more flawed, more deserving of criticism, the lesson is not, I think, that they should be abandoned as without value, but that literature tends to be more manageable than life. Claiming the Jewish anti-racist and progressive tradition that I learned about when I was growing up involves, then, looking at it from a number of perspectives.

Because of my own upbringing and my ex-Communist stepmother who entered my life when I was 18; because I have read—and heard—enough of the social and political situation in the late Twenties and Thirties, when a quarter of American workers (and 60 percent of those in Harlem) were unemployed, to appreciate the attraction the Communist Party had for radicals of the time; and because I know enough politically active Jewish lesbians who are Red Diaper babies, the children of one-time CP members, who regret not their parents' early commitment but their more recent political inactivity, I take some pride in the knowledge that an estimated "40 to 50 percent of the [CP] membership in the later 1930s was Jewish."[5]

At the same time, I am aware that for Jews the price of such membership was adherence to a CP "Americanization" policy that supported the assimilation of all white ethnic groups and "demonstrated a negative attitude toward Jewish culture, history and Yiddish."[6] In the Twenties, as part of the Party's anti-religious ideology, "Jewish organizations in the Communist orbit held mock *seders* on Passover, social affairs on Rosh Hashonah, lectures on Yom Kippur"; "some CP members were even expelled for attending religious services."[7] As the Popular Front policies of the late Thirties tried "to draw the Jewish community as a whole into the 'united front against fascism'," new CP positions

> had two immediate consequences: first, the Party as an organization began to devote an important part of its efforts to combating anti-semitism in the United States, and secondly, it encouraged the Jewish subculture attached to the Party . . . to promote a "progressive Jewish identity" as a positive good.[8]

After establishing itself as militantly anti-fascist, the CP profoundly affected its relationship with many of its Jewish supporters as a result of the 1939 Nazi-Soviet Pact, in effect until the 1941 invasion of the Soviet Union.[9]

Strongly critical of the Party's male chauvinism, its homophobia, and many of its tactics, I have ambivalent feelings about the role that many white Communists, disproportionately Jewish, played in organizing in Harlem and other Black communities.[10] They brought *their* interpretation of Marx and Communism to a people whose lives they could see only through the lens of their own whiteness, their own first-generation American or immigrant experience. Beginning in the early Thirties, their work built on Communist International resolutions which "endowed the black struggle with unprecedented dignity and importance," instructed the CP in this country to work against "'lynching, Jim Crowism, and segregation'," to make "'the Negro problem ... part and parcel of all and every campaign'," and to combat "white chauvinism" in Party ranks through "a 'thorough educational program'."[11] So I retain my appreciation of a Left which directly confronted institutional and personal racism during a period when doing so was a far more radical act for white people than it is today; which adopted so many other progressive positions; and which fostered the activism and writing of such Jewish women as Olsen and Rukeyser.

Part of this progressive Jewish history involves the knowledge that, despite totalling less than 4 percent of the American population, "in the summer of 1961 Jews made up two-thirds of the white Freedom Fighters who traveled into the South to desegregate interstate transportation. Three years later Jews comprised from one-third to one-half of the Mississippi Summer volunteers."[12] They engaged in teaching literacy skills to Blacks, registering voters, and doing other political work amid the threat and the reality of bombings, jailings, beatings, shootings. Synagogues as well as churches were bombed during those years for their support of this campaign. Two of the civil rights workers slain in 1964 were Jewish.

However, as with the involvement of Jewish CP members in various anti-racist struggles, the relationship of white Jews to the civil rights movement had its limitations. Some Jewish liberals fully supported the civil rights movement but, like their non-Jewish white allies, knew little of Black people, little of racism more subtle than that manifested by separate drinking fountains, back-of-the-bus seating for Blacks, and the denial of voting rights. In addition, politically active whites—Jewish and non-Jewish—brought to the civil rights struggle their own assumptions about race, expressed in some instances as paternalism or as the romanticizing of Black lives.

A central issue is how to hold onto a Jewish progressive and anti-racist tradition without ignoring the areas in which its intent or action has not been what it might have. Again, the issue involves joint identity, the way in which white-skin privilege—and the assumptions that can accompany it—exist side-by-side with that tradition. How, for example, can the anti-racist work done by white Jewish people be acknowledged—and criticized—without being either dismissed or glorified? How can we get beyond the ways in which that history has been used and reinterpreted to see what was actually there?

The role of white Jews in the civil rights movement has been viewed from a number of perspectives. In the late Sixties, for example, some Black Power advocates saw the involvement of whites in that earlier movement as almost entirely negative, as an attempt to dominate their politics. In some instances, they expressed their anger, however justified, against someone white and Jewish as anti-Semitism, not as anti-white rage or a diatribe against the actions of a specific white person. The publication of the Afro-American Research Institute in New York City, *The Liberator,* for instance, ran a series of 1966 articles that describe the activism of Jews in this movement as "this diseased Zionist influence" intended to control Black activism.[13] And in *The Crisis of the Negro Intellectual* (1967), Harold Cruse scapegoats Jews in the civil rights movement and elsewhere for many of the problems faced by Black people, and even for *causing* anti-Jewish prejudices among them.[14]

Neither of these publications went unchallenged within the Black community. Both James Baldwin and Ossie Davis resigned from *The Liberator's* advisory board, decrying the immoral, "wild and unsupported contentions" made in the series; Davis argued against the idea that there was "a gigantic plot to dupe and take advantage of Negroes, a deliberate agreed-upon 'Zionist,' 'Jewish Community,' 'Semitic' plot against Negroes."[15] Robert Chrisman, editor of *The Black Scholar*, objected in his review to the "vicious anti-Semitism throughout...[Cruse's] work."[16] But for some Black political leaders, as well, no doubt, as for some Blacks who were not public figures, the concerns expressed by Baldwin, Davis, and Chrisman remained unimportant compared to the opportunity to criticize white Jews in terms of their Jewish identity, rather than in terms of the skin-privilege that unbalanced their relationship within and outside civil rights organizations.

For the Northern Jews who had gone South out of the belief, in part, that racism was *there*, the political shift from a Southern to a national focus underscored far more than their intense anti-Southern bias. Returning to the changing political landscape of their own neighborhoods, some of these Jews found themselves on the sidelines of—and even occasionally opposed to—Black demands for quality education, job opportunities, and community control of local services and institutions. Even for those who maintained their political activism in other arenas, the *option* remained for them because of their race to leave the movement to go back home—to college, to jobs—and make it, or attempt to make it, as people who were both Jewish and white.

If rage at the exercise of white-skin privilege, during and after the civil rights movement, has resulted in some expressions of anti-Semitism by Black people, the active role of Jews in the civil rights movement has been misused by some Jews in ways that are clearly racist. So Rabbi Jay Kaufmann wrote in 1969:

> Jewish organizations labored alongside of and for a period *even prior to* Negro organizations to combat anti-Negro prejudice, to break down employment barriers, to gain equal rights for Negroes. Jews had already learned, *and subsequently helped Negroes understand*, that the democratic creed notwithstanding, neither freedom nor liberty nor equality are automatically granted to the out-groups . . . so Jews *volunteered* their experience, energies, expertness and together with Negroes were *comrades in combat* in a long and vigorous association in behalf of the Negro advance. (my emphasis)[17]

In just a few patronizing sentences, Rabbi Kaufmann manages to overlook several centuries of Black people *initiating* anti-racist activities that go back to the very beginning of the slave trade. He ignores both formal organizations and spontaneous protests: petition drives for legal redress, slave revolts, Underground Railroad networks.[18] He suggests as well that a people brought here as slaves actually need a people who never had that status in this country to teach *them* to be wary about "the democratic creed"; he subsumes under the term "comrades in combat" any distinction between the day-to-day danger faced by Blacks and by white Jews in this country.

Unfortunately, Rabbi Kaufmann's words are only one variation on a theme. A Jewish friend told me the following story: A friend of hers went to a synagogue where she heard a rabbi expressing disappointment and anger at Black people's lack of support of Jews on a given issue; he argued that Jews deserved support because they had stood up for Blacks during the civil rights period. The congregation listened attentively, occasionally nodding in agreement. After he had gone on for some time, her friend got up angrily and asked people in the crowded room to stand if they had actually gone South to participate in the civil rights movement. Nobody stood up.

As I move into a more detailed discussion of racism and anti-Semitism within the women's movement itself, the above exchange, as well as the general issues of history, politics, and tradition, raises, I think, central questions, especially for those of us who are Jewish and white. In terms of Jewish oppression and racism, when *do* we stand up and *how* do we do so? Do we fully comprehend the differences between having confronted either oppression yesterday or in 1963 and our readiness to do so tomorrow? Do we have expectations of people of color in terms of their response to our anti-racism in a specific instance or over an extended period of time? How can we acknowledge that we have done something anti-racist while recognizing both our white-skin privilege and the possibility that we did not confront racism as effectively as we might —because of our limited insight or self-awareness, our inability to act as we wanted, our failure to work cooperatively with one or more individuals with whom we might be in full or partial agreement?

How do we raise issues of anti-Semitism with non-Jewish people of color in ways that have the best possible chance of being heard and acted upon? Can we do so in ways that do not reflect our own racism and that avoid placing racism and Jewish oppression in competition with each other? How do we view earlier political movements that appear flawed to us—in a major or a minor way—but which included a notable number of white Jews who were seriously and actively committed to combatting racism? What steps do we take to create a feminist theory that fully incorporates anti-Semitism and racism into its analysis of woman-hating? How do we engage in political activism that rests on such theory?

VI. THE MALE ENEMY/ THE LEFT ENEMY

The Cold War and the anti-Communist witch hunts of the late Forties and early Fifties devastated the progressive community in ways that scarred subsequent years of activism. As Anne Braden, a white Southern woman with decades of anti-racist work behind her, has said, "The new [Civil Rights] Movement developed with no direct links to its predecessor movements. Without doubt, it was impoverished by that fact."[1] I believe that in many ways the women's movement shares that lack of connection, that impoverishment. It might be more accurate to say that, even where direct links with past struggles exist, the tendency has all too often been not to see them, not to acknowledge them, or, in some instances, to acknowledge them only for the sake of angrily denying their usefulness. The practical effect of such responses on feminist opposition to anti-Semitism and racism has been significant.

In some parts of the women's movement, it is anathema for women to claim a tradition which involves men as well as women. In others, radical politics which are not an integral part of the women's movement are not seen as containing value, or men are not seen as anything but oppressors. In "Sisterhood—And My Brothers," Rima Shore raises one challenge to these assumptions:

> As the politics of identity play an increasing role in our community, I find myself baffled at conflicting claims on my loyalty. We are being urged, and urging each other, to acknowledge and to reclaim the cultures from which we have emerged. . . . Am I to value the culture from which my family came, while dismissing the family itself? Do I seek to identify with Jews in the abstract, but not with the brothers I have loved all my life?[2]

Outside of a family context, these questions are equally pertinent: Am I to value the "culture from which my family came while dismissing" anything men in that family have done? "Do I seek to identify with Jews in the abstract," but not identify with Jewish men who, on a personal and political level, might very well enrage me with their woman-hatred, their homophobia? Women of color confront parallel questions. For women of both groups, the answers inform our most basic analysis of racism and anti-Semitism, and affect our first steps in formulating opposition to these oppressions.

Many women who identify themselves as "radical feminists" have based their theory on the idea that woman-hating is the primary oppression, the one which most fully explains other oppressions.[3] As with any politics based on a hierarchy of oppressions, the resulting schema implies that oppressions which are less than "primary" are of subordinate importance and political urgency. While an understanding of men as oppressors of women is an absolutely essential and major part of any analysis, an approach which concentrates almost solely on sexism can skew the overall picture.

Thus far, objections to such formulations and their practical impact have been made primarily in relation to racism. The political beliefs of the Combahee River Collective, for example, challenge the validity of any theory based on the concept of a "primary oppression":

> We believe that sexual politics under patriarchy is as pervasive in Black women's lives as are the politics of class and race. We also often find it difficult to separate race from class from sex oppression because in our lives they are most often experienced simultaneously. We know that there is such a thing as racial-sexual oppression which is neither solely racial nor solely sexual, e.g., the history of rape of Black women by white men as a weapon of political repression.
>
> Although we are feminists and lesbians, we feel solidarity with progressive black men. . . . We struggle together with Black men against racism, while we also struggle with Black men about sexism.[4]

In "An Open Letter to Mary Daly," Audre Lorde comments more directly on radical feminist theory:

> The oppression of women knows no ethnic nor racial boundaries, true, but that does not mean it is identical within these boundaries. Nor do the reservoirs of our ancient power know these boundaries, either. To deal with one without even alluding to the other is to distort our commonality as well as our difference.
>
> For then beyond sisterhood, is still racism.[5]

Kalpana Ram is likewise strongly critical of a white Western radical feminist theory which locates women's oppression solely within *"the patriarchal psychology of the male,"* without reference to *"the complex interactions between patriarchal and non-patriarchal social forces which have shaped the position of women in Third World societies."*[6] Prior to discussing sexual violence in the lives of the Dalit and Adivisi women of India, Ram writes about radical feminism:

> *A feminist analysis should be capable of theoretically incorporating a recognition that there is a real intermeshing of these different forms of oppression, and that women located at the intersection of these forms have more than one struggle on their hands.*[7]

Ram's comments have implications too for the way in which radical feminist theory subsumes Jew-hating beneath woman-hating. Daly's *Gyn/Ecology*, for instance, insufficiently incorporates an understanding of racism into its analysis and fails to take account of the full lives of women of color. Daly's writing also effectively reduces the power of anti-Semitism *in itself* as a motivating force in the attempted annihilation of the Jewish people. Speaking of the Nazis, Daly points out that, "although their victims—mental patients and Jews—were of both sexes, all were cast in the victim role modeled on that of the victims of patriarchal gynocide, which is the root and paradigm for genocide"[8]; men could thereby rationalize the killing of other men *if* the victim was first forced into a powerless, and therefore feminized, role. Might we at least consider the possibility that the Nazis *began* with a deep loathing of their victims, initially saw them as defective and subhuman, and *therefore* cast them into "the victim role"? Or the possibility that, in relation to the Jews, the Nazi's Jew-hating meshed with their woman-hating so that the feminized victim role seemed the "appropriate" one for Jewish men?

In the conclusion to this section of *Gyn/Ecology*, Daly writes:

> The Holocaust of the Jews in Nazi Germany was a reality of indescribable horror. Precisely for this reason we should not *settle* for an analysis which fails to go to the roots of the evil of genocide. The deepest meanings of the banality of evil are *lost* in the kind of research which *shrinks/localizes perspectives on oppression* so that they can be *contained strictly within ethnic and "religious group" dimensions.* The sado-rituals of patriarchy are perpetually perpetrated. Their plane/domain is the entire planet. The paradigm and context for genocide is trite, everyday, banalized gynocide. (my emphasis)[9]

I hardly think that it "shrinks/localizes perspectives on oppression" to contend that the "context" for the Holocaust is not gynocide, but "trite, everyday, banalized" anti-Semitism: specifically the German variety which goes back to Martin Luther and earlier, constituted a major strain in German political life from the late 19th century on, and was codified into German law after Hitler took power. What are the implications for acknowledging Jewish oppression as a significant and dangerous issue in times less extreme than the Nazi era if *even* the Holocaust is seen as inadequately described by the repeated statements of Nazi leaders and generations of political theorists before them which express loathing of Jews simply because we are Jews?

My comments here on *Gyn/Ecology* are less important than the fact that Daly's discussion of the Holocaust, published in 1978, has, to my knowledge, not been criticized by the many reviewers and feminist authors who have written about the book. While working in 1980 on "Racism and Writing: Some Implications for White Feminist Critics," which contained an examination of racist assumptions in *Gyn/Ecology*, I privately noted the objections I've just raised, but chose not to include them in my article. Both Daly's analysis and the lack of critical attention it received underscore the fact that in the writing of those years the issue of anti-Semitism was raised far less frequently among feminists, Jewish and non-Jewish, than it is now.

Unfortunately, the radical feminist assumptions of Daly's work continue to be found in a considerable amount of writing by white feminists. Such theory has been accepted by some women *as a given*, so that neither its assumptions nor its implications are subject to examination and possible reconsideration. In a 1982 review of Sylvia Plath's collected poems, for example, Mary Kurtzman notes:

> *As so many modern women writers remind us,* we are Jews in a Nazi world. (Some critics are outraged that Sylvia would feel as oppressed as a Jew. Not only are half of all Jews women, but as Daly, Rich, Barry, Chernin, Dworkin, and the rest of the feminists writing on violence against women have shown, *men's violence against women is the ultimate in violence.)* (my emphasis)[10]

The Holocaust is here reduced to a convenient metaphor. Plath's very real oppression as a wife and a mother, as a woman poet trying to make it in a man's world, is thereby portrayed as equivalent, at least, to that suffered by "Jews in a Nazi world." The accuracy of such a comparison does not need to be explored: a certain kind of white feminist theory has already assured us that the "ultimate" oppression is men's violence against women. It will, no doubt, be good news for the massacred Indian, the lynched Black, the gassed Jew, the A-bombed Japanese to know that they have suffered something less than "the ultimate in violence."

Both the assumption that violence against women is the ultimate in violence and the subsequent devaluation of violence against males of oppressed groups are fundamental even to the radical feminist theory propounded by Andrea Dworkin, a Jewish feminist who has spoken and written about the dangers of anti-Semitism.[11] In *Pornography: Men Possessing Women,* Dworkin analyzes the situation of Jewish women in particular and then broadens her comments to include Blacks and other groups of people. Writing about "the concentration camp woman, a Jew," Dworkin says:

> It is her existence that has defined contemporary mass sexuality, given it its distinctly and unabashedly mass-sadistic character. The Germans had her, had the power to make her. The others want her, want the power to make her. And it must be said that the male of a racially despised group suffers because he has been kept from having her, from having the power to make her. He may mourn less what has happened to her than that he did not have the power to do it. When he takes back his manhood, he takes her back, and on her he avenges himself: through rape, prostitution, and forced pregnancy; through despising her, his contempt expressed in art and politics and pleasure. This avenging—the reclamation of masculinity—is evident among Jewish and black males, though it is in no way limited to them.[12]

Dworkin simply assures us that these men "*may* mourn less what has happened to . . . [Jewish women] than that they did not have the power to do it" (my emphasis). Dworkin's statement is surrounded by what we know to be true—"The Germans had her"; by supposition presented as fact—"The male of the racially despised group suffers because he has been kept from having her"; and by what we know to be true of some Jewish men in "normal" times—the victimization of Jewish women through "rape, prostitution, and forced pregnancy . . . ." Is this sufficient to convince us that countless Jewish men felt no anguish for the pain, the very survival of their mothers, their wives, their daughters, their lovers, their female comrades, but felt only sexual jealousy of the Nazis who had the power to rape them? When she says that Jewish male inmates "want the power to make her," Dworkin is speaking of desire not only for sex but for rape. Doesn't this characterization of *all* Jewish male inmates deserve to be supported by something stronger than conjecture?

Dworkin's reference to Black males suggests that she would argue in much the same way about their view of Black women, *even* in situations in which Black people have suffered most deeply from white barbarism.

As a feminist who has counseled rape victims, has spoken with and found shelter for battered women, and who, like women all over the world, knows women among those I love who have been raped and abused by men, I have no illusions about the physical danger to women of the male-female power dynamic in this or other societies. But I fear the practice emerging from a theory which, in the attempt to object loudly and strenuously and justifiably to woman-hating, skims lightly over other oppressions.

It is quite different, as Melanie Kaye/Kantrowitz has done, to find heroes in those Jewish women who fought against the Nazis in ghettos or concentration camps, or, as Paula Gunn Allen has done, to celebrate a tradition of spiritually powerful Indian women.[13] Neither negates the woman- or dyke-hating within the oppressed group *itself*. Neither diminishes the level of violence visited upon all Jews, all Native Americans, regardless of sex, by those who consider them less-than-human and therefore more-than-expendable. Neither denies that, as victims, the women in these groups suffer additionally *as women* at the hands of the male of the dominant race, the dominant religion. And certainly the complexity of identities, of oppressions, gets addressed in Elana Dyke-womon's yet unanswered question—how to say:

> . . . I am a lesbian and I am a jew, and I am fighting back. Without giving any encouragement to jewish men, without making them feel like they still have a claim and a right to you, without denying them in such a way that it causes you to be self-hating.
>   That question.[14]

"That question" is critical, and not just for those who share Dyke-womon's separatist politics. As a feminist, as a lesbian, I know that I do not want to assert my Jewish identity, to oppose a range of oppressions, in a way that encourages any men to feel like "they still have a claim and a right" to me. But I will support a politics that mourns all of the Jews locked in Soviet prisons, all of the Palestinians massacred at Sabra and Shatila—regardless of sex—even though such politics are shared by men whose sexism and homophobia I have also to confront.

The focus on woman-hating in radical feminist theory represents a necessary and valuable attempt, too often marred by white and Western solipsism, to grasp the global meaning of women's oppression. Yet this theory has also helped create such an atmosphere of hostility to the men on the left and men working in progressive causes that they end up looking practically indistinguishable from the men of the right. The equation of left with right has become something of a radical feminist stock in trade. In the middle Seventies, I heard a well-known lesbian-feminist say offhandedly at a workshop that the male left is the same as the male right. Her point was not simply that rampant sexism exists among men of all political perspectives or that woman-hating is totally unacceptable from men with otherwise progressive politics (both positions I share), but that left and right are the same in the sense that one is no more positive than the other. This ideology has persisted through the Seventies and on into the Eighties. Dworkin, for instance, one of the most vocal anti-leftists among radical feminist theorists, uses "left" as a pejorative term, sometimes accurate, sometimes not, to describe some of those men whose woman-hating is a matter of public record. In *Right-Wing Women*, she manages to mention no more than a half-dozen male leftists, but goes on for pages about "the left."

The "boys of the Sixties" have a well-documented record of sexist actions and words. Sara Evans, Robin Morgan, Marge Piercy, and others have described the dynamic between white "Movement" women and men in the late Sixties.[15] Although the women's movement has had an impact on a huge number of women and some men since then, sexism within the left is still alive and kicking—and women are still being kicked. But the fight against sexism is not helped by presenting a skewed picture. That Dworkin quotes two male leftists, one white, one Black, who oppose abortion does not mean that the left *per se* opposes abortion, any more than a couple of well-chosen examples of *virulent* anti-Semitism or racism within the women's movement would *prove* that the movement as a whole maintains such values.[16] Dworkin is not deterred from making generalizations by events which contradict her views: the presence of women and men from *some* left groups at pro-choice demonstrations against President Carter's Secretary of Health, Education, and Welfare Joseph Califano, and their presence at the protest in Cherry Hill, New Jersey at the National Right-to-Life Convention; the membership of a number of left groups in the Reproductive Rights National Network; the stated pro-choice position of many single- or multi-issue left or progressive groups. "Men do not have principles or political agendas not congruent with the sex they want," Dworkin writes about "the left."[17] And, if, as she assures us, they are *all* like that, feminists are wrongheaded to seek alliances in that quarter.

Within parts of the women's community, the male enemy/left enemy formulation serves as a handy deterrent to women's stepping out of line and considering issues in ways which involve serious political criticism of radical feminist theory. When I discussed the racism in *Gyn/Ecology* in *Sinister Wisdom 13*, for example, I received letters which accused me of "male modes of thinking" and suggested that I had "left sympathies." My failing, as far as I could tell, was that I *assumed* that the racism affecting men—the Asian men victimized by Western stereotypes and U.S. bombs, the Afro-American man randomly shot because of his color, not his sex—was both dreadful in itself *and* an inherent part of the racism which affects women of color on a day-to-day basis. Tossed like rotten tomatoes to splatter all over my argument, the terms "male" and "left" were clearly meant to obliterate any validity in what I had written.

Such responses have, in fact, silenced me, and, I suspect, other women. In 1981, when *Sinister Wisdom* published an excerpt from *Pornography*, I objected strongly to Dworkin's distortions of the left. The inaccurate picture she presented undercut the possibility of effective organizing against the right wing in this country. I was angry enough to write, but I chose to send the letter to the editors as a personal correspondence, not for publication. I was not willing, as the Native American poet Chrystos has written at the beginning of an article about lesbian separatism, "to declare . . . [my] purity and credentials—number of years a lesbian, number of women loved, sufferings encountered as a result of, etc.,"[18] or to offer any analogous declaration in order to avoid having my argument consigned to the scrap heap of work by those who are clearly anti-woman pawns of the male left.

My caution was not misplaced. After reading a copy of that letter, a co-worker who strongly supported Dworkin's work and was well aware of my feminist activities over the years suddenly asked me what I thought of the recent charges of sexual harrassment made by several women in Boston against leftist professor Sidney Peck. I was a bit astounded, since I had never considered believing anybody but the women. But the implication was clear: making anything short of a blanket condemnation of the left makes one immediately suspect; criticizing someone who has so consistently equated the male enemy with the left enemy raises grave suspicions.

At the center of much feminist anti-leftism rests the familiar hierarchy of oppressions with sexism/gynephobia sitting unchallenged at its pinnacle. In practical political terms, this theoretical tenet implies that the pain of sexism justifies dismissing the left and seeing it as a monolithic political movement in which woman-hating and homophobia are constants. Ironically, that part of the left which sees class at the pinnacle of *its* hierarchy dismisses the women's movement wholesale for classism and for the failure to share a particular left political schema. In both instances, "other" oppressions tend to slide through the cracks.

The history of the women's movement, for instance, is certainly as replete with racism and classism and Jew-hating as the history of the left is replete, in addition to these biases, with sexism. Yet within those spheres of the women's movement which are overwhelmingly white and lesbian, largely middle-class in background or current lifestyle, heavily populated by women whose own *central* experience of oppression has been sexual, one movement is damned for its sexism and the other accepted with its flaws and the belief that work will continue to be done on its own prejudices. I fully support continued strenuous criticism of the left—by feminists who define themselves as leftists and by those who do not—both for acts of individual oppression by men against women and for group failures to take strong, active, consistent pro-woman stands based on political principle, not on opportunism. But I distinguish such responsible criticism from the kind of knee-jerk anti-leftism which can play into the hands of the right-wing powers that control this country.

Too often both feminist theory and feminist activism have developed in isolation from work that men—or women working in groups with men—are doing. What effect does theory which presents the world in dichotomized terms—good women vs. bad men—have on the fight against Jewish oppression and racism? At one level, I think that such theory can discourage some women even from *learning* about issues which have been central concerns of the left, concerns which are central as well to groups of Jews, people of color, and others who might not define themselves as leftists: apartheid, the Israeli-Palestinian conflict, police brutality, U.S. policy in Central America. On another level, I think that it can discourage some women from *learning* about mixed groups which are combatting racism and anti-Semitism: the National Anti-Klan Network, New Jewish Agenda, the Southern Poverty Law Center, and other organizations. Additionally, it can discourage some women from *considering* participating in demonstrations organized by groups or coalitions which include men, whether these demonstrations are against the closing of Sydenham Hospital in Harlem, against the Israeli invasion of Lebanon, or against the not guilty verdict in the Greensboro shooting by the Nazis and the Klan. What gets categorized—and dismissed—as the "left" includes any number of mixed groups whose politics can be called left or progressive or radical. While major political differences might exist between these groups and any number of women's organizations, as well as between individuals in each group, the differences do not cancel out the fact that on the right-to-left spectrum of U.S. politics, where power is clearly in the hands of the right, women's interests are far better served by politics that fall definitively on the left of that spectrum. Reagan administration policies have illustrated this all too painfully.

I am assuming here that each woman needs to decide where and how to be most politically effective. As someone who has worked almost entirely in all-women's groups, I am well aware of the impact that such groups can have, both within the women's/lesbian community and as a visible feminist presence in progressive coalitions. And I know that many issues central to women's lives have only been addressed because of the presence of an autonomous women's movement. But I do not believe it is harder for me to cope with the sexism I encounter at a demonstration, meeting, or conference attended by men than it is for a woman of color to cope with the racism of an all-woman's group or demonstration. Classism, anti-Semitism, and other oppressions can present equally severe obstacles to participation in certain groups. Yet I have spoken to a number of white women who, though they would not consider working in organizations with men, *assume,* for example, the positive value of women of color participating in groups that would require them to work closely with white women. Again, the implication that sexism is more painful, more damaging, and more central affects political theories, expectations, and actions.

While one prevalent strain of anti-leftism within the women's movement results from a critique of sexism, another strain results from a critique of Jewish oppression. Within the women's movement, the latter represents a more recent public development, and is the consequence of the growing amount of discussion, writing, and activism on the part of Jewish women regarding anti-Semitism. Some Jewish women who support the anti-leftism emerging from this concern with anti-Semitism might also see sexism as the primary oppression. Others might have long defined their politics in terms of a *simultaneity* of oppressions. Still others, in the course of working out the ramifications of their own Jewish identities, seem to be in some process of rethinking and rejecting a radical feminist theory which gives insufficient weight to Jewish oppression (as to racism).

Regardless of the history of each woman's perspective on the left, it is unlikely that she has remained unaffected by the anti-leftism of so much feminist writing.[19] She might also have been influenced by the early anti-Communism and more recent anti-leftism expressed in parts of the Jewish establishment, which has itself been motivated by genuine concern about left anti-Semitism, together, in some cases, with the desire to keep as much distance as possible from unpopular, government-investigated, and/or radical politics.

Whatever the political background and motivation of individuals, a consequence of such anti-leftism in the women's movement has already been felt. A number of statements have been made which, in their opposition to Jewish oppression, present the left as a bloc and totally ignore the existence of a Jewish left which is quite different from the New Left. In a letter to *off our backs* protesting its publication of Women Against Imperialism's anti-Jewish statement, Bat Deborah comments: "Left-wing politics, *exactly like* right-wing politics, has *always* been rabidly anti-Semitic . . ." (my emphasis).[20] Her statement ignores the organizing against anti-Semitism by Jewish socialist movements in Europe and by Jewish socialists in this country: those who began the *Jewish Daily Forward* in 1897; those who established the Workmen's Circle in 1892 and made it a national organization in 1900; those who formed "the first American branch of the [Jewish Labor] Bund . . . in 1900."[21] Her statement also excludes Jewish-identified radicals from the left, including, for instance, those Jews who, as Communist Party members during the Popular Front period of the middle- to late-Thirties, supported a law which would make illegal "the propagation of anti-Semitism"[22] and militantly opposed Nazism.

Outside of the Jewish left, a "radical" ideology which has been hostile to religion and many forms of ethnic identification has intersected with societally prevalent anti-Jewish attitudes.[23] Historically, left political analysis has tended to portray class or, in some cases, race and imperialism, as primary. Within this framework, the oppression of Jews *as Jews* gets, at best, subordinated to these concerns, at times to the point of invisibility. Sometimes the argument is used that Jews who do not suffer economic or racial oppression cannot "really" be oppressed. The value of being strongly Jewish-identified is challenged, and common anti-Jewish stereotypes are incorporated into a particular left analysis. Communist Party policies changed dramatically, so that the CP moved directly from the Popular Front period to support of the 1939 Nazi-Soviet non-aggression pact; many members of the CP did not know, while others chose not to see, the tremendous extent of Soviet repression of Jews. More recently, a John Brown Anti-Klan Committee pamphlet makes no mention of Jews as targets of Klan hatred and violence; although *Big Mama Rag* has "both written and spoken" to Committee members about "their very obvious omission . . . they have never responded."[24] A woman from a left group maintains at a public forum that the onus for the anti-Semitism of progressives is on "the Jewish community" itself because it is, she says, racist and reactionary. She apparently thinks it quite acceptable to blame Jews for the oppression *they* suffer and to make general statements about the entire Jewish community based on the politics and actions of some of its members. The All-African People's Revolutionary Party distributes an anti-Zionist leaflet depicting Jews as arch-capitalists, arch-imperialists, arch-racists: "It was Jewish mercantile capital which financed the voyages of Columbus and da Gama. It was Jewish capital which financed slavery and the slave trade. It was Jewish capital which financed the invasion and colonization of Africa, the Middle East and the Western Mediterranean."[25]

As with the women's movement, a number of such examples do not illustrate that the left as a whole—or all its adherents—maintain anti-Jewish attitudes or would be unwilling to condemn their expression. Certainly anti-Semitism on the left is no more excusable than that on the right. But it does not benefit Jewish history and our understanding of Jewish oppression to paint the left as *uniformly* anti-Jewish and to ignore that part of the left which, in both Europe and the United States, has been created out of a "consciousness of uniquely Jewish needs and dilemmas."[26]

Some of the complexity of this situation is suggested in "That's Funny, You Don't Look Anti-Semitic: Perspective on the American Left," published in the 1977 anthology of the Chutzpah Collective, a group that is part of the Jewish left. Steven Lubet and Jeffry (Shaye) Mallow write:

> In this article we refer to a Left with an apparent majority which is hostile to the Jews. We must point out, however, that we ourselves are leftists . . . . Some individual leftists have . . . expressed to us their disgust at the anti-semitic attitudes of many "progressive" organizations. Thus, we are not referring to our allies and potential allies when we excoriate "the Left" in this article, rather, we hope that our analysis will help others speak out more clearly against the anti-semites.[27]

Still, given the presence of anti-Semitism on the left, it is relatively easy to understand why such distinctions are not necessarily made in critiques of left anti-Semitism, as, for instance, analogous distinctions are not necessarily made by women of color in critiques of white feminist racism. As Irena Klepfisz has written in an excellent article, "Resisting and Surviving America":

> There is a danger, I believe, from the Left as well, and this includes the Jewish Left—especially those in the Jewish Left who are embarrassed about being Jewish. Who will only say that Jews are guilty of this or that. Who never express any pride or love or affection or attachment to their Jewishness. Who only declare their Jewishness after making an anti-Semitic statement, as if ending such a statement with "Well, I'm Jewish" makes it all right, acceptable. That too enrages and frightens me. Those of the Left, Jew and non-Jew alike, seem to believe what the Right has always maintained—that Jews run the world and are, therefore, most responsible for its ills. The casualness, the indifference with which the Left accepts this anti-Semitic stance enrages me. It is usually subtle, often taking the form of anti-Semitism by *omission*. Its form is to show or speak about Jews *only* as oppressors, never as anything else. That is anti-Semitic.[28]

I am in fundamental agreement with the main points of this statement:

that the serious danger of anti-Semitism can come from the left as well as the right; that some Jews within the left contribute to this danger. And recently I attended two events at which at least a dozen leftists identified themselves as Jewish just before making some vigorously anti-Jewish statement. But Klepfisz' comments are so sweeping that they seem to reflect a far different attitude toward it from that of Lubet and Mallow, one which implies that the left is both monolithic and bad.

At least as troublesome for me is the implication that "the Jewish Left" is the same as "Jews in the Left." Since Klepfisz has written elsewhere about the role of the Jewish left in the Warsaw Ghetto resistance and spoken at events organized by sectors of today's Jewish left, this equation seems inadvertent. Still, the reader of her critique is very likely to come away without knowing that a Jewish left presently exists and that it should not be confused with Jews who identify with segments of the sectarian or independent left which are anti-Jewish.

I don't think that those of us who are Jewish need to identify as part of the Jewish left to find something positive in the knowledge that it does, indeed, exist, and that it is, among other things, concerned in a major way with Jewish oppression. We do not have to embrace the left to benefit from knowing that there are independent left or progressive Jewish groups committed to fighting racism, supporting women's and lesbian and gay rights, favoring affirmative action, backing Israeli and Palestinian self-determination, opposing military and trade assistance to South Africa, and combatting the arms race, U.S. militarism and intervention in the Third World. And it is valuable to know, even when we might not be in agreement with all of their political positions, that, among other periodicals, we can read *genesis 2*, "an independent voice for Jewish renewal," publishing since 1970; *Israel & Palestine*, since 1971 "an independent monthly providing free expression for all those who did not share the official positions of the Israeli Establishment and the Palestinian Establishment, as reflected in the PLO Charter"[29]; *Jewish Currents*, pro-Israel, non-Zionist magazine that has been publishing independently since 1956; *New Outlook*, "dedicated to the search for peace in the Middle East and to cooperation and development of all the area's people"; and *shmate*, a new "journal of progressive Jewish thought."

The dismissal of the left, the paucity of information about the Jewish left in many sectors of the women's movement, does not assist any of us in seeking to criticize Jewish oppression and racism in ways which recognize the uniqueness and danger of each. As those of us who are white attempt to combat racism, we have much to learn from the ways in which some left groups have already done so. Similarly, the commitment within the Jewish left to oppose anti-Semitism and racism in a responsible way that minimizes neither can provide those of us who are Jewish with models which can be adapted to the political circumstances in which each of us finds herself, even where we think that a group has not adequately reached its political goal or is lacking in committed opposition to sexism or homophobia or other oppressions.

Working outside of a framework in which the words and actions of those in the Jewish left can be scrutinized for what can be learned from them, Jewish feminists run the risk of neglecting valuable models which are not specifically feminist. A consequence is a certain amount of "reinventing the wheel" which tends, I think, to affect the women's movement in a number of areas: the belief that something totally new has been developed when a similar version, relevant to a feminist context, has long been in existence, but outside the women's movement. Certainly, Jewish feminists bring to politics an unprecedented commitment to issues affecting us directly as Jews, as women, and, for many of us, as lesbians. But the dismissal of the Jewish left means that this political work has a far shakier foundation than is necessary.

The dominant society would have us believe that racism and anti-Semitism are oppressions to be pitted against one another, that opposition to one precludes serious opposition to the other, that Jews and people of color should be at each other's throats—and that Jews of color don't even exist. We cannot afford to dismiss any potentially useful models of ways to reject these destructive dichotomies and move beyond them to creative political action.

VII. BREAKING A CYCLE

The pitting of anti-Semitism and racism against each other, the pressure to see opposing them in either/or terms, arguments about the degrees of oppression, degrees of opposition—all are part of a cycle of competition which is oiled by the powers that be, and is often played into by those of us with relatively little power. The tension lurks at or just below the surface, ready to break out when some balance is not achieved, when some full acknowledgment is not granted to one group or the other. Sometimes the comparisons, the contrasts, the weighings are unavoidable. Sometimes they are done in ways that reflect one person's racism, another's anti-Semitism.

The cycle is fueled, in part, by what Melanie Kaye/Kantrowitz has called "the 'scarcity' theory of political struggle,"[1] the false assumption that ultimately one must choose which of the two oppressions to confront, that one cannot choose to oppose both. A Black woman ends an article on racism with a footnote that gratuitously explains why, in contrast to Blacks, Jews cannot properly be called an oppressed group.[2] Some Jewish women resent the visibility thus far of Third World women in the movement, the attention they see given to racism as opposed to Jewish oppression. Women Against Imperialism, a group of non-Jewish and Jewish white women, argues against "putting more energy into the issue of Jewish oppression than into the much more basic issue of support for [Third World] liberation struggles."[3]

Despite these arguments, despite the tangle of issues and the tensions within and between groups, feminists—Jewish and non-Jewish, Third World and white—have in the last few years increasingly acknowledged the ways that Jewish oppression and racism intersect; how, together and individually, they anger, hurt, endanger, divide us. In the process, strong feminist statements have been made which have refused the divisions.

Writing about being fired from a large Southwestern state university, Melanie Kaye/Kantrowitz has described how the anti-Jewish attitudes in the women's studies program merged with the specific "assumption, that to be a strongly identified Jew *meant* being less anti-racist, as though the struggles were mutually exclusive or, worse, antagonistic . . . ."[4] The subsequent dismissal by the white Christian coordinator of Kaye/Kantrowitz, "the only identified Jew in the program—and the only out dyke,"[5] left her clear about the various strains of bias—including classism—which had combined to get her fired. It also left her clear about her own belief that "there is no contradiction between being a proud Jew and a fighter against racism. I fight against racism because I am a Jew; because my Jewish parents taught me to hate injustice and cruelty; and because I know danger when I smell it."[6]

A similar argument is asserted by the lesbians from the Necessary Bread Affinity Group, "northern Black and southern white; Anglo, Jewish, daughters of engineers and domestic workers . . . . first- and tenth-generation Americans, Cuban immigrants, transplanted Chicanas." In a statement prepared for the massive June 12, 1982 disarmament demonstration in New York City, Necessary Bread said:

> We know the fear of violence, not just from the Klan and the American Nazi Party, but from the less readily visible, the more "respectable," those who share the anti-Semitism and racism and queer-loathing of these groups, and could find in us "appropriate" targets for hatreds supported by every Establishment institution in this society.
>
> We know too that these threats, these acts of violence are meant to divide us, to make us see each other as the enemy. We refuse to accede to such pressure, regardless of its source.[7]

And the Jewish lesbian group Di Vilde Chayes has written:

> We do not accept the idea that our fight against anti-Semitism robs political energy from our fight against racism. To maintain that all our energy must be devoted to only one of these oppressions is divisive and strategically unsound.[8]

For all of us, Jew and non-Jew, white women and women of color, statements are, naturally, a lot easier to make than to act on. Words on the page are inevitably clearer than the words we must come up with when we have only seconds for a response and probably no time for rethinking or revisions, for putting the emphasis on *this* part of the sentence rather than on *that* one so that our intent is as precise as we can make it.

Surely, statements are far clearer than the plans we make for outreach; the rap we prepare for streetcorner leafletting; the proposals we first make for political action and then reconsider, revise, perhaps defend, probably compromise on at a meeting at which everyone shares neither our individual identity nor our specific political perspective and priorities. And, in any event, we do not yet know how to raise the issues of Jewish oppression *and* racism in the best possible way, or, given the history and complexity of both, in ways that will assure us not only that we have done it well, but that we are likely to be heard.

Certainly, *I* do not know how to do it, especially when the issues intersect: when, for example, my stomach knots up as I pace back and forth, phone in hand, as I struggle for the words that will explain to a woman of color that I am not being "obstinate," as she charges, when I insist that I want to know what work on Jewish oppression another woman of color has done before I agree that she would be a good addition to a racism and anti-Semitism panel; when I struggle for the words that will, at the same time, acknowledge that our discussion is necessarily affected by my being white, by her history of dealing with white women who want simply to exercise power in such a situation. Or when, at a meeting between a Jewish and a Black community group, I search for the language that will respond adequately to a Black man who wonders whether I am not asking an awful lot when I insist that, although he suffers frequently from the racism of people who are white and Jewish, he direct his anger at the whiteness that can allow us certain privileges, not at our Jewishness.

I do not think I am alone among Jewish women in the uncertainty of my reactions, in my frustration at being unable to pull out the exact words at the precise time I need them; in my anger at prejudices that render ineffective the most cogent argument; in my desire to do a better job of fighting Jewish oppression, of confronting racism; in my tendency to play and re-play interactions to try to figure out what I could have done better. Too often the dynamic is so complex that I am lucky to be able to pull apart the strands and look at them in the clear light before I am called upon for a response. Too often the strands will simply not be parted.

While ideally, we should all be actively opposed to every oppression, the reality is that it's exceedingly hard, sometimes near impossible, to work against the oppression of someone whose foot we feel on the back of our neck. The optimum political goal is, I think, quite clear. It is exemplified by the Combahee River Collective statement: "We struggle together with Black men against racism, while we also struggle with Black men about sexism."[9] Achieving a concrete political realization of that formulation is more complicated. The reality is that the racism of many white Jewish women discourages many non-Jewish women of color from strongly confronting Jewish oppression; the anti-Semitism of many non-Jewish women of color discourages many white Jewish women from being strongly anti-racist. The prejudice of each group is often affected by the other's actions. But it is not caused by these actions. Each has a life of its own. Each is the inevitable by-product of the society in which we live. And if a non-Jewish woman of color responds with anti-Semitism to my racism, she is no less responsible for her words and actions than I am for my own; if I counter her anti-Semitism with my own racism, I too play into a cycle that must, at some point, at every point, be broken.

The tendency for feminists to fall into this trap does not single out our movement from the rest of society as any less able to deal politically with these issues. Rather, it marks the women's movement as an extension of the larger society in which the same conflicts get raised with depressing regularity. A Black man objects that when a handful of Jews are killed the news gets front-page coverage in the daily papers, whereas when hundreds of Africans are murdered, the item gets tucked away in fifteen lines on page five; he focuses his anger on the Jews whose suffering has, for the moment, been recognized, rather than on a media that responds to Western political priorities, values the lives of those in the West over those in the Third World, and should be pressured into seeing as equally deplorable, equally newsworthy, deaths anywhere on the globe. A Jewish man objects to affirmative action quotas on the grounds that his Hungarian-born parents managed to pull themselves out of poverty without any such assistance; he focuses his anger on the people of color who benefit from such efforts, rather than on the institutional racism that has kept them from more than token representation in many jobs and professional schools.

For white Jewish feminists, breaking this cycle of competition involves, in part, how we perceive the racism *and* the anti-racism of the women's movement. From a white perspective, it is not all that difficult to overstate the commitment to fighting racism within the movement, and, as a consequence, to skew our expectation of what we can expect from it in opposition to Jewish oppression. Much of it is a question of our angle of vision. For over a decade, many parts of the women's movement have, after all, at least acknowledged racism as a critical issue; in some instances, the opposition to it by white women has gone well beyond acknowledgement. Yet this is a far cry from a movement that is fully dedicated to fighting racism.

The belief that a staunchly anti-racist women's movement exists does not take into account the *major* limitations of the anti-racist work done thus far by those of us who are white. Too often the steps we take are positive, but ultimately or potentially only cosmetic: the inclusion of racism on a list of organizational concerns; the Third World keynote speaker at a largely white feminist conference; the mailings of announcements by a white to a Third World group. Too often we magnify the mostly superficial gains made by women of color within a predominantly white women's movement, and forget their day-to-day encounters with racism.

One example from the 1981 National Women's Studies Conference on racism at the University of Connecticut: Going off campus with a half dozen women, I entered the local ice cream parlor immediately behind a dark-skinned Black woman. As she reached forward to open the restaurant door, she said quietly, but loud enough for me to hear, "Here I come, white folks!" I was momentarily startled, muttered something inane and hardly supportive, and realized that I was quite unprepared for this particular venture into white America. The moment I walked through the door, *my* skin-color did not grab the attention of the white person sitting over a sundae in the booth furthest away from where we entered. A few hours after I had been on a panel on racism in the lesbian community, I could imagine going out for an ice cream as a simple and uncomplicated act.

The world out there brings me up short, reminds me not just of what I have failed to accomplish, but of *why* I am even trying to do anti-racist work. It raises for me too the broader question as to why *anyone* who does not share the most immediate impact of some oppression makes a commitment to combat it. I find one answer in the link between ethics and self-interest. The most effective work by white Jews against racism, for instance, emerges, I think, from some combination of the two, the belief that racism is simply wrong *and* the belief that struggling against it will benefit us personally and politically, that such work, as Black feminist Alice Walker has said about opposition to any oppression, "lightens the load on all of us."[10]

Anti-racist activism by those of us who are white and Jewish in ways that make us visible *as Jews* who are also strongly committed to fighting anti-Semitism has the potential for *supporting* Jewish survival and Jewish concerns through our involvement in coalitions in which anti-Semitism can become integrated into political action and analysis. Such work can make non-Jews look at assumptions in ways that may lead them to rethink stereotypes and reconsider the impression that racism and Jewish oppression are at loggerheads, that one must select one or the other as a political priority.

Although ethics and enlightened self-interest together form an effective motivation for political work, separately they are sorely wanting. Done purely for others without a strong sense of its general benefits, such work can subsequently lead to the expectation of "repayment": "I'll focus on anti-racism in organizing this demonstration, so that later on I can get you to work against Jewish oppression." A consequence can be a surface commitment to the issues, so that they function as bargaining chips in a larger political game. Done solely as a means of raising consciousness, of assuaging guilt, of sharing feelings, the work is dead-ended, a form of political self-improvement quite alien to the kind of activist political perspective described by Mab Segrest when she writes, "whatever consciousness I arrive at through language must also find its expression in activity in the world."[11]

An analogous situation occurs when a non-Jewish woman of color includes anti-Semitism in a list of oppressions and sees Jews as a useful group with whom to work in anti-racist coalitions, but, perhaps talking about *other* women's anti-Jewish attitudes, does not consider her own, and, perhaps accepting without question references to historical and current anti-Semitism, does no work to attain more than a surface knowledge of it. In both cases, the issues remain abstract, picked up in an attempt to be "politically correct," to avoid criticism, to be politically expedient. In both cases, the question is deferred as to how doing such work will change not just the individual, but her relationship with everyone with whom she comes into contact, Jewish and non-Jewish, Third World and white.

Whatever our motivation, we need to begin with a clear sense that the two oppressions operate in the women's movement in different ways, that these differences will affect both analysis and strategy. Historically, as now, women of color in the movement have been excluded, tokenized, placed on a pedestal, and, when they work in autonomous Third World feminist groups, ignored by many white feminists. Frequently inclusion comes late: white women with the economic resources and institutional access to start a project seek Third World feminists to participate only when things are well under way; an issue is defined by white women who then ask women of color to provide input within already established parameters. In these kinds of situations, the women of color function more as political symbols than as individuals: when the participation of one or two or more women of color is used by white women to "prove" to themselves or others that Third World women *as a group* have "endorsed" a particular project or political stance; when white women apply a "dancing dog" double standard to women of color, the wonder being not that they are doing their work well, but that they are doing it at all.[12]

Anti-Semitism in the movement operates differently. Jewish women in the U.S. have been central in the women's movement since its inception, though often not as identifiable Jews. The fact of centrality is difficult even to acknowledge because the standard anti-Jewish response is to see more than token Jewish visibility as a bid for "Jewish control": at the 1981 Women in Print Conference, all of the Jewish women were asked to stand. About a third of the women rose. But the pleasure those of us felt was dashed some time later when a report on the conference cited it as a place where the writer "learned that feminist publishing is controlled by JEWISH-WORKING-CLASS-LESBIANS and the 4-H,"[13] an attempt at humor that simply recalls the stereotype of Jews as in control of the media. For white Jewish women, unlike for women of color, the initial question is not presence but visibility.[14] "The question is," as Evelyn Torton Beck has said, "can Jewish women have a voice as Jewish women? Or is the price of being active and respected to be white but not Jewish?"[15]

While the Women in Print example illustrates an external pressure for Jewish women to be silent as Jews, Jewish oppression also manifests itself in what Letty Cottin Pogrebin has described as the "self-hatred and denial of a part of oneself or one's origins [that] is a kind of *invisibility imposed from within*,"[16] Pogrebin's discussion places this invisibility squarely within a societal context of anti-Semitism that actively fosters self-hatred, rewards assimilation, and defines any visible Jewish presence as "too much." The relative silence among Jewish feminists about Jewish oppression must, I think, be seen within this framework.

It is essential not to fall into the trap of "blaming the victim." However, the responsibility for any silence regarding anti-Semitism has to be shared by those of us who did not *ourselves* raise it. This point is critical because one way in which white Jewish women have seen women of color in competitive terms has to do with the fact that racism is now acknowledged in many parts of the women's movement where Jewish oppression is not. Going from competition to strategizing involves some historically-based understanding of the role of the oppressed in crying out against her oppression, in insisting that it be confronted. While it would be terrific for women to take the initiative to learn about oppressions that do not affect each of us most directly and to be active in opposing them, the unfortunate political reality is that the impetus has almost always come from those groups—lesbians, the disabled, older women, poor women—who suffer the oppression immediately and *demand* that other women pay attention.

Whereas white Jewish women usually have had the option of being in the movement as white women, not as *visible* Jewish women, women of color, except for those relatively few whose skin color, features, and accent allow them to "pass" for white, have *had* to be there as who they were. Certainly whatever attention has been paid to racism by white feminists has resulted from over a decade's worth of women of color consistently and loudly raising that issue inside and outside the women's movement. Although I have long held the idea, for instance, that racism, like other oppressions, was wrong, I have no illusion that I would have even begun to *act* on that anti-racist belief in the absence of the work of women of color. Only later did I develop some sense of how often they spoke, and in how many different ways, before I was able to hear. Repeatedly I notice how often I continue to get caught looking over my left shoulder when the racism is clear as day over my right one.

So, while I want the responsibility for dealing with Jewish oppression to be taken up by non-Jews, I do not expect a whole lot to happen quickly. Anti-Semitism is too deeply ingrained for that. Additionally, I have no reason to believe that non-Jewish women—white women and women of color—learn any faster than I or any of the white women I know. Nothing I have read, nothing in my personal experience, has taught me that anything more than the most superficial acknowledgment of an oppression's presence—and sometimes not even that—will occur without years of groundwork by those on whom it weighs most heavily.[17] As a lesbian, for instance, I have been in many settings— feminist academic, community activist, progressive Jewish—where it remained for the dykes among us to remind people that we were there, that recognizing our existence and concerns in some serious way was not a divergence from the "real" issues. Eventually, where we have stood up often enough over the years, we have not always had to be the ones to remind, to prod, to object.

From this perspective, I am a lot more concerned about the willingness of non-Jewish women to identify and confront Jewish oppression now that it is being raised with considerable consistency within the feminist community by Jewish women. Women need to deal with both racism and anti-Semitism on a day-to-day basis regardless of the actual presence of women of color and/or Jewish women. This is especially critical in the many places in this country where non-Jewish women have little or no contact with Jews and white women have little or no contact with women of color. Although the attendance of only two Jewish women at the 1982 Womanwrites: Southeast Lesbian Writers Conference, for instance, resulted in an extremely small Jewish women's caucus, the non-Jewish women had no less responsibility for addressing the issue of anti-Semitism than if many Jewish women had attended; the responsibility was taken, in part, by a Black woman who, at the conference's closing session, offered an impromptu overview of Black-Jewish relations in the South.

How those of us who are Jewish and white perceive the women's movement—who is definitively in it and who is not, whose presence we experience most immediately—has major implications for the political work we do. We create obstacles to such work when, in the course of arguing for strenuous opposition to anti-Semitism, we do not accurately describe both the degree of the movement's anti-racist commitment and the steps which remain to be taken. One facet of this problem can be illustrated in a 1982 interview with Evelyn Torton Beck. Beginning with the observation about racism that " . . . we have taken a stand as a movement against it, although I don't think we've eradicated it by a long shot," Beck adds:

> I've thought a lot about why our movement has been able and willing to dedicate itself so fully to fighting racism and so unwilling to cover Jewish issues. I think it has partially to do with the fact that Jews have not been so segregated. You can dedicate yourself to fighting racism, because there are groups that have been left out. But Jews *are* very much in the movement; so, if you're going to commit yourself to fighting anti-Semitism, you have to deal with it immediately, on a daily basis—in a way that most white feminists still don't have to deal with women of color because there is still not that much working together. Immediately taking this into your life appears to be somewhat more threatening.[18]

Beck builds on her assumption of full anti-racist dedication by white women a competitive argument that itself illustrates how limited this anti-racism is. The fact that the women's movement is still at the point at which inclusion of women of color is a vital issue is itself a measure of the inadequacy thus far of any movement-wide dedication to anti-racism. From this perspective, Beck's failure to describe as "very much in the movement" the many women of color who are active as feminists, *regardless* of whether she or other white women are doing political work *with them*, reflects this larger problem. Such a political view perceives the "movement" as white and defines women of color as, at best, on its periphery, at the same time that it presents in overstated terms the movement-wide dedication to anti-racism.

From an activist perspective, bringing in "groups that have been left out" is only an initial step in a complicated process. Beck's contention that "you can dedicate yourself to fighting racism, because there are groups that have been left out" implies that one can be seriously committed to anti-racism while doing far less than one has to do to be equally committed to opposing anti-Semitism; that, in some ways, it is *easier* to be anti-racist because that involves most white women only with women who are out there, clearly Other, rather than with women who are a daily part of our lives. Some non-Jewish feminists are, indeed, reluctant to deal with Jewish oppression out of the fear that doing so will negatively affect their personal relationships with Jewish women; that fear can override the awareness that their refusal to deal with it can itself badly hurt such relationships and thereby prevent them from doing necessary work not just on a political but on a personal level. But others might find it far more pressing to deal with anti-Semitism *because* of their personal commitment to specific Jewish women. Similarly, a significant motivation for white women to confront racism is the interaction with women of color that, among other things, allows for an understanding of their identity and oppression which simply cannot be gained without personal contact.

Clarifying one's motivation for opposing either oppression involves pulling back from one's anger at the other group to look at the larger political picture, the larger stakes. For non-Jewish women of color, it means questioning the kinds of assumptions that led one woman of color at a workshop for Jewish women and women of color to state "that she would not deal with Jewish women until we 'dealt with' Zionism."[19] For Jewish women, it means avoiding the kind of tit-for-tat mode of thinking that contends that the anti-racist work done by white Jewish women obligates women of color to reciprocate. Writing in this vein, Letty Pogrebin says:

> many Jewish women specifically resent that, for years, they have talked openly about "confronting" their racism, while with a few noteworthy exceptions black women's anti-Semitism has been largely unmentionable.[20]

Although Pogrebin does not depict white Jewish women as having gone beyond the level of "talk," her message to those women is clear: if we have done this, we have done enough. And her message to Black women is: because we have done this, you owe us something which you have not paid.

Ignoring in her discussion of "Black-Jewish Relations" responsibility on the part of Jewish women for the breach in relations, Pogrebin appears to accept without question the appropriateness of some Jewish women's years of resentment. In doing so, she casts doubt on the political motivations of Jewish women who do—or have done—anti-racist work. As Alice Walker has written in a published response to Pogrebin's article:

It depressed me that Pogrebin imagines Jewish women's work for "civil rights, welfare rights, Appalachian relief was work that did not necessarily affect [their] own lives." Meaning, logically, that this work was charity, dispensed to the backward, the poor, and the benighted, and that Jewish feminists should now be able to expect "payment" in the form of support. Fortunately, I have worked with too many Jewish women in social movements to believe that many of them think this—rather than that any struggle against oppression lightens the load on all of us—but if they do, we are worse off than I thought.[21]

We are just as badly off when, having overstated the extent of white anti-racism, those of us who are Jewish and white fall into the trap of over-stating the extent and intransigence of anti-Semitism among non-Jewish people of color. Doing so contributes to the competitive cycle: while white Jewish women have taken racism seriously, non-Jewish women of color do not take anti-Semitism seriously. Thus the cycle moves on apace, political strategizing gets done in far greater isolation than is either necessary or desirable, the possibilities of coalition seem increasingly remote, and the people who benefit certainly don't come from any of *our* communities.

For me the issue is not whether to confront Jewish oppression, but how to do so. With comparatively few exceptions, non-Jewish women of color—like non-Jewish white women—have neither sufficiently explored their own anti-Semitism nor actively opposed it. In terms of non-Jewish women of color, no less than of non-Jewish white women, personal and political interactions must be based on the belief that, as Irena Klepfisz has written, "anti-Semitism, *like any other ideology of oppression,* must *never* be tolerated, must *never* be hushed up, must *never* be ignored, and that, instead, it must *always* be exposed and resisted."[22]

For Jewish women, the rage at the anti-Semitism of non-Jewish women of color sometimes seems far greater than at the anti-Semitism of the non-Jewish whites who have immeasurably more power. For white Jews who were raised with a belief in some "special relationship" be-tween Jews and Blacks, the recurrence of anti-Semitism among Blacks can seem a final sundering of that perceived link, more painful than the anti-Semitism of whites and thereby drawing on a deeper level of anger. For Jews of color, the pain of such anti-Semitism is especially sharp, coming as it does from within their own group, perhaps even from non-Jews within their own immediate family.

Perhaps the intensified anger stems from *their* failure to meet *our* expectations, our assumptions that their gut-level experience of their own oppression will provide them with a ready store of empathy for others. When, for instance, I am dyke-baited on my block by teenagers, white and Black, I am, in total defiance of logic, angrier at the Black kids than at the white ones: *they*, I mutter to myself, should know better! Sometimes rewarded, more often not, these expectations are put into perspective by Cherríe Moraga's comment: "Oppression does not make for hearts as big as all outdoors. Oppression makes us big and small. Expressive and silenced. Deep and dead."[23] On every side, it makes us deep and dead.

Unrealistic expectations can skew how Jewish women define the issues, attribute responsibility. Pogrebin's article, for example, left me with the impression that I would be hard put to find more than four or five Black people *in the entire country* who thought Jewish oppression a serious issue. What does it mean that she chooses to end an article on anti-Semitism in the women's movement with "Problem 5: Black-Jewish Relations," a litany of examples of anti-Jewish statements by Black people, including several women who would probably not identify as feminists but who *do* have anti-Jewish things to say?[24] What does it mean to single out Black people in this way, as no other racial/ethnic group is singled out? What is the impression left on the reader? Reversing this situation can put it in useful perspective. How might Pogrebin, or another Jewish woman, respond to an article by a non-Jewish woman of color on racism in the women's movement that concluded with a section on "Black-Jewish Relations," placed responsibility for the breach on white Jewish women, and rattled off a series of racist statements made by white Jews?[25] Would this not illustrate Pogrebin's statement: "That this game of blacks versus Jews is continued in the Women's Movement is one of the gravest failures of feminism"?[26]

The fact of Third World anti-Semitism—like the fact of white anti-Semitism—is undeniable. A problem is how to acknowledge it, deplore it, oppose it, *and* place it in some kind of context. How to hear Barbara Smith say, "I have seen some Black women be blatantly anti-Semitic with a self-righteousness they would probably not exhibit in any other case,"[27] *and* know that this statement presents only part of the picture. How to read Gloria Z. Greenfield's description of the 1981 New England Women's Studies Association workshop for Jewish women and women of color at which the presence of working-class Jews "was ignored with remarks that 'all Jews are rich' and 'there's no such thing as a poor Jew',"[28] *and* know that the women who made these anti-Jewish remarks were not representative of all the women of color present, that four Third World women, Cherríe Moraga, Julia Perez, Barbara Smith, and Beverly Smith wrote in response to the confrontation at that conference:

We are not trying to side-step the pervasive fact of color oppression in this country and are committed to confronting white racism, whether practiced by Jews or non-Jews. However, we feel it is critical for women of color not to fall into the trap of countering racism on the part of Jews with anti-Semitism.

The issue is not a simple one and as women of color who have struggled for nearly a decade in a white-dominated feminist movement, we understand and empathize with the tendency to react to racism with despair. We feel that this is not a time for viewing this one event as an impasse, but rather as a moment of harsh enlightenment—reckoning with the extent and depth to which we are separated from each other.

We don't have to be the same to have a movement, but we *do* have to admit our fear and pain and be accountable for our ignorance. In the end, finally, we must refuse to give up on each other.[29]

Within and outside the women's community, we are faced with the question of whether we *will*, in fact, give up on each other, whether we will generalize from our worst experiences and proceed in a climate smoggy with a distrust so thick that effective political work cannot take place. Examples of anti-Semitism among people of color—as among non-Jewish whites—are depressingly easy to locate. The 1981-1982 issue of *Jazz Spotlite News,* a Black publication, includes, "as a public service by The Third World Institute," an "excerpt from the 'Protocols of The Learned Elders of Zion'," on Jewish "control of the press."[30] Jewish protests of a fall, 1982 program on Israel on *Like It Is,* a Black WABC weekly show, gave WABC an excuse to try to crack down on its independence, and led Reverend Calvin Butts, head of the Organization of African American Clergy, to characterize the "affair as 'a pound of flesh' . . . extracted from our community"; when Black protests succeeded in quashing WBAC's attack, host Gil Noble "said nothing about the anti-Semitic undercurrents of that protest . . . [and] repeated the infamous 'pound of flesh' line from *The Merchant of Venice,* adding that the Blacks, in response, had 'extracted eight pounds of flesh!'"[31]

Without doubt, non-Jewish people of color—like non-Jewish whites—exist for whom no amount of Jewish history and information on Jew-hating will be enough for them to rethink their anti-Semitism. When challenged about the "Protocols" excerpt, for instance, one Black woman denied that they were a tsarist forgery and, indifferent to this information about their actual history, supported her argument with such sources as *The Black American,* a New York City newspaper which has supported the 1980 presidential candidacy of the notoriously anti-Jewish Lyndon Larouche and has printed articles maintaining that the Holocaust did not happen.[32]

Such resistance, however, is not uniform. When asked about the anti-Jewish "pound of flesh" reference, for example, a Black woman first defended Butts on the grounds that he "didn't know" that the reference was anti-Jewish and then, after some discussion, admitted that, even if Butts and Noble had acted out of ignorance, they were, in fact, perpetuating anti-Semitism. For this woman, information and political dialogue did make a difference. Neither of these examples cancels out the other. Nor are they affected by the existence of other Blacks, by other non-Jewish people of color, who would have *immediately* identified as anti-Jewish both the "Protocols" reprint and the "pound of flesh" quote from *The Merchant of Venice.* They do, however, illustrate a diversity that needs to be acknowledged.

The goal of acknowledging opposition to anti-Semitism is definitely not to express gratitude or to single out a few individuals as "good" representatives of their group. Opposition to anti-Semitism, as to racism and other oppressions, is not a favor that merits thanks, nor is it a means to establish a token few who are "politically right-on," while everyone else lies mired hopelessly in "political incorrectness." Such an acknowledgement is, however, part of a political strategy, a means to break a cycle in which silence begets more silence. It will help make clear to white Jewish women that interactions and alliances with non-Jewish women of color are not by definition a dead end, though, like other work that crosses lines of significant difference, they are bound at times to seem overwhelmingly difficult. It will help provide non-Jewish women of color with the sense that they are not necessarily alone in their opposition to Jewish oppression, that other women like them have begun to take public and private stands against it. Without exaggeration, without minimizing the extent of Jewish oppression or racism, each of us benefits, as we oppose one or both, from knowing that we are not working in isolation. The greater the sense of isolation, the more formidable the task appears and the more likely we might be to wait until someone takes it on first.

On all sides, the barriers seem, at times, insurmountable, the cycles of competition seem impossible to break. The way out of the impasse involves challenging our own assumptions, checking them for accuracy, scrutinizing them for political implications. It certainly involves examining those areas where, practically before we know it and often against our desires, Jewish women and non-Jewish women of color become embroiled in competition, shut out the world beyond the women's movement, and view each other with enmity. Without such examination, non-Jewish women of color and Jewish women will not break fully out of our current situation. Like Jews and the Polish Underground in the

Warsaw of 1943, we will remain, as Irena Klepfisz has written, "two oppressed groups facing a common enemy unable to overcome ancient hatreds, struggling separately."[33]

VIII. SEMITE VS. SEMITE/ FEMINIST VS. FEMINIST

> *If God as some say is now dead, He no doubt died of trying to find an equitable solution to the Arab-Jewish problem.*
> —I.F. Stone, "Holy War"*

If I could simply argue that Israelis and Palestinians had a "common enemy" against which they should unite, I would find it far easier to think about the Palestinian-Israeli conflict and its impact on relations between women in the United States and elsewhere. I could more readily step outside the cycle of suspicion, fear, and escalating tension that profoundly affects feminists, Jew and non-Jew, Arab and non-Arab, Jew and Jew, white women and women of color. But the competing claims, the century-long conflicts, the on-going killings, have historically been conceived of and experienced in adversarial terms. So, even before writing a word of this section, I chose a title reflecting the clash of assertion and rebuttal.

My main concern here is to look at how the issues of racism and Jewish oppression raised by the Israeli-Palestinian confrontation play themselves out in the women's movement. I will examine only briefly the ways in which both the maneuvers of superpowers acting out of their own strategic interests, not those of either Israelis or Palestinians, and the conflicts between Middle East states and factions affect regional events. Yet, in practical terms, I cannot limit my discussion to the women's movement. Most frequently, information about the Middle East comes to me from the world outside the women's movement, through the morning newspaper and through a steady stream of books and articles by men. Far less often have I been able to find writing which links the regional issues with feminist politics. It is, however, primarily these attempts at analyzing the problem that I want to address.

What Israel does—and what is done to it—reverberates in my life: in newspaper headlines, political reports, passing comments, the anti-Jewish and anti-Arab climate in my community. The problem is immense. And I am no Middle East scholar. I neither speak nor read Arabic or Hebrew. I visited Israel so long ago that it is almost inaccurate to say I have any first-hand knowledge of the country. As I choose now what to read and say, I know that I am selecting and presenting only part of the picture.

As a Jew, I have a special relationship to Israel. That relationship will remain whether I embrace it or rage against it. Attempting to ignore it is like trying to ignore my Jewish identity: someone is bound to remind me of it, out of solidarity or hostility. However I define the connections, I am affected by some people's assumptions that, because I am a Jew, I support not only Israel's existence but the policies of its government and have only minor, if any, criticisms of Israel's role—and that of pre-statehood Zionists—in creating the current impasse. I am affected too by assumptions that, because I am a radical, I not only reject Israel's right to exist but back, without significant reservations, the actions of Palestinian nationalists.

In my writing and my activism, I support *both* the Palestinian and the Jewish national movements, the continued existence of Israel within pre-1967 borders and the establishment of a Palestinian state on the West Bank and Gaza Strip.[1] My preference to see the need for two sovereign states as *equally* pressing places me outside of both the most common Zionist and anti-Zionist positions, the first of which affirms a belief in Israel's survival and then, depending on politics, might move on to a statement of support for the formation of a Palestinian state in the Occupied Territories, while the second would replace the Jewish state with a democratic secular one. I see the present situation in the Middle East as one of fundamental imbalance: a Jewish state exists whereas a Palestinian one does not; the Palestinians live everywhere in the region at the sufferance of Israel or of Arab states. I disagree strenuously with those who maintain that criticizing Israel is necessarily anti-Jewish or, if the critic is a Jew, self-hating, though I certainly agree that such criticism *can* be anti-Jewish. Similarly, criticism of acts by Palestinians or other Arabs can reflect anti-Arab racism. But, as I will argue later, these general positions of mine—like those of anybody else—have meaning primarily in terms of how they get translated into concrete analysis and political action.

As an "out" lesbian, I also have a special relationship to Israel.

It is, after all, one more place in the Jewish community where the "dykes need not apply" sign is up and visible. As a lesbian, I am ineligible for the automatic citizenship which the Law of Return is supposed to confer on all Jews.[2] I have no guarantee that, if Jewish oppression escalated to Jew-killing in this country, the Orthodox rabbis who have disproportionate power in Israel would support offering sanctuary to me—or to other Jewish lesbians and gay men.

As a lesbian, my skepticism runs deep. Even as I recognize Israel as a potential refuge for other Jews, its official position defines me as an outsider, unwanted and unmissed. Like my relationship as a lesbian to the American Jewish community, and indeed to the world in general, this reality is painful. But it does provide me with some additional understanding of others who are outside or on the fringes of Israeli society—Palestinians, Israeli Arabs, Oriental Jews.[3]

Although my focus here is on the conflict between Israelis and Arabs, I am also aware of the effect of Ashkenazi racism on Oriental Jews, *Adot Ha-Mizrach*, those originating from Asia and Africa.[4] Now more than half the Israeli Jewish population, Oriental Jews emigrated in greatest numbers after the 1947 United Nations partition of Palestine.[5] Except for Palestinians in the Occupied Territories and Israeli Arabs, the ethnically segregated Oriental Jews have the biggest families, the worst schools and mortality rates, and the most people on welfare.[6] For Oriental Jews—as for Palestinians and Israeli Arabs, lesbians and non-Jews, women and non-Orthodox Jews—Israeli society needs to change radically.[7]

Inside and outside the women's movement, political debate about the Middle East often begins with the assumption that one is concerned either with racism *or* with Jewish oppression. That the same language reflects different political perspectives is part of the problem. For Di Vilde Chayes, *"Zionism is one strategy against anti-Semitism and for Jewish survival."* Letty Cottin Pogrebin maintains that *"Zionism is simply an affirmative action plan on a national scale."* Marcia Freedman, an American-born Israeli feminist and former Knesset member, says, "to be pro-Zionist in Israel today is a kind of jingoism or superpatriotism." I.F. Stone, whose book describes his going "underground to Palestine" with Holocaust survivors after World War II, writes about "the other Zionism" of Ahad Ha'am (Asher Ginzberg), Judah P. Magnes, A.D. Gordon, Martin Buber, and Henrietta Szold. In contrast to mainstream Zionist thinking, these Zionists hoped for a bi-national state in which Arabs and Jews could live together.[8] On the other hand, Rabbi Meir Kahane, head of the Jewish Defense League and of the Kakh Party in Israel, interprets Zionism as justification for driving Palestinians and other Arabs out of Israel and the Occupied Territories. Menachem Begin finds his Zionism in Genesis, "I give this country to your posterity from the river of Egypt up to the great river, Euphrates" (XV:18), seeing in the Biblical imperative a justification for Israeli expansion.

Those who challenge Zionism offer quite different definitions. Writing about "Zionism from the standpoint of its victims," Palestinian Edward Said analyzes it "as practical systems for *accumulation* (of power, land, ideological legitimacy) and *displacement* (of people, other ideas, prior legitimacy)." Lebanese-American Malea Kiblan argues that "Zionism is a political ideology that does not admit Palestinian self-determination." "Zionism," says Arab-American feminist Helen Samhan, "by its very nature is discriminatory and promotes dehumanization of the people it displaced." "Zionism is *the direct opposite* of all that constitutes Judaism" and delays the coming of the Messiah, according to the Neturei Karta, Orthodox Jews living mostly in Jerusalem who reject the authority of the Israeli state. The non-Zionist Israeli political party *Shasi* contends that, since "neither Zionism nor Israel has insured physical security to the Jews who have come to Israel . . . the problem of Jewish physical security in Israel, like the problems stemming from anti-Semitism, remains on the agenda of the revolutionary movement." Jewish Women for a Secular Middle East believes that "although the primary victims of Zionism are the Palestinian people, . . . Zionism is not in the interests of most Jews either." The All African People's Revolutionary Party asserts: "ZIONISM is a well organized and financed, international conspiracy which controls the economic and political life of the United States and Europe."[9]

Some anti-Zionists adopt the current Palestine Liberation Organization call for a democratic secular state, but support Yasser Arafat's stated willingness "to live in any part of Palestine from which the Israelis withdraw or which will be liberated".[10] Some, like Palestinian feminist Raymonda Hawa Tawil, favor an "interim solution": "a state of our own, side by side with Israel, as envisaged in the 1947 partition plan. Later, we might be able to join up with the Israelis and form a unified state . . . ."[11] Others still hold to Nasser's aim in the 1950's to "drive the Jews into the sea," refuse to consider the possibility of negotiations, and speak of how Israel "will be destroyed one day."[12]

I see Zionism as having two distinct and opposing meanings: first it is a desire for a Jewish homeland, a refuge for Jews oppressed in Europe, in Arab countries, and throughout the world; and second, it is a movement which has displaced large numbers of the Arab residents of this homeland, and a political theory which, in practice, applies different systems of justice to Jews and non-Jews, Arabs and non-Arabs. Seeing truth in both definitions, I find myself unable simply to select "Zionist" or "anti-Zionist" as the appropriate description of my politics. I prefer the stated views of Arab-American feminist Azizah al-Hibri, who suggests that "we forget about labels and ask how we feel about various policies," and the implicit one of New Jewish Agenda, whose national platform statement on the Middle East stands in the absence of a political label.[13]

My skepticism makes me particularly wary of slogans which imply that one single theory and practice—Zionism *or* anti-Zionism—is beyond reproach, and its contrary, beyond redemption. Each with its piece of the truth, slogans like "Zionism is racism" and "anti-Zionism is anti-Semitism" can freeze not just dialogue but thought. One member of the Chutzpah work group on anti-Semitism has articulated something very close to my own belief in the need to consider what is, in fact, accurate about the criticisms lodged against each political stance:

> As a non-Zionist organization, we don't have to figure out if anti-Zionism without anti-Semitism is possible. That's the anti-Zionists' struggle to develop, their act to clean up . . . . Neither do we have to argue that, as we often hear from the Jewish communal leadership, all anti-Zionism must be anti-Semitic. If the left claims that's a myth, fine; maybe so. Our role is to expose where it *is* anti-Semitism, just as we criticize Zionism where it's chauvinist. We've begun to hear anti-Zionist groups stating, "We oppose anti-Semitism." The extent of their opposition in practice is to make that statement. Then they go on to say that anti-Zionism has nothing to do with anti-Semitism. That's the anti-Zionist left's myth.[14]

Regardless of one's political perspective, this statement provides a useful framework. It supports criticism of both Zionism and anti-Zionism, seeing as "myth" the argument that "anti-Zionism has nothing to do with anti-Semitism" and implicitly disagreeing with those who would argue that Zionism "has nothing to do with racism or chauvinism."

While anti-Zionism may be espoused by those deeply concerned with the survival of the Jewish people, it is far more often expressed by those who exhibit, at best, indifference to Jewish oppression or ignorance of Jewish history. As Chaia Lehrer has said:

> . . . to simply say that "Zionism is Racism" is to say that the motivation that drove the Jewish people to Palestine was their racism. If we know our history, and live in the aftermath of the Holocaust and the pogroms all over the world, we know the motivation of our people was our survival. It is the intent of the U.S. and Israeli *governments* that have proven to be imperialistic

and racist.[15]

In some instances, the anti-Jewish attitudes are reflected in the equation between Jewish identity and support for Zionism or in the denial of the existence of anti-Semitism. Within the women's movement, for example, an anti-imperialist collective acknowledges that it has been anti-Jewish in applying a double standard to articles written by Jewish women; the collective has held such articles, even those having nothing to do with the Middle East, until an anti-Zionist piece could be found to "balance" them.[16] An anti-Zionist group calls Jewish women's criticisms of anti-Jewish statements and actions "spurious charges of anti-semitism and internalized self-hatred"[17]; the group does not even consider the possibility that at least some of these charges might have validity and that anti-Jewish expressions are common.

At the same time, the history of Zionism frequently reflects attitudes toward the Palestinian people which range from indifference to hostility and which have shaped state policy. As a Jew, I would prefer the founding of Israel to have been motivated only by the idea of a country safe for Jews to live as Jews, and not to have been influenced by European imperialistic aspirations and racism which simply overlooked the dark-skinned, non-Western people already inhabiting the land.[18] A year after the 1896 publication of Theodor Herzl's *Der Judenstaat* (1896), the beginning of "modern political Zionism," the German Zionist Max Nordau said to Herzl: "But there are Arabs in Palestine! I did not know that! We are committing an injustice!"[19] As one Zionist historian observes, "The moment of doubt passed quickly."[20] Israeli Amos Elon writes that 20 years later David Ben-Gurion, despite his awareness of Arab nationalism, "made the astounding suggestion that in the 'historical and moral sense' Palestine was a country 'without inhabitants'."[21] This conception of the Palestinians as invisible, as non-persons, was both reflected in and reinforced by the language of the Balfour Declaration (1917) which expressed Great Britain's support, however questionable in motivation and inconsistent over the years, for "the establishment in Palestine of a national home for the Jewish people." Although they constituted 90 percent of Palestine's population, Arabs were described by the British policy statement simply as "non-Jews."[22]

These colonialist conceptions, together with the enmity between Jew and Arab which built up over the following decades, contributed to later Israeli politics and actions. Chaim Weizmann, Israel's first president, declared the flight during the 1948 war of 750,000 of the 900,000 Arabs living in pre-partition Palestine "a miraculous simplification of Israel's task."[23] A 1950 Israeli government publication maintained that "it would be folly to resurrect artificially a minority problem which had been almost eliminated by the war."[24] Not only did Israel confiscate the land of those Arabs who fled during the 1948 war, but it has taken land from Arabs who remained in Israel, became citizens, and wanted to continue to own and cultivate their property.[25] As non-Jewish citizens, Israeli Arabs are today totally excluded from owning the 90 percent of land in Israel which is state-owned and is controlled by the Jewish Agency and the Jewish National Fund.[26]

Knesset member Shulamit Aloni has written that Palestinians in the Occupied Territories are subject to the same "Defense Emergency Regulations that the British had enacted against the rebellious underground Jewish organizations . . . which the leaders of the Yishuv (the Jewish population in Palestine)—among them Menachem Begin . . . termed 'Nazi laws'."[27] Aloni explains:

> All the laws circumscribing human liberties: those allowing the government to employ Emergency Regulations in the framework of administrative arrests or to sell off areas; to impose the obligation to accommodate soldiers, to hold closed trials without respect for the principle of *habeas corpus*, to prevent publication of a newspaper or weekly, to impose arbitrary censorship—particularly in the Arabic language—to prohibit demonstrations, to confiscate or destroy property—all these remain valid.[28]

All of these policies reflect an attitude, held by some Israelis, that Palestinians are, as Begin has said, "beasts with two legs."[29] Former Israeli Chief of Staff Rafael Eitan has stated, "When we have settled the land, all the Arabs will be able to do about it will be to scurry around like drugged roaches in a bottle."[30] Eitan was found in breach of duty for his failure to stop Phalangist activities in the Sabra and Shatila refugee camps even after reports indicated the Phalangists "were perpetuating acts of slaughter."[31]

The hatred of Arabs by some Jews has its counterpart in the Jew-hating of some Arabs. While both attitudes are, in part, reactions to the other group's violence, the terrorism of armies and guerrilla fighters, they are also, in part, outgrowths of pre-Zionist attitudes and history. In "The Jews and the Koran," for instance, Abdul Sattar El-Sayad writes:

> According to the descriptions provided of the Jews in the Koran, they stand as an enemy which is devoid of any human feelings. They are rather a pest or a plague that is cursed like Satan who was expelled by God from the realm of His mercy. . . . The Jews wherever they existed [sic] act like poisonous thorns and chronic diseases that spread germs into the body of their neighbors and continue to do so unless the thorns are uprooted and the diseases are eliminated.[32]

Although noting that "Muslim law guarantees to Jews and Christians the free exercise of their religion provided that it is not offensive to Muslims," S.D. Goitein also acknowledges that "preachers of hatred never had great difficulties finding quotations in . . . [the Koran] for their purposes."[33] As Goitein has written about Jews in Arab countries:

> . . . the position of the Jews inside the Arab Muslim society was relatively better than that enjoyed by them in Medieval Europe. But only relatively. In principle, they and other non-Muslims were second-class citizens and consequently their position was always precarious, often actually dangerous.[34]

In addition to restrictions on travel, dress, and place of residence (applied also to Christians), Jews suffered periodic massacres, forcible conversions, destructions of their synagogues, and emigration bans. Early in the Muslim Era, "the yellow badge for Jews was known in Muslim countries centuries before it was introduced into Christian Europe."[35] In 1012 in Syria and in 1474 and 1721 throughout Palestine and Syria, synagogues were destroyed. In 1517 the Egyptians accused the Jews of siding with the Turks and sacked the Cairo Jewish quarter. In 1679 Jews were expelled from Yemen, recalled the following year, and then denied the right to emigrate; those who managed to leave forfeited their property. Arabs plundered the Jewish settlements in the Upper Galilee in 1604, 1628, 1656, 1660, 1834, and 1838.[36] Arab Muslims collaborated with European Christians in the 1840 Damascus Affair in which Jews were "imprisoned and tortured to make them confess to a ritual murder," a European-inspired accusation that Jews murder Christians and use their blood in Passover rituals.[37] The Damascus Affair "inspired" a similar charge against Jews in Jerusalem in 1847.[38]

After the beginning of Zionist settlements in Palestine and especially as tension between Arabs and Zionists increased, Jews living in Arab countries fared badly. "In June, 1941, in Iraq," writes Tunisian-born Jew Albert Memmi, "six hundred people killed, one thousand seriously wounded, looting, rapes, arson, one thousand houses destroyed, six hundred stores looted . . . ."[39] After the creation of Israel, some Arab countries used Jew-hating propaganda to stir opposition to Israel's policies. Excerpts from the Protocols of the Elders of Zion were published by the United Arab Republic Information Services in a 1965 English-language pamphlet, "Israel, the Enemy of Africa," which it then distributed throughout Africa.[40] After the 1967 war, the Arab Information Center in Cairo put out an Arabic *Mein Kampf*. The edition was annotated by Luis Heiden, "a former Goebbels associate and high official of the Nazi Propaganda Ministry . . . one of a number of former Nazi and

SS leaders attracted to important posts in Egypt's ministries during the late forties and early fifties."[41] In 1968 Kuwait published and distributed an edition of the Protocols in English, French, and Spanish, and a new edition was listed as a 1970 non-fiction best-seller in *Al Anwar,* a Lebanese newspaper.[42] In the absence of alternative information about Jews, these publications dispense the dregs of European anti-Jewish ideology to the Arab population. They support the notion, believed by some Arabs, that Jews are bent on taking over the world.

Yet to speak only of Arab-hating and Jew-hating is to ignore the ways in which attitudes and acts are conditioned by the drive for survival, safety, and control over one's life. Isn't the fervent Jewish nationalism of the Polish Jew who, after living through the Nazi camps, escaped death in post-War Poland, and then traveled illegally to Palestine, in large part, simply a desire for survival? Isn't the nationalism of the Palestinian whose home has been destroyed by Israeli troops, who has been living in a refugee camp which was attacked by Phalangist militia, and who wants to return to her childhood home in the Galilee, an expression of a similar impulse to live in a state in which she is not in danger? Can we automatically dismiss one as anti-Arab, the other as anti-Jewish, because one sees Zionism as providing a home and the other as having taken her home away?

In the light of competing claims and a century of conflict, the need is not just to hear the other side, but to speak for the other side. Perhaps in that way we can contribute to bridging the chasm, lessening the sense of the Other. Nobody will argue as forcefully against anti-Jewish bias as Jews. Nobody will argue as strongly against anti-Arab prejudice as Arabs. Certainly we must work politically out of who we are. But I do not believe that those of us who are Jews will convince Arab people to recognize our struggles, our oppression, our aspirations, if we are not also ready to recognize—and speak out about—their own. By the same token, Jews want to hear recognition coming from Arabs. Once again, the question is whether we will break a cycle or perpetuate it. I am less interested in who does this first, than that it happen.

When a statement by Di Vilde Chayes, for example, strongly objects to Jewish oppression but almost entirely fails to mention the Palestinians, an opportunity is lost for showing that the choice is not either/or.[43] When a Palestinian-Jewish dialogue in *off our backs* focuses on the repression of Palestinians, but does not even mention anti-Semitism—in relation either to emigration to Israel or to Jewish fears of a democratic secular state—the same opportunity is lost.[44] The non-Jewish woman who refuses to discuss Jewish oppression with someone supporting Israel's right to exist contributes to the deadlock as surely as the Jewish woman who is capable only of invective or silence until she has been assured that she is engaged in a dialogue with another Zionist.

For white, non-Arab women, Jewish and non-Jewish, beginning to break these cycles involves overcoming the anti-Arab racism that is deeply engrained in Western culture. Anti-Arab racism reveals itself, as does racism generally, in the simple failure to *see*—that the other is there, that the other is very much like oneself. As a white person, an Ashkenazi Jew, a non-Arab, a Westerner, I do not, of course, approach anti-Arab racism with a clean slate. When I began teaching in 1965, a favorite essay of mine was a short one by George Orwell about Morocco.[45] In it he used the image of "firewood passing" to underscore the inability of the British colonialists to see the people under the wood who, too poor to own pack animals, themselves served as beasts of burden. I taught this essay always with indignation at the white Europeans who could not *see* a country's brown-skinned inhabitants. Yet when I visited Israel in 1972, I failed to see in any meaningful way its Arab inhabitants. While I recall noticing Arabs on the streets of Jerusalem, Netanya, and elsewhere, I never wondered who they were, where or how they lived. Putting them into a narrow slot in my mind marked "Arabs" required of me no more thought than if I had seen them laden with firewood and classified them as "bundles of wood." Nor did it occur to me that some of the people I looked at and registered as "Arab" might actually have been Oriental Jews who had lived for centuries in Arab countries.

Nearly a decade later, when my daughter returned from a month's visit to Israel to see her paternal grandparents, I had a sharp and immediate reaction to her observation that the Arabs seemed to be "treated well," but I did not respond. Although she was wrong in her assessment, and at 11 lacked the tools to make a more accurate one, she knew, as I had not when I was more than twice her age, that the status of Arabs in Israel needed to be considered. On a later day, when she mentioned that in Israeli schools non-Arab students must study Hebrew and English, I was able to explain in some detail how much better it would be if they all learned Hebrew and Arabic.

What was most striking about my growth in consciousness was how far it lagged behind what I learned about people of color in the United States and in some other parts of the world. My response is not, I think, unique. It reflects, in part, the frequent resistance of Westerners—whites and people of color—to learning about societies whose language, cultures, and social mores are very different from our own. It reflects, in part, the

desire of many Jews in this country not to admit, except maybe super-
ficially, the true complexity of what is happening in the Middle East.
This admission necessarily involves perceiving Israel as it is, not as we
might like it to have become, and exploring how, although "the Arabs
bore no responsibility for the centuries-long suffering of Jews in Europe
. . . in the end, the Arabs were punished because of it."[46] Considering
these issues involves those of us who are non-Arabs in confronting anti-
Arab racism in ourselves.

Almost never has the need to combat racism against Arabs been
included in the concepts of anti-racism put forth in the women's movement. Certainly *I*—who live within two miles of one of the largest Arab-
American communities in the United States—have not thought of this particular form of racism when I have spoken out against racism generally.[47]
I would have agreed, had someone said something, that depicting Arabs
in general as terrorists or sheiks or OPEC ministers was wrong. But it is
only recently that I have begun to notice not only the omissions but the
active anti-Arabism in the media all around me. A spate of books and
movies centers on the plans of "Arab terrorists" to blow up buildings or
take someone hostage; these depictions further the equation of Arab
with terrorist, and are especially dangerous because they provide most
people in this country with nearly everything they know about Arab
life.[48] A sports report on a rookie placekicker begins, "You might
think that Ali Haji-Sheikh is a sheikh or oilman," just because this University of Michigan graduate is an Arab-American.[49] A *New York Times*
article on the Rothschild family says that its members "created the first
multinational bank and seemed as *exotic* in mid-19th century as Saudi
Arabia's sheiks did in the 1970's" (my emphasis).[50] Implicitly anti-
Jewish in the analogy between the "exotic" Jewish banker of a century
ago and the "exotic" Arab sheik of the 1970's, the statement is explicit
and unselfconscious in its anti-Arab racism; the two stereotypes—the rich
Arab and the rich Jew—reinforce each other.

I have been taught not to see these connections. In many ways, my
adult attitudes have grown out of what I was taught in a family, a community, and a country that considered Jews alone as Semitic people and
saw Arabs solely as obstacles to Jewish survival, of little interest in themselves, and certainly not worth speaking up for. The lesson I learned
about Arabs was either to ignore them or to oppose them. Mostly I have
chosen the former option. At first the choice was not conscious: for
years I unthinkingly accepted the view that had been presented to me of
Arabs and of the Middle East. At one time, when I did not identify as a
Jewish feminist, I felt no greater compulsion to inform myself about
the Middle East than about any number of other areas of the world.

Later the choice was a conscious one, and I often rationalized it by saying to myself that other Jewish issues seemed more pressing, closer to home, and that I would deal with *that* later.

Only recently have I felt able to look at how "close to home" the issues really are. A review in *Chutzpah* of *The Disinherited* by Fawaz Turki, a Haifa-born Palestinian exile who grew up in a Beirut refugee camp, notes

> the many parallels between the present situation of the Palestinian people and the historical situation of the Jewish people. Dispersion is of course the most obvious, as the Palestinians now live not only in Syria, Jordan, Israel, Lebanon and Egypt, but also all over the Mid-East and the rest of the world. Turki communicates a strong sense of family, and some scenes lend themselves to *deja vu*. Mother says, "Eat your hommes, it's good for you, and remember all the people still in the camps." The Palestinians have the highest literacy rate in the Middle East, and between 1948-1967 trained 64,000 university graduates (which was only 3,000 less than Israel, and represents a higher percentage). They are discriminated against in many ways and places in the Middle East, and elsewhere. Like us, or any oppressed group, self-hate runs deep. Palestinians are, like Jews, greatly over-represented in middle person economic roles (teacher, civil servant, small shopkeeper) in all the countries of their present settlement. Also, there is a strong sense of solidarity. "Whenever Palestinians met in those days we would reach out to touch the vibration of intimacy, the sharing of pain now blinding the eyes, and the intangible qualities of mind that made 'us' and excluded 'them'."[51]

In the closeness of these parallels, in the divisions of the world into "us" and "them"—the results of love and exile, personal strength and political powerlessness—Jews can find much that, despite differences, is indeed close to home.

As a feminist, I need especially to understand how Arab women conceive of "us" and "them." Once I hear Arab women's voices, I need to recognize how their varied perspectives have been shaped by family history, country of origin, class background, religion, skin color, sexual preference, age, their relationship to an Arab or Arab-American nationalist and/or feminist movement, and their connection to a women's or lesbian community. Achieving this recognition, in large part, involves pushing beyond stereotypes and unfounded assumptions of which I may not even be aware. When, for instance, an Arab-American woman mentions to me that all but one of the women on a panel on Arab feminism are

Christian, not Muslim, I realize that I have given no thought to precisely *who* these women are, except, of course, that they are Arab-Americans.[52] However, I realize that, even when given the information about their religious backgrounds, I cannot immediately formulate more than the most general thoughts about how these might influence their approach to the issues, what they are most likely to stress, ignore, or de-emphasize.

Even when Arab and Arab-American women speak for and about themselves, I must question who the women are whose viewpoints, conveyed in print or in person, are most available to U.S. feminists. I need then to balance the words of middle-class, light-skinned, well-educated, Christian women like Palestinian Raymonda Tawil and Lebanese Etel Adnan—whose books have been translated, respectively, from Hebrew and French into English—with those of poorer, often darker women living in far different material circumstances, women who do not write for publication, whose words have rarely been translated from Arabic into English.[53] As in other situations, the intersection of class with skin color and with religion/ethnicity affects who is most likely to be published, translated, and read, as well as who is most likely to be invited to speak at conferences and who can afford the cross-country or transcontinental trip. I learn what I can from the resources available to people who do not read Arabic.

Even Arab women who have had access to the media may have their words altered by white Westerners. Egyptian Muslim author and gynecologist Nawal El Saadawi, for example, has spoken angrily of Gloria Steinem's having solicited an article for *Ms.* on clitoridectomy and then having deleted without permission Saadawi's "political, social and historical analysis."[54] Her lengthy preface to the U.S. edition of *The Hidden Face of Eve: Women in the Arab World* was also cut by her publishers, leaving her feeling "exploited and . . . [her] ideas distorted."[55]

Arab women themselves may also make the political decision to present Westerners with a less than full picture of the role of Islamic women. At the beginning of an article on "Western Ethnocentrism and Perceptions of the Harem," for example, Egyptian-born feminist Leila Ahmed describes how she learned why Islamic women might choose a particular mode of self-presentation in front of a U.S. audience. Commenting on the 1980 National Women's Studies Association panel on Islam and Feminism, Ahmed says:

> . . . [I] found myself hotly speaking up from the audience because the panel of three Arab women were, it seemed to me, presenting an unwarrantably rosy picture of Women in Islam. Islamic societies were, if anything, surely rather remarkable— so had been my thought—for their unequivocal placement of

women under the control of men, and their equally explicit
licensing of male sexuality and exploitation of women....
   But this was over two years ago and before I'd lived in
America. Now that I have, I see perfectly why the women
making the presentation took the stand that they did. For if one
is of Arabic or Islamic background in America, one is almost
compelled to take that stand. And what compels one is not only
that Americans by and large know nothing at all about the
Islamic world, which is indeed the case, despite America's heavy
embroilment in the area and despite the fact that Muslims
constitute something like one quarter of the world's population:
it is, rather, that Americans "know," and know without even
having to think about it, that the Islamic peoples—Arabs,
Iranians, whatever they call themselves—are backward, uncivilized peoples totally incapable of rational conduct.[56]

At the same time that they explore the ways in which Arab women's
lives are shaped by their particular cultures, studies by and about Arab
women must assess the distorting effect of Western bias. Ahmed, for
example, describes the harem not only as it is almost universally perceived in the West—as a bastion of male control—but as an area of female
autonomy from which Western feminists could learn.[57] In another
discussion of feminism in the Middle East, she examines the role of
women in each Arab society as it reflects both that culture's attitudes
toward women *and* its "attitudes and relationship to feminism's civilization of origin, the Western world."[58]

Women's lives and women's oppression cannot be considered outside the bounds of regional conflicts in which it matters deeply whether
one is Arab or Israeli, Muslim or Christian, Palestinian or Arab national,
Jew or non-Jew. In her novel *Sitt Marie Rose,* Etel Adnan explores some
of the intermeshings of these identities through the fictional account,
based on a real incident, of the abuse and final death of a Christian
Lebanese woman, a supporter of Palestinian struggles, at the hands
of anti-Palestinian Christian Lebanese men.[59] Her fate is linked not
only to the internecine warfare within her country but to the dynamic
between male predator and female victim. Making similar connections
between sexism and regional politics from its own perspective, the Israeli
feminist group Women Against the Occupation links Israeli militarism
with the view of woman as subsidized "baby machines" for regiments
of future soldiers; it quotes Dr. Haim Sadan, advisor to the Minister of
Health, as saying, "Abortions have resulted in the loss of twenty divisions
since the creation of the state."[60]

These brief examples suggest not only the complex connections
between women's oppression and the male-controlled politics of the
region, but also the difficulty of deciding whether a single struggle

should take priority and, if so, which. Samiha Khalil Salameh, for instance, answers an "invitation to speak on Palestinian women by commenting that women suffer the occupation like all Palestinians, and do not demand to be singled out for special attention."[61] A Palestinian woman living in Southern Lebanon says in response to two Swedes who want to interview women: "Really, it's about time, too. Strong traditions are keeping the women down, although we are the ones to make the greatest sacrifices. All the time we are the ones who sacrifice and suffer the most . . . ."[62] Another young woman, responsible for the General Union of Palestinian Women in her area, exclaims: "We want to return to our homes! We are stateless. Compared to that, all other problems seem to shrink. The women, the women's struggle, has a long way to go when the whole people is oppressed."[63] Later in the same day, she offers a somewhat different view:

"Palestine, you see, was a very patriarchal society, and my people are still in the firm grip of those traditions . . . Unfortunately, the women have to sacrifice themselves to make it easier for the men. Look at our Palestinian leaders, they are all men! They think that women's liberation is something that will have to wait, it mustn't get in the way of the national liberation struggle. They seem to believe that one excludes the other, but I think they could both go hand in hand. But it's *not* easy!"[64]

Rashideyeh, the camp in which this woman lived, was destroyed on the first weekend of the June 1982 Israeli invasion.

A standard feminist argument is that our links as women contain the possibility for us to talk and work together and are a source of political change. Some articles by white Jewish women on anti-Semitism in the women's movement emphasize the power of this connection, but without including Arab women. The message of this and other writing is clear: Palestinian (and other Arab) women are different. Palestinian women are the enemy. They have no true understanding of feminism. They are pawns of Arab men. They are ungrateful recipients of Israeli progress. And they hate us. Much analysis stemming from these various assumptions goes beyond political differences to reflect anti-Arab racism.

The argument that women's issues should come first, that they should never be compromised, that they can and should be separated from other struggles, reveals an ignorance of Palestinian women's lives and concerns. This belief is implicit in Annette Daum's article about attempts to guarantee that the 1985 United Nations Decade of Women Conference focus on "the economic, health and education needs of *women* and avoid extraneous political matters."[65] It also comes across in Israeli feminist Joanne Yaron's praise of the workshops she attended at the 1980 Copenhagen conference on women because they "put women's issues above all else" and avoided "topics that only serve to divide women."[66] Neither considers the possibility, raised by a Lebanese woman at a 1983 meeting on the forthcoming conference, that some mid-point be sought in which both "women's" issues and "Palestinian" ones be dealt with.

The assumption that for Palestinian women separate issues do, in fact, exist and that they can realistically be divided implies not only a particular perspective on the plight of Palestinians, but a refusal to recognize the interlocking nature of oppression. Although Letty Pogrebin writes about how "the feminist's world-view needs to be expanded to recognize times when sisterhood must bow to 'peoplehood' for blacks and Jews," she does not recognize that the depth and seriousness of oppression which makes such a priority necessary might also affect Palestinian women. While she can also say that she now feels "more vulnerable in America as a Jew than as a woman," Pogrebin does not expand her analysis to consider that Palestinian women might feel more vulnerable as Palestinians than as women.[67] Yet, though the circumstances differ, Palestinian women share today the justified fear for physical and cultural survival which Jewish women have felt at different times. Within this context, it is useful to note that, during the late Thirties "Jewish feminists left [Women's Suffrage] Alliance and other women's groups to devote themselves full-time to helping European Jews."[68] Then, as now, the voices which might characterize such a decision as divisive, not in the "best interests" of women, have belonged to those with relative power. They were not the voices of the homeless, the stateless, those living in the Diaspora or in the *ghourba,* as the Palestinian Diaspora is called.

It would be a dangerous mistake, however, not to recognize that the arguments made by Daum, Pogrebin, Yaron, and others come out of fear and anger, of concern for Jewish survival. Pogrebin lists a chilling series of statements and incidents at the 1980 Copenhagen women's conference: Sonia Johnson tells how, "I heard, ' The only good Jew is a dead Jew. ' I heard, 'The only way to rid the world of Zionism is to kill all the Jews'."[69] E.M. Broner quotes a Thai woman as saying, "'The Israeli woman is not a human being. She is poisoned by the worm of Zionism. She can only be reached with the sword'."[70] The Program of Action of the official U.N. conference adopts a resolution whose goal is "to *purify* Palestine of the Zionist presence'."[71] Reading through these and other such examples, I am hard pressed indeed to feel anything but that "they" want me dead.

Yet, rather than holding Palestinians and their supporters fully responsible for their role at the conference, these Jewish feminist responses depict Palestinian women as firmly under the control of men and as lacking autonomy. Cited approvingly both by Daum and by "Regina Schreiber" (a pseudonym) in her own conference report, a statement by the National Coalition of American Nuns characterizes Palestinian women participants as "hostages to the perverse nationalistic hatred of the PLO . . . pawns in the game of politics . . . ."[72] Schreiber describes the speech of a Palestinian refugee as having "nothing to do with women" and as "clearly written" for her.[73] The report does not consider that this woman might herself be part of what Rosemary Sayigh has described as "a broad national consensus"—"the priority of national struggle over women's 'rights'."[74] Instead, these articles and statements implicitly contrast pro-Israel, anti-PLO feminists, Jewish and non-Jewish, who have freely arrived at their political positions, with pro-PLO women who, "in the bondage of Arab male supremacy,"[75] are unable to think for themselves. The National Coalition of American Nuns can, ironically, continue to claim Palestinian women as sisters only by describing them as helpless victims who have allegedly been coerced by a PLO which "has not shown any signs of joining the human family, as they are still pledged to 'liquidate' the State of Israel . . . ."[76] This sisterly concern for the oppression of Arab women unfortunately extends only to situations where the oppressor is an Arab man.

These conference reports assume that Palestinian women are dishonest. This attitude is hardly startling when one considers that a 1983 *New York Times* poll on relations between Jews and Arabs living in Israel showed that over 2/3 of respondents from each group would not "necessarily believe anything" said by a member of the other group.[77] The Pogrebin article includes a report by Barbara Leslie of the International Council of Jewish Women. Leslie writes that when at a conference workshop, "a Palestinian said, 'I was never a prisoner but here is how Israelis torture our women'," Tamar Eshel, "a member of the Israeli parliament and chair of its subcommittee on police and prisons," denied that charge, comparing it to "'Goebbels' technique of the big lie'."[78] Certainly, given the charged anti-Jewish tenor of the workshop, it was very difficult for Jewish women to identify the statements which at least deserved examination. But it is typical of the pervasive problem here that, in such an exchange between a Palestinian and an Israeli, the former is assumed a liar.

An additional obstacle to exploration is the perception that not only do Palestinians lie, but they hate Jews. In this particular example, the message is clear: since the Palestinian woman's statement reflects nothing but Jew-hating, Jewish women don't have to give a second thought to whether Palestinian women are tortured by Israelis. Critical questions which might be asked in a less polarized context are not raised: critical questions about the likelihood that Eshel or any other Knesset member will be *shown* signs of prisoner mistreatment when visiting prisons; about the pressures on an Israeli not to look for or follow up on instances of mistreatment of Palestinian prisoners who have been jailed for acts ranging from possessing banned books to distributing pamphlets to throwing stones to shooting hostages; about the chance that, in addition to its political repercussions, speaking up for Palestinian prisoners' rights can bring a swift banishment from the mainstream of Israeli life.[79]

In the rare instance where these articles present a picture of a Palestinian woman which is not totally negative, the omission of central information about her politics implies that she would not have major disagreements with the politics being set forth. The result is tokenization. Inge Lederer Gibel of the American Jewish Committee is quoted by Pogrebin as regretting that Raymonda Tawil was not at the conference. Described only as "a prominent Palestinian feminist . . . left home for daring to suggest that not only should there be mutual recognition between Israel and the PLO but also Palestinian women had faced oppression within their own ranks,"[80] Tawil is useful in demonstrating that the PLO is sexist and politically restrictive.

Neither Gibel nor Pogrebin mentions anything further about Tawil. Nothing is said of her writing about Israeli treatment of Palestinian women prisoners—of, for instance, her account of how her friend Rada al Nabulsi "told the judges how her [Israeli] interrogators had tried to rape her,"[81] and of the experience of Rasmiyah Oudeh whom the Israelis "threatened to rape . . . with a metal rod."[82] Tawil writes that on the West Bank:

> The first large protest action by women took place in 1968, after the Israeli authorities arrested a large number of resistance members, including some thirty women, mostly girls in their late teens or early twenties. The women were brutally tortured under interrogation.[83]

For Tawil, herself "kept at times in an unlit cell, blindfolded during interrogation, subjected to threats," and beaten in 1978, such abuse is a fact of life under Israeli occupation.[84] When she takes a position compatible with the particular concerns of pro-Israeli feminists, she is praised. When she speaks also as a Palestinian nationalist—a supporter of Palestinian self-determination, a backer, despite her criticisms, of the

PLO, a strenuous foe of Israeli policies—she is ignored.

An important issue here is how Jewish feminists define sisterhood and what we perceive as its boundaries. While some Jewish feminists, such as the Israeli group Women Against the Occupation, are working to stop the physical and psychological mistreatment of Palestinian women prisoners, others assume that such reports are simply propaganda.[85] The possibility that a report is unreliable cannot automatically be ruled out. But I am bothered when feminists reject our usual belief that a woman is telling the truth when she says she has been abused. *Without additional evidence,* some women conclude that she has made up a story for political purposes. Some Jewish women at an International Women's Day event responded with disbelief when a Palestinian woman spoke of her own experiences in an Israeli prison; they complained that she was not *even* a feminist, as though that fact made the brutality of the treatment she'd received less relevant.

As feminists we must consider that some Israeli men might behave in ways men as a class often do when they have power over women, particularly over women from a despised ethnic and political group. To give credence to reports of abuse in Israeli custody—or at least to seek further information before dismissing their accuracy—would not require us to believe that Jewish men or Israeli men are any worse than other groups of men. Immediately denying the validity of such reports—even when we thoroughly deplore the anti-Jewish framework in which some are presented—raises critical questions about the meaning of feminism and the possibility of bonds of sisterhood not just across lines of difference, but in the face of major political disagreement.

Understanding the position of Palestinian women involves, for non-Arab feminists, perceiving that the current conflict cannot be reduced to one between Good and Evil. For example, rather than arguing, as the National Council of American Nuns does, that the PLO is "still pledged to 'liquidate' the State of Israel," a position that prevents their "joining the human family,"[86] it would be useful to consider the *far* less extreme statements made by PLO leaders and Palestinian elected officials. Pogrebin's discussion, however, reflects some of the NCAN assumptions. She details the virulently anti-Jewish statements of a number of anti-Zionist women, but nowhere discusses those Palestinians or their supporters who reject Jew-hating as a stance. At one point, she writes:

> I long for a PLO counterpart to the Israeli peace groups so that rational dialogue may begin. But PLO moderates, rare as they are, seem to have been silenced by their own violent hard-liners. I have heard that many—including some peace-seeking women— fear for their lives. In the absence of peace initiatives and open

sisterhood, I am left to assume (according to PLO sentiment expressed in Copenhagen) that the average Palestinian woman would wish me dead.[87]

Rather than discussing PLO moderates, thus making their ideas more concrete to her readers, Pogrebin only makes the point that PLO "hard-liners" have silenced them. Certainly some moderates have been silenced by hard-liners who are intransigent, strongly nationalistic, and/or Jew-hating, including some whose anti-Zionism has as "its bottom line . . . an end to the Jews."[88] But Pogrebin does not mention those who have been silenced by the Israeli government in acts specifically designed to subjugate the Palestinians. Shortly before the appearance of her article, in the winter of 1981-1982, the Israelis dismissed four West Bank mayors, including Ibrahim Tawil of El Bireh, a PLO supporter who has "advocated a Palestinian state that would coexist peacefully next to Israel."[89] Several months later, two other deposed mayors joined with the two remaining West Bank mayors to issue a statement calling for mutual recognition between the PLO, which they regard as their legitimate representative, and Israel.[90] Ignoring such Palestinian calls for recognition and coexistence leaves the impression not only that the two sides are hopelessly polarized, but that *all* responsibility for the polarization rests with the Palestinians.

Pogrebin finally describes Palestinian women as implacable enemies of Jewish women, women who "wish us dead." It is significant to note that this is not the perception of a conservative or right-wing Zionist, but of an American Jew who takes moderate positions—supporting a two-state solution, recognizing that criticism of Israel is not "automatically anti-Semitic," acknowledging the situation as "a conflict between two national movements with complex historical origins."[91] Like some other feminists, Jewish and non-Jewish, Pogrebin does not analyze her gut-level response to Jew-hating in a way that would allow her to question her entrenched anti-Palestinian position. In her response to Pogrebin's piece, Alice Walker provides some balance and helpful political perspective when she writes:

> . . . my Jewish friend went to visit the Palestinian camps. She did not assume Palestinian women "wished her dead," and she was happy to discover that they did not. She did discover she looked a lot like them (*dark* and *Semitic*; "cousins, my ass," she said, "*sisters,* or somebody's mirror is lying"), that they shared many historical and cultural similarities, and that Palestinian women were no more wedded to the notion of violence than she was. But this was during the sixties, and perhaps everything *has* changed since then . . . .[92]

Pogrebin prefers to use only this specific forum at Copenhagen as the basis for her sweeping generalizations about Palestinians. She makes no reference to other conferences, to meetings she or other Jewish women have attended with Palestinian women, to Palestinian women's writing. She makes no reference to political activities in Israel or in the United States in which Palestinian and Jewish women are working together. She describes a particular frightening situation in which the rhetoric of Jew-hating was right out there. And she shuts down, instead of deciding she has to learn more, read more, hear more, before stating so definitively that the average Palestinian woman wants her dead, before holding Palestinians *as a group* responsible for the words and actions of some Palestinians and their supporters.

When the subject is the Middle East, the critical stance fundamental to feminist analysis can disappear entirely. Thus Annette Daum wisely urges a skeptical approach to mainstream, non-feminist organizations. But she does not bring that skepticism to bear on the portrayal of Palestinian women by a mainstream Jewish group, Americans for Peace and Democracy in the Middle East. The organization's ad featured a picture of a young Palestinian girl and the headline, "Thanks to Israel, she won't grow up to be mutilated, flogged or beheaded."[93] As Helen Samhan has written, "the image is of Arab women being liberated by Israel from their own civilization."[94]

Daum takes a different view, placing a particular Jewish feminist stamp of approval on this depiction of Palestinian women:

> Americans for Peace and Democracy in the Middle East had adopted an innovative approach to bring information to the American public about the position of Palestinian women and girls in Israel which is far superior to the position of Palestinian women in Arab countries. The infant mortality rate is 22 per 1,000 in Israel, compared to a range of 86 to 156 per 1,000 in Jordan, Syria, Egypt and Saudi Arabia. Nearly twice as many Arab Palestinian children attend school under Israeli administration. The chances of growing up literate are only 3 in 10 in Jordan and one half that in Iraq. Arab Palestinian women gained the right to vote in democratic elections in Israel in 1976, a right that does not exist in Arab countries. While reaching readers of prestigious publications like *The New York Times* is necessary, it is even more imperative to reach feminist leaders and to reach third world women who made a charade out of the U.N. Decade of Women conference and who themselves lack the opportunities in their own native lands that Israel provides for Palestinian women.[95]

Daum accepts the method commonly used by strong supporters of Israeli policies to evaluate the gains made by Palestinians under Israeli administration. The lives of Palestinians are compared to those of Arabs living in Arab countries, rather than to the lives of other people whose rights and services are determined by Israel. This yardstick is roughly equivalent to measuring the achievements of Haitians and Salvadorans in the United States, refugees and U.S. citizens alike, on the basis of whether they are doing better than people still living in Haiti or El Salvador, rather than comparing their status with that of white U.S. citizens.

Daum leaves unchallenged the incredible paternalism of this ad and its description of the status of Palestinians under Israeli rule. The implication is that Palestinian women should be grateful for what the Israelis have done for them, rather than that some good things might have inadvertently emerged from Israeli military control of its Palestinian non-citizens. The enfranchisement of Palestinian women, for instance, was, according to Raymonda Tawil, instituted by the Israelis "to show the world how they were 'bringing civilization and democracy to the Palestinians'."[96] Tawil indicates some of the ambivalence with which Palestinians received news of

> a decree amending the [Jordanian] electoral law in such a way that all households—even those that did not own property—were enfranchised if they paid any kind of municipal tax; moreover, with each household entitled to as many as four votes, the male head of the family was empowered to grant some of these votes to his female relatives. Although there was still much to criticize in the form of the law and its humiliating aspects—for women especially—its practical effect was a sweeping social revolution: For the first time, the vast majority of the adult population—women as well as men—was entitled to vote! Our feelings were mixed. The Geneva Convention forbids an occupying power to alter the legal structure of the territory it administers. Although this particular modification was beneficial, there was a question of principle involved: If we welcomed the Israeli move in amending one law, would this not serve as a precedent, giving them a pretext for changing our entire legal system?[97]

When the ad lauded by Daum was published, only a single elected West Bank mayor remained in office. Certainly the removal of these elected officials rendered moot the question of whether women, even with male approval, had been given the vote in 1976. And in 1980, as the Israeli newspaper *Al-Hamishmar* notes:

> The Military Government has forbidden *all the women's organizations* in the West Bank and Gaza Strip to have anything to do with politics. The order was issued after a clash between Israeli

soldiers and a group of Palestinian women holding a sit-in opposite the three houses sealed in Nablus last weekend . . . [after
some of the inhabitants'] sons had been accused of having thrown
stones at an Israeli car. In the course of the confrontation, which
was accompanied by sharp arguments, one of the women spat at
an officer. Seven women were arrested . . . The women will be
forbidden, among other things, to hold assemblies, publish
information or make public declarations. (my emphasis) [98]

Simply mentioning the right to vote without placing it in this broader
context has the practical effect of using women to make a spurious
political point.[99]

A further misunderstanding of issues basic to Palestinians is inherent
in Daum's argument that knowledge of "the opportunities . . . that
Israel provides for Palestinian women" will have a major impact on Third
World women, an impact so strong that they will rethink their negative
view of Israel. This misunderstanding is not new. Writing in *A History of
Zionism*, a standard pro-Zionist study, Walter Laqueur criticizes similar
assumptions held by Yishuv Jews during the pre-World War I period and
the Twenties:

> From a purely economic point of view, Arab resistance to
> Jewish immigration and settlement was inexplicable and un-
> justified. But then *the economic aspect of the conflict was
> hardly ever of decisive importance.* For that reason *the Zionist
> hope,* shared by Marxists and non-Marxists alike, *that economic
> collaboration would act as a powerful stimulus towards political
> reconciliation, was quite unrealistic. The conflict was, of course,
> basically political in character, a clash between two national
> movements.* (my emphasis)[100]

Although Laqueur recognizes that the issue which must be addressed is
nationalism, in terms of their assumptions relatively little difference
exists between the situation Laqueur depicts and the argument made by
Daum and the Americans for Peace and Democracy in the Middle East.
The virtues of economics and higher standards of living have been re-
placed by feminism and women's rights, but the premise remains that
Jews can bring—have, in fact, brought—to the Middle East "the blessings
of modern civilization"[101] and that, if these "blessings" are only emphasized enough, the desire for Palestinian self-determination will eventually die down. This assumption differs significantly from that behind
Helen Samhan's criticism of the ad mentioned above. She writes: "I
know I am not alone in admitting that certain traditions in Arab societies
are oppressive and perhaps barbaric. But no one can convince us that our
people's emancipation can ever come from the occupation of Arab land

and suppression of its people's right to self-determination."[102]

Challenging these Zionist assumptions and finding in them resonances of the European belief in the "white man's burden" and other ideas fundamental to colonialism, I do not presume that Israel is worse than a good many other countries in the world. And I do know that in its provisions for the democratic rights of Jews, particularly Ashkenazim, Israel strives for "institutions that guarantee political participation and human rights,"[103] which, as Edmund Ghareeb has written, are largely absent in the Arab world. But I do question the impact of separating the concerns of Palestinian women from their national political struggles on potential dialogue with Arab and other Third World women, including women of color in the United States.

Women who hold to a far different ideology than that of these Jewish feminists are equally likely to present a partial picture, to engage in rhetorical overkill, and to express their own bias. I have, for example, heard that some Arab women contend that "real" anti-Semitism, the European variety, has affected only Christian Arabs, and that no anti-Jewish feeling existed in Palestine before Zionist settlements began in the nineteenth century.[104] These positions seem intended in part to distinguish between the historical situation of Jews in the Arab world and their much more dangerous one in Europe. However, the first statement overlooks the willingness of some Moslem Arab leaders to spread European-created propaganda designed to inspire hatred and distrust of Jews, as well as its impact on some Arabs. The second ignores the history of anti-Jewish acts during the centuries preceding Zionism, thus distorting Jewish history. It also implies that, because Zionism took root in an area "free" of anti-Jewish attitudes, the subsequent development of such attitudes among Arabs was caused by Zionism.

The argument that Israel's responsibility for events extends farther than that of other countries expresses a common anti-Jewish attitude. The Wallflower Order, a feminist and progressive dance group, has charged Israel with committing "the worst crimes of any country since 1945."[105] I consider, for example, the Israeli use in Lebanon of U.S.-provided cluster bombs to be horrible and indefensible, and I believe that we must denounce this action as strongly as we can.[106] But the assertion that these acts make Israel *worse* than any other country since the Nazis is fallacious. For one thing, it ignores the United States' role in Vietnam. It also overlooks, among other mass killings, those "in Indonesia in 1967,

Burundi in 1972-73, Kampuchea in 1975-76, East Timor in 1975-76, Uganda in 1976-78, Argentina in 1976-80, the Central African Empire in 1978, and Equatorial Guinea in 1977-79."[107] And this list is of course terrribly incomplete. In no way does it excuse what Israel has done. But it does make clear that to say Israel's crimes are the "worst" in recent memory has little to do with facts and a great deal to do with anti-Semitism. The equation between Israel and Nazi Germany, implied in the Wallflower Order's use of 1945, the end of the Nazi era as a reference point, and made explicit in its description of Israel as "the new Nazi state," compounds the offense.[108]

An Alliance Against Women's Oppression statement singles out Israel in a similar way, citing it as "*the* principal source of war and impediment to progress in the Middle East region" (my emphasis).[109] The statement manages to overlook the large number of Arabs killed, since 1948, in fighting between Arab states or between factions within these states or, for the past four years, the nearly a million people estimated killed in the war between Iraq and Iran, a Persian Gulf state; the "impediment to progress" created by reactionary policies and state repression of some Arab regimes; and the destructive role of the superpowers in playing factions and governments off against each other.[110] That Israel has had a special role in keeping the Palestinian people homeless and without self-government (and that the United States has supported Israel in its policies) is clear. But the AAWO position is typical of others which wrongly single Israel out for blame.

By glossing over the role of Arab states in the Palestinian-Israeli struggle, the statement neglects, among other things, the fact that from 1948 to 1967 Jordan controlled the West Bank and Egypt controlled the southern part of the Gaza Strip. Neither government supported the autonomy or independence of Palestinian residents of those regions; the Egyptians, according to Fawaz Turki, "proceeded to treat the people worse than their Israeli counterparts did across the border."[111] On the West Bank, "political parties were banned [by Jordan], labor unions made illegal, and expressions of critical views were punished with imprisonment."[112] Jordan "in 1951 prohibited the use of the word Palestine to refer to those portions under its jurisdictions, substituting for it the term West Bank."[113] In Arab states, as well, Palestinian refugees were badly treated. Writing about his childhood in a Lebanese refugee camp, Turki notes how

The irony of my plight was that as I grew up my bogeyman was not the Jew (despite the incessant propaganda that Radio Cairo subjected us to), nor was he the Zionist (if indeed I recognized the distinction), nor was he for that matter the imperialist or the Western supporters and protectors of the state of Israel, but he was the Arab. The Arab in the street who asked if you'd ever heard the one about the Palestinian who . . . The Arab in the Alienes Section who wanted you to wait obsequiously for your work permit, the Arab at the police station who felt he possessed a carte blanche to mistreat you, the Arab who rejected you and, most crucially, took away from you your sense of hope and sense of direction.[114]

Describing the years after he and his family left Palestine in 1948, Turki recalls how "the Arab governments continued to oppose schemes for integration on the grounds that these would be tantamount to admission of defeat by Israel," but that "the price paid for this intransigence and inflexibility was paid by the Palestinians alone and not by the Arabs."[115] In 1970, for example, King Hussein, with U.S. backing, defeated the PLO in a Jordanian civil war in which many civilians died, while no other Arab states provided the Palestinians with support; in 1983, with Soviet arms and Syrian support, a faction of the PLO defeated Arafat loyalists in and around Tripoli, again with high civilian casualties among the Palestinians.[116]

The type of analysis that places responsibility for events almost solely on Israel contributes to an atmosphere in which Israeli actions are condemned more strongly than similar actions by other groups or countries. Although Bethlehem Mayor Elias Freij, for example, "denounced the reciprocal massacres in Lebanon and said they 'sully the name of Arabs throughout the world',"[117] the pro-Palestinian, anti-imperialist movement in the United States remained silent when two Palestinian refugee camps outside Tripoli were destroyed in the fighting between PLO factions. Pro-Syrian PLO forces attacked the camps; under fire, pro-Arafat forces remained in the camps longer than warranted by military considerations as they maneuvered for political survival. U.S. groups which marshalled themselves to protest vehemently the massacre by Phalangists with Israeli complicity at Sabra and Shatila were quiet during—and in the aftermath of—this killing of Palestinian and Lebanese noncombatants. Similarly, the U.S. media has taken little notice of the destruction caused by U.S. battleships lobbing shells into the villages around Beirut.

This double bookkeeping is apparent in Israel's attitudes as well. Its government rejects talks with the PLO on the grounds of PLO "terrorism." Yet Israel's last two prime ministers were leaders in pre-Israel

Palestine of groups routinely characterized as "terrorists" by pro-Zionist historians. Begin was a leader of the Irgun, which in 1946 blew up the King David Hotel in Jerusalem with many British, Arab, and Jewish casualties. Shamir was prominent in the Stern Gang, which assassinated United Nations Mediator Folke Bernadotte in 1948. Both participated in the joint Irgun-Stern massacre of Palestinians at Deir Yassin in which 250 men, women, and children were brutally killed.[118] While calling for the PLO to recognize Israel's right to exist, Shamir declares, "All we want from the P.L.O. is that it disappear from the face of the earth."[119] The consequence is the polarization deplored by the Israeli-American Civil Liberties Coalition in a post-invasion ad headlined:

> Some Palestinians think that calling Jews "Zionists" justifies the killing of Jews.
> Some Jews think that calling Palestinians "terrorists" justifies the killing of Palestinians.
> We do not.[120]

This voice is, unfortunately, that of a minority, both within the women's movement and outside it. Polarization has been far more common. After objecting to the anti-Jewish comments in a newsletter published by white radical South Africans, New Jewish Agenda's racism and anti-Semitism taskforce (Brooklyn chapter) received a reply stating that, because of its support for Israel's existence, the taskforce was incapable of doing anti-racist work in the Brooklyn community. The deadlock was absolute. Nothing those of us on the taskforce could say, including reiterating once again our complete condemnation of Israel's support for South Africa, could make dialogue possible. Nothing we could say would make them consider the possibility that, despite our disagreements, we might be seriously and actively concerned with racism. It was easier to dismiss us totally, to assume that we had nothing to contribute to progressive politics, and to treat us as indistinguishable from reactionary forces.

Similar interactions have occurred in the women's movement. And similar conclusions have been drawn. An International Women's Day panel in Madison, Wisconsin was disrupted by Jewish women after the Israeli woman scheduled to speak was "disinvited" following the last-minute discovery that she was a Zionist; the possibility that she might strongly support Palestinian rights was never considered.[121] The multiracial collective which edits *Spare Rib*, the London-based feminist monthly, decided that it would print none of the letters it has received from Jewish women in response to the statement of an Israeli woman, "if a woman calls herself feminist she should consciously call herself anti-Zionist"; the implications, as Dena Attar, daughter of an Iraqi Jew, has written, is that "*all* of those letters were Zionist and/or racist."[122] Jewish women's identification as Zionist was immediately characterized as racist and the right to object to anti-Zionist statements was rejected on the grounds of real or alleged Zionist identification.

In mentioning examples of polarization, I assume that some positions are thoroughly incompatible. The anti-Zionist who actually favors driving Jews into the sea and the Zionist who condones any violence against Palestinians as acceptable in protecting Eretz Yisrael, all of Palestine, have nothing to say to each other. Sometimes "the other" actually is "the enemy." Too often, however, assumptions about beliefs behind a label and the tendency to see written statements as carved in stone lead feminists and others to condemn someone from whom we could learn, someone whom we might also be able to teach. Too often we dismiss out of hand a position about which we need to learn more.

Felt painfully in the women's movement, such responses parallel in their righteous anger that described by Jacobo Timerman in *The Longest War: Israel in Lebanon,* an extremely critical look at recent Israeli policy. Timerman writes:

> The government appears to be girding itself for a typical Israeli political debate, in which accusations require no proof and weigh more than ideas or analysis. Israel is a country of great verbal violence. Anybody familiar with the history of Jewish institutions knows the phrases of lament and accusation that have divided the Jewish people for thousands of years. But it seems to me that more than verbal violence affects Israelis in their debates. It is almost verbal cannibalism. Words must, before demonstrating the rightness of one's own judgment, eradicate the existence of the opponent, devour him.[123]

One such eradication of Timerman occurs in the neo-conservative Jewish journal *Commentary,* whose review of his book concludes with a comment on both Timerman, who had escaped persecution as a Jew in Argentina to live in Israel, and Ephraim Sevela, a Russian emigré who has been critical of Israel: "Israeli democracy is much stronger than these two men claim if it has been able to weather such consequences of the Law of Return as they."[124]

We can find equally scathing responses within the women's movement, in personal and group relationships, in the letters columns of our publications, in the individual and collective statements circulated locally or nationally. Verbal annihilation is hardly limited to a single political perspective. In a June 1982 letter to *Gay Community News,* a Jewish woman, Janet Gottler, objects to "the assumption . . . that anti-Zionism is anti-Semitism and that any Jew holding an anti-Zionist position must be a self-hating Jew." She compares these accusations and implications to those made by the Jewish Defense League "back in 1972 and 1973, when [she was] organizing public forums of Jewish-Israeli, Palestinian-Israeli, and Jewish-American activists."[125] Rachael Kamel responds to Di Vilde Chayes' "letter defending Zionism [which, she says] takes as its central point the idea that Zionism is a 'strategy for Jewish survival'," by characterizing this position as "a psychotic fantasy."[126] In this atmosphere, it is noteworthy when a woman in a *Gay Community News* Speaking Out column makes clear her assumption that the pro-PLO, strongly anti-Zionist column with which she strenuously disagrees has been motivated by a serious concern for peace in the region and refrains from applying to its author any number of defamatory adjectives.[127]

While written exchanges are a critical part of work on the Middle East, they lack the give-and-take which can most effectively encourage rethinking of one's position. Almost always one-shot interactions of statement and response, they seem to lend themselves to criticism of group or individual motivation. In the absence of personal contact, little room exists to say simply, "Do you really believe X?" or "Don't you think you should have been more emphatic about Y?" Rarely does the opportunity present itself for an individual or group to agree that some criticism of its position has validity or even to acknowledge that a statement written months before no longer reflects its current thinking on this issue. In the absence of such response and counter-response, questions of motivation, frequently near the heart of the criticism, remain unclarified. So the impression remains that someone is truly unconcerned with Jewish oppression or indifferent to Palestinian rights, that someone is unalterably racist or anti-Jewish, *rather* than that she might have done a better job initially of stating her politics or that, with minimal prodding and added information, she might expand her politics in a substantive way.

The writing of position papers can be done, if not individually, then in homogeneous, often rather small groups which offer a valuable base of support. Other activism necessarily involves working—even appearing publicly—with people whose politics we don't fully share, as well as with people whose biases might deeply offend and anger us. Nothing is simple about the choices one makes in terms of coalition politics. While I have done work related to the Israeli-Palestininan conflict as a member of Jewish groups—with the Brooklyn chapter of New

Jewish Agenda and with a group of Jewish feminists and lesbians—I have also participated in coalition actions and workgroups in which anti-Jewish attitudes are sometimes expressed and have to be confronted, and in which Jewish oppression is not immediately assumed by all participants to be a significant issue.

I have, for example, attended demonstrations where it has been necessary to object to anti-Jewish slogans and placards: "Hitler and Begin are the same, the only difference is their name"; a rectangular sign with a star of David on the far left which, through a series of repositionings of its lines, emerges as a swastika on the far right side. And I have been told of a speaker at a rally against the invasion of Lebanon saying, "I'm tired of hearing of this Holocaust trip"; of an audience member at a literary event soon after the invasion calling out, when a Jewish man read a poem about Anne Frank, "Is that why Begin is doing what he's doing?" This turning the Holocaust metaphor back on the Jews was not made one whit more palatable by Begin's unprincipled use of the Holocaust to justify any conceivable action during the invasion and subsequent occupation of Lebanon.[128] So I have chosen *not* to go to some demonstrations, to some political events, because I didn't want to deal with the signs and slogans, because of my anger at the anti-Jewish attitudes of some people who, sharing my abhorrence of Israel's actions, might otherwise have been my allies.

Sometimes the demonstration has been organized by a Jewish group which I know will make me feel well supported. At other times, when I go, I do so selectively, I check out the sponsors, read the leaflet carefully, and make sure I go with Jewish friends. Then I prepare for the possibility of directly objecting to the words on someone's homemade placard or, *if* we have a sign indicating our presence as Jews, of coping with questions about why we have chosen to protest *as Jews*. When the occasion has stirred me deeply—the invasion, the Sabra-Shatila massacre —the choice has not been between the comfort of staying home and the pain of attending a demonstration where I might have to face anti-Jewish sentiments, but between the pain of remaining silent and the pain of going to the demonstration. At these times, I have often gone, desiring to protest not just Israeli policies but the U.S. support for them that my tax dollars finance.

Political forums are no less perilous arenas. The quick history, the passing comment, the political rhetoric, all contain the possibilities for anti-Jewish assertions or inferences. At forums and panels, encounters are brief, the chances for exchange limited, and follow-up usually impossible. At an International Women's Day panel featuring two Palestinians and one Israeli, the American Jewish moderator began with an anti-Zionist history of the region. It covered the Thirties and Forties without reference to the Holocaust. At a forum on Jews and the Rainbow Coalition, an Asian-American woman was greeted with enthusiastic claps when she remarked that criticizing Israel is not anti-Jewish. Although I agreed with her statement, I feared that some of the audience interpreted it as meaning that one can say anything about Israel—in any way—without being anti-Jewish. A subsequent speaker talked passionately about "Jewish reaction" and "Jewish influence" before launching into a condemnation of Israel's relations with right-wing regimes in Latin America and South Africa—a criticism I fully agreed with. But the speaker had laid such a solid anti-Jewish base for her comments that my gut-level response to the entire statement was that it was anti-Jewish.

In the context of long-term work, political differences and personal prejudices can be confronted on a regular basis. The individual or group is more than a presence at a demonstration, a participant with only a few minutes to speak, an endorsement at the bottom of a leaflet. Ongoing work on any aspect of the Middle East conflict is unlikely to occur without tension and disagreement. Rarely will we find ourselves in a group where unity exists in analysis *and* strategy. Often the initial goal is not total unity, but agreement on certain issues. Often individual and group decisions must be made through compromise: some Jewish women might decide to alter a statement about anti-Semitism in relation to the Middle East so that the women of color with whom they are working feel able to support it publicly; some anti-Zionist Jewish women might be willing to work in a coalition in which their anti-Israeli views are not fully expressed so that they can participate in a Jewish-Latin American unity event.

When I speak of compromise, I am not talking about abandoning our most basic political principles or remaining silent about the oppression(s) we see most sharply. I am, however, talking about the flexibility necessary for political work to go on. For Jewish women like myself who do not define themselves as anti-Zionist, for example, working politically with Arab women will almost always involve differences which have to be negotiated, and in some cases simply accepted as irresolvable. Much will depend on the tolerance for difference. If, for instance, I assume that someone who defines herself as an anti-Zionist, as Palestinian or Arab nationalist, is, by definition, my enemy, we have no grounds for meeting. If she assumes that my support for Israel's existence defines me as the enemy, she will have no reason to work with me. If we can survive the tension of having different analyses, we can perhaps begin to consider what, as feminists and as political activists,

we can work on together—opposition to the general repressiveness of
the Israeli occupation, its specific effect on Palestinian women, the building of more Israeli settlements in Occupied Territories, Israel's role as
arms seller to right-wing governments, the danger of conventional warfare
in the Middle East escalating to nuclear confrontation, the United States'
self-interested role as arms merchant to countries on both sides of the
conflict.

The direct contact involved in such joint organizing efforts can
also provide Jewish women with a keen sense of the disparity between
the lives of Palestinians and Israelis. When I read an Arab-Jewish dialogue in which both Palestinian and Jewish women agree that the "realistic" position, the reasonableness of some American Jews about the
Middle East is a "privilege,"[129] I was confident that I understood clearly
the argument being made. And, in fact, I did. But I did not reach a more
basic understanding until several months later when I sat at meetings
with women whose relatives have been under bombardment by U.S. ships
off the Lebanese coast, with women whose relatives are under military
control on the West Bank, when I listened to a woman who cannot visit
her family in the West Bank city of Nablus. I know that, despite a series
of civilian-aimed bombings in Israel, a machine-gun and grenade attack
on Jerusalem residents, a bus hijacking by one or more PLO factions, *my*
relatives—my daughter's paternal grandparents—sit in comparative safety
somewhere north of Tel Aviv where she will spend her upcoming summer
vacation.

Even in this situation of fundamental imbalance, it is, of course,
imperative to confront anti-Jewish assumptions, statements, and actions.
It is vital to resist the pressure to remain silent and the implication that
the charge of anti-Semitism is a diversion from the "real" issues. At times,
it will be necessary to address the anti-Jewish bias of a group which,
despite stated opposition to anti-Semitism, has a limited idea of its manifestations and impact, as well as how actively to protest it. At times,
it will be necessary to deal with the assumption that concern with Jewish
oppression marks one as being unconcerned with Palestinian rights (as
in other settings, people might believe that any concern with Arab
oppression marks one as indifferent to Jewish oppression).[130]

In doing this work, Jewish women need to acknowledge Arab
women as one possible source of support in opposing Jewish oppression.
Lebanese-American Tina Naccach, for instance, has spoken out about
"the realistic fear" of anti-Semitism in the United States.[131] After
arguing for the need to "resist, challenge and defeat racism against all
peoples," Helen Samhan has drawn parallels between "racist cartoons
of fat bankers strangling the German economy in the 1930s . . . [and]
racist cartoons of the fat greedy oil sheikhs of the 1980s strangling the

American economy."[132] When a woman explains that she backs Palestinian rights because, "the Jews are taking over where I live," a Palestinian woman objects. When a right-wing group sends an anti-Jewish pamphlet to an Arab woman because it assumes that, working for an Arab organization, she too hates Jews, she angrily throws it out.

We can also find support for our work in ongoing organizing. In Israel, joint Arab-Jewish efforts have protested the continuing occupation of southern Lebanon, the destruction of Palestinian houses and the building of Jewish settlements on the West Bank, the discrimination against Arab students at Haifa University, the violence by Jewish settlers directed at Palestinian residents of Hebron, racism in Upper Nazareth, prison conditions of Palestinian prisoners, restrictions on academic freedom at Bir Zeit University on the West Bank.[133] Women Against the Occupation, Committee to End the War in Lebanon, East for Peace, Committee in Solidarity with Bir Zeit University, and Peace Now are among the Isareli groups which have been working with Palestinians and with Israeli Arabs.[134] In addition, a committee of Jews and Arabs has been formed to oppose MENA, "Defenders of Upper Nazareth," a group seeking to prohibit sale of apartments to Arabs in that region. The American-based Interns for Peace sends Israeli Jews, Israeli Arabs, and Diaspora Jews to live and work in Arab villages, helping in such areas as childcare and adolescent recreation and encouraging contact between neighboring Arabs and Jews. Four Bir Zeit professors have engaged in unprecedented public dialogue with Israeli Jewish faculty. Prominent West Bank leaders have condemned recent terrorist attacks on Israeli civilians. Members of Yesh G'vul ("There's A Limit"), Israeli army reservists, have been jailed for refusing to serve in Lebanon. Deposed West Bank mayors, all PLO supporters, have met with delegations from such Jewish groups as the International Center for Peace in the Middle East, have toured in the United States with a representative of Peace Now, and have called on both sides to recognize each other's rights.[135]

This listing, although incomplete, undercuts any tendency to view Israeli Arabs, Israeli Jews, or Palestinians as a monolithic group unwilling to work with people whose identities and/or politics differ from their own. It illustrates well the risks people on all sides—Jew and non-Jew, Arab and non-Arab, Zionist, anti-Zionist, non-Zionist—take in the course of their work for peace and co-existence. Jewish feminists in this country need to ally ourselves with the people taking these risks, both in the Middle East and in the United States; the people who know the limits of an either/or political approach; the people less concerned with debating history and labels, and more concerned with organizing in the context of the current political situation.

IX. OPENINGS

In the year and nine months I have been working on this article—intermittently, sometimes taking time to do paid work, too often taking time to be sick—I have felt driven. Early on I had dreams of concentration camps. Later I dreamed of the Middle East. The work did not stay neatly contained in the hours I had allotted to it. I thought of it as I jogged through the park, sat on the subway, observed a high school math class. Even when I caught some virus, my ready excuse to crawl into bed and away from my typewriter, I could not escape. Across the room from my bed, next to my desk, a makeshift edifice had arisen—four milk crates, two cinderblocks, three boards from an old bookshelf. It reached the maximum safe height, a bit shorter than me, and began to expand horizontally, milk crates stacked above the adjoining dresser and atop the single properly-constructed bookshelf I had begun with. Books, pamphlets, newspapers, overflow onto the floor, into and on top of cartons. The process of writing has not been tidy.

Perhaps the mess is inevitable. Racism and anti-Semitism are not neat subjects. They do not lend themselves to simple emotions or pat answers. But, as long as they exist, we must work toward solutions. So I come back always to strategies, to strategies and activism. I return to the questions: What to do? How to do it? And whom to do it with?

The recent growth of a Jewish feminist movement has, for many of us, opened up possible responses to these questions which we would never have thought of a few years ago. And, as I consider these questions, I am impelled to consider what influences us to select one strategy rather than another, what makes a particular approach harder to consider than it might be; to consider how the recent growth of a Jewish feminist movement has both opened up and hampered certain kinds of activism.

Many Jewish feminists come from backgrounds of assimilation which continue to be a source of pain and potential tension. It can be tempting, especially for those of us who have emerged from years of silence and self-denial, to distance ourselves from our histories, particularly when we see them reflected in someone else's process of coming to self-awareness. The distancing, the failure to acknowledge the relative newness of an insight or political identification, can prevent constructive interaction. A white Jewish woman responds to the criticism of a non-Jewish woman of color by asking whether she has *always* shown sufficient concern for Jewish oppression in her anti-racist work, when the Jewish woman herself had begun to speak out against anti-Semitism only a few years before (and had not always spoken out against racism). A Jewish woman calls another one "self-hating" because the second woman doesn't agree with a political position which the first woman had arrived at recently.

In part, these responses may be the growing pains of a movement, but they also reflect a long-standing tendency in the Jewish community to separate the "real Jews" from those who are not. At one point, I considered using as an epigraph to part of this article a remark by an elderly Jewish man quoted in *Number Our Days*: "If you don't put out your hand against injustice, I don't care if you pray all day. You may be religious, but by me this isn't a Jew."[1] It was only my realization that he too was determining who was and was not a "real Jew" that made me decide to leave it out.

This problem also takes the form of distinguishing Good Jews from Bad Jews. A Jewish woman angrily characterizes Jewish women working in one racially mixed group as "Good" Jews, supposedly currying favor with women of color and insufficiently concerned with Jewish oppression; she numbers herself among the "Bad" Jews, because of her membership in a feminist group which has made opposition to Jewish oppression its priority. From this perspective, a Good Jew is actually a *bad* Jew.

Within the Jewish feminist movement, the proponents of the Good Jew/Bad Jew formulation often attempt to define others' motivations —as do those who employ such slashing characterizations as "self-hating" or (for women of color) "white-minded." Motivation is, of course, an easy target, sometimes attractive when the substance of the disagreement has been exhausted and a closing personal swipe seems irresistible. What we need are ways in which we can disagree with the substance of what a woman says, with the emphasis she has chosen, with the analysis and strategy she has outlined, without calling into question her political and personal integrity or attacking her sense of positive Jewish identification.

I believe that my work stems from my politics and sense of ethics. I know too that, faced with a huge number of possible political projects, equally deserving of time and energy, I choose in part because of what *I* will gain, not simply what I will give back; I choose in part because my connection with the people involved serves as its own motivating force. But this does not constitute all of what motivates my political work. I am not immune to feeling "the old competitiveness, the wanting recognition, 'success'," which Mab Segrest pinpoints as one dynamic in "a movement working on liberation."[2] The desire for approval from any number of quarters—Jewish and non-Jewish, white and Third World—might also serve as a motivation for political work. Since I cannot even swear to the absolute purity of my own motivation, I think it is much more useful to focus on what someone *does* and how she does it. Maintaining this perspective is part of the work of politics. It keeps the emphasis where it belongs—on actions intended to move toward a specific goal.

If we choose the work of politics, we need to figure out how differences, sometimes relating to Jewish oppression, sometimes to racism, sometimes to both, can be discussed without inhibiting dialogue. Melanie Kaye/Kantrowitz describes one attempt to do this in a meeting with part of the hiring committee at a university where she was denied reappointment:

> I raised the issue of antisemitism, of cultural clash; and was again ridiculed. One woman, L., a Chicana, said that to many Chicanas, Jewish people were just white; just *landlords;* that Jewish people came here and took land from the Indians. I said that to many Jews, Chicanos were just Catholics, and she knew what Catholics had done to the Jews. I said that the few Jews who came here—to the Southwest—had been kicked out of Spain. I should have said that all non-natives took the Indians' land, though in truth I don't know if Jews took land or not. One condition of the American Jews is ignorance of our history, and an absorption of this history into the history of white people, so that whatever is said of white people is said of Jews as well—and sometimes blamed on Jews. *Anyway, this woman and I looked at each other with some understanding.* "Hear other people's prejudice—and our own?"
>
> At one point the wasp coordinator left the room. L. talked about her anger at white lesbians from a white community, ignorant of the experiences of lesbians of color. I said my community in the Southwest wasn't an all-white community. L. said she'd assumed it was. L. and P., a Black lesbian, said they wanted a woman of color to teach the Heterosexism class. I was upset that they had no interest in representing Jewish women in

the program, but I understood their feeings; I said this. *At least we were talking.* (my emphasis)[3]

In this exchange, Kaye/Kantrowitz appears to have made some difficult decisions, the first of which was not to respond simply by labeling the ridicule as anti-Jewish. She chooses instead to engage, replying with information that might undercut stereotypes of Jews, and with statements highlighting the similarities between biased assumptions about Jews and biased assumptions about (Chicano) Catholics. She recognizes that, regardless of her individual actions, the women she is talking to might see her as typical of and responsible for the white lesbian community; she may be seen—and cannot help but operate—as both oppressor and oppressed. As a result of their willingness to keep talking, Kaye/Kantrowitz and L. and P. begin, however tentatively, to reach "some understanding" of each other's situations. Each paragraph concludes with the acknowledgment that some advance, however, slight, has been made; "at least," as Kaye/Kantrowitz writes, they "were talking."

Doing such work involves not confusing our emotional community with our political arena, or, as Bernice Johnson Reagon says, our home with our coalition. In each place, the expectations are quite different. As Reagon writes:

> Coalition work is not work done in your home. Coalition work has to be done in the streets. And it is some of the most danger-ous work you can do. And you shouldn't look for comfort. Some people will come to a coalition and they rate the success of the coalition on whether or not they feel good when they get there. They're not looking for a coalition; they're looking for a home! They're looking for a bottle with some milk in it and a nipple, which does not happen in a coalition. You don't get a lot of food in a coalition. You don't get fed in a coalition. In a coalition you have to give, and it is different from your home. You can't stay there all the time. You go to the coalition for a few hours and then you go back and take your bottle wherever it is, and then you go back and coalesce some more.[4]

Reagon assumes, as I do, that politics involves working in coalitions and having a "home" to go back to. In her way, she is positing a "We/They" framework of home vs. coalition. The critical issue is to find the home, to find the base from which to do political work. This is neither a purely personal dilemma nor one faced only by those who, like me, are Jewish feminists. Audre Lorde expresses the same yearning as she writes of the time before she was generally known to be a lesbian when, as she entered the room, her

>   ... eyes would seek out the one or two black faces
>   for contact or reassurance or a sign
>   I was not alone
>   now walking into rooms full of black faces
>   that would destroy me for any difference
>   where shall my eyes look?
>   Once it was easy to know
>   who were my people.[5]

Having worked at different times in organizations of "my people"—all women, all lesbians, all Jews, all Jewish feminists—I know well the attraction and uses of such groups. They have—and do—provide me with a ground from which to move out into the larger world. When they have offered me the greatest support, it has been the combination of shared identities *and* compatible politics, rather than the simple fact of shared identities, which has made communication possible. While we often think of coalitions as *crossing* lines of identity—women of color and white women working together, Jews and non-Jews, lesbians and non-lesbians—the interactions Reagon describes as typifying "coalition politics" do, in fact, exist within each identity group. Certainly this is true in those situations where the politics of those involved differ sharply. Working with non-Jews also involves identifying those areas where we can work together and those in which we cannot. For efforts arising from our common politics to be successful, I need to decide which points to raise, which to push, and which to leave in the background. My ability to do effective political work depends both on finding allies and on keeping a sense of home. Out of the larger "lesbian community" or "women's community" or "Jewish feminist community," we carve a smaller, more personally and politically compatible one made up of "those among whom we can sit down and weep, and still be counted as warriors."[6]

As I have thought increasingly about the issues of home and community, I have found myself coming up with questions, not with answers.[7] So I made a list of questions (included in the Appendix) which might provide a framework for each of us to analyze how we see ourselves in relation to the Jewish feminist movement, to the women's movement as a whole, to other progressive movements; and then to look at how we interrupt—or might interrupt—racism and Jewish oppression, at how we do—or could do—political work on both issues; at how we work in coalitions.

I begin with many assumptions. I believe, for instance, that our choices both of political priorities and of strategies are influenced by our definitions of our community and our home, by the people we can trust are beside us and those we see only across the room or down the block. Our analysis and activities will necessarily be affected by our lack of contact with other Jewish women, with non-Jewish women of color and with those who share our general political perspective. When I ask myself who *I* define as my most immediate community, I come up with answers which are not nearly as broad as they might be. I am aware, for instance, that, when my personal connections to women of various identities are extremely limited, these limitations are reflected in my thinking, my words, and my activism. On the other hand, my links with some Jewish women, almost all Ashkenazi, all themselves struggling with the issues of racism and Jewish oppression, have informed my work, even when we do not fully agree with each other; in the absence of these women, I would have ceased writing this piece long ago. Taking stock can show us the parameters of our most immediate community. It can also show us how our individual political work has, over the years, both focused within these boundaries and transcended them; how we have both stayed with what we know best and stretched ourselves to learn about—and connect with—women whose paths do not necessarily cross our own.

We might explore a host of questions about how we have confronted either racism or anti-Semitism; how we would like to have done so; what kind of support we have gotten, or failed to get, from others present; how the identity of the person we confront and the circumstances in which the interaction takes place affect what we do. We make choices. And sometimes we are not all that happy with them. At a workshop on anti-Semitism, for example, the Jewish participants discussed various responses to Jewish oppression: rage, rationality, reasoned explanation that acknowledges anger, silence. A week later, when one woman described the workshop to members of our anti-Semitism and racism taskforce, she mentioned that, though everyone at the workshop agreed that silence was unacceptable, it had also been the most common response. Everyone laughed, recognizing in that statement our own failures, our own political frailty. Each of us has been silent in response to racism and Jewish oppression, each of us has tried to confront them in nonconstructive ways; rarely can any of us look back without feeling that she might have done it better. When we consider our experiences of confronting anti-Semitism and racism, we do so primarily to learn how to do it better.

Within a broader organizational framework, we need to ask questions about who confronts Jewish oppression or racism or who argues that these issues need to be discussed; about the response of other group or coalition members to such discussions and confrontations; about what is "acceptable" to raise in a given setting; about how a group's attitudes toward racism and anti-Semitism affect politics vis 'a vis the Middle East; about how a group or coalition achieves unity and works out compromises, as well as about what to do when unity and compromise prove impossible. In each setting we might consider further questions about whom we identify as our constituency; which goals are essential, which most realistic; what allies exist for us to seek out for coalitions. At every step along the way, as we join a group, form a coalition, or put our names on a flyer, we also ask whom we are prepared to work with: Jewish lesbians, Jewish feminists, progressive Jews, feminists or radicals from different backgrounds. The answers to these questions, different from group to group, from year to year within a group, can tell us something useful for our work.

The questions I ask are not comprehensive, and are not meant to be. If we apply them broadly, they may help define both individual and group analyses of a range of issues—militarism, economics, imperialism—which I have touched on only in passing. They may help us judge ways in which these major forces intersect with institutional racism and anti-Semitism. These questions are not a standard way of ending a piece of this length. Yet they seem to me the right way to end. They emphasize how slow personal and political change is—how hard, and how necessary. They underscore the fact that political work is more complicated than we often think. More complicated, no doubt, than I have made it out to be.

So I resist the temptation to end with a closing burst of optimism, a reference to sisterhood, unity, or revolution. I am neither a visionary nor an optimist. I have sat in too many meetings and been in too many groups to be either. But I do believe in the absolute necessity of fighting anti-Semitism and racism and in the possibility of political change. And I do know that there is much work to be done.

August 1982-May 1984

APPENDIX: QUESTIONS

Since my primary focus in writing has been on ways for Jewish women to confront Jewish oppression and racism, I assume here a reader who is herself Jewish; at the same time, I hope that the following questions will be used by—and, where necessary, adapted to—non-Jewish women, Third World and white. I assume as well that there are no correct answers to these questions. Rather, they are intended to challenge, to reveal changes in attitudes and strategies over time, to underscore how much each of us still has to learn.

Since many Jewish women have engaged in consciousness-raising about Jewish identity and anti-Semitism and many white women have done so about racism, I have skipped over a basic avenue of inquiry: essential CR questions about one's earliest recollections of racism and anti-Semitism; about parental attitudes toward people of color and Jews; about the ways in which economic issues affected what each of us was taught about Jewish oppression and racism. Yet, responding fully to some of the questions I *do* ask might also require considering these other questions, so that the lessons of childhood and growing up which remain part of us can illuminate the work we do in the present.

I have divided the questions into three sets: 1) Communities; 2) Confrontations; and 3) Groups and Coalitions. I recommend that each be used in a different fashion. The "Communities" questions lend themselves to being considered by one's self, as a means of self-clarification, or perhaps with one or two friends. The "Confrontations" questions can be used as exercises in workshops or as focuses for discussion in any small-group setting. The "Groups/Coalitions" questions can be used by ongoing groups, whether or not their primary focus involves racism and/or anti-Semitism, as well as by individuals who work in such groups.

COMMUNITIES

A. List five Jewish women, five women of color, and five non-Jewish white women whose politics you respect, and consider what it is about their view of Jewish identity, racism, and anti-Semitism that made you select them.

Do any of them have significant differences from each other?

If so, what made you list them all?

If not, what common aspects of their perspective do you feel positively about?

B. List five Jewish women, five women of color, and five non-Jewish white women whose views of Jewish identity, racism, and anti-

Semitism you regard negatively, and consider what it is about
their views that impelled you to select them.

Do any of them have significant differences from each other?

If so, what made you list them all?

If not, what common aspects of their perspectives do you dislike?

C. What kind of activist work against Jewish oppression and/or racism
have these women done?

Consider both lists in terms of the following: age, racial/ethnic
identities, class background and current economic lifestyle,
region, sexual preference/orientation, religion and religious
upbringing, nationality.

Are any of those on the women of color lists Jewish and/or Arab?

Are any of those on the Jewish lists women of color?

How do the Jewish women on the lists fit into the entity you see as
"the Jewish feminist movement"?

How do the women of color on the lists fit into the entity you see as
"the Third World feminist movement"?

Do you know the women on each list personally or only by reputation?

Do you know some of the women well and others only slightly?

How do you think the women listed whom you know personally feel
about your own political perspective and work?

How is your own political activism regarding racism and/or anti-
Semitism affected by your relationship (or lack of relationship)
to these women?

Consider both lists in terms of how you think each woman would
define her political perspective.

How would these lists have been different if you had made them
one, two, five, ten years ago?

Do you see these women as peers, as women you want to emulate, as
women from whom you want to disassociate yourself?

For each group, consider how your lists would differ if you were to
list women you respected/did not respect regarding racism *or*
anti-Semitism instead of racism *and* anti-Semitism.

CONFRONTATIONS

A. For each of the following situations, consider these questions:
How did you feel?

What did you do?

Would you like to have acted differently?

What was the response of the individual(s) you confronted?

What were the responses of the other people present—Jewish and

non-Jewish, white people and people of color, Sephardim and
Ashkenazim, Arabs and non-Arabs, working-class people and
non-working-class people, lesbians and non-lesbians, women
and men?

How was the interaction affected by the sex, class, or sexual
preference/orientation of the person you confronted?

How did what happened relate to your expectations of what was
going to happen?

1. Recall a situation in which you confronted the anti-Semitism
   of a non-Jewish white person.

   Were there any differences between your response and action
   in this situation compared to one in which a non-Jewish
   person of color said or did something anti-Jewish?

2. Recall a situation in which you confronted the anti-Semitism
   of a non-Jewish person of color.

   Were there any differences between your response and action in
   this situation compared to one in which a non-Jewish white
   person said or did something anti-Jewish?

3. Recall a situation in which you confronted the internalized anti-
   Semitism of another Jew.

   Were there any differences between your response and action in
   this situation compared to one in which a non-Jew said or did
   something anti-Jewish?

4. Recall a situation in which you confronted the racism of a white
   Jew.

   Were there any differences between your response and actions in
   this situation compared to one in which a non-Jewish white
   person said or did something racist?

5. Recall a situation in which you confronted the anti-Arab racism
   of a Jewish person.

   Were there any differences between your response and action in
   this situation compared to one in which a non-Jewish white
   person or a non-Arabic person of color said or did something
   anti-Arab?

6. Recall a situation that you participated in or observed in which
   a person of color was anti-Jewish in response to the racism of
   a white Jew.

7. Recall a situation that you participated in or observed in which a
   white Jew was racist in response to the anti-Semitism of a
   person of color.

B. For situations 1-7, recall an instance in which:

   1. you identified the racism or anti-Semitism but said nothing;

2. you only later became aware of it;

3. you were present when someone else confronted it.

C. For situations 3-5, recall an instance when you have been the person confronted and consider both your responses and those of others present.

GROUPS/COALITIONS

The following questions can apply to groups/coalitions whose focus is racism and/or anti-Semitism and groups/coalitions doing Middle East organizing, as well as those whose focus is *not* Jewish oppression and racism (e.g., groups working on abortion rights, tenant organizing, conference planning). Some questions may be more relevant to one type of group than to another. While questions are addressed specifically to group interactions and politics, many are applicable to coalitions.

A. To what extent have racism and/or Jewish oppression been discussed/ confronted in the group?

What pressures or values have increased the difficulty of raising/ confronting anti-Semitism and/or racism?

What members have initiated those discussions/confrontations?

What effect has it had on the group and on its members if one or two individuals have always been the ones to raise/confront these issues?

How have the issues been raised? How was a member's racism or anti-Semitism confronted?

What kinds of responses, supportive or not, have been made by other group members?

How have these interactions been resolved?

When you have initiated such a discussion/confrontation, what kinds of expectations, fears, concerns did you bring?

To what extent have these been realized?

What has been the effect of such discussions/confrontations on the ongoing work of the group? on group membership? on coalition efforts?

What has been the effect of any lack of discussion/confrontation on the ongoing work of the group? on group membership? on coalition efforts?

B. To what extent has raising and exploring the issues of anti-Semitism and/or racism been affected by the members':

religious/ethnic and racial identification?

class background and current economic lifestyle?

political affiliations or affinities?

identification as Zionist, non-Zionist, anti-Zionist?

C. When racism and/or anti-Semitism have been discussed, to what extent have they been analyzed in relation to:
interactions among group members?
coalition work?
economic factors?
institutions?
international events?

D. When Jewish oppression and/or racism have been raised in a group, to what extent have they been dealt with in relation to the Middle East conflict?
What effect has raising this issue had in groups whose focus is not Middle East organizing?

E. How has the group dealt with situations in which it felt it necessary to choose between opposing anti-Semitism or opposing racism, between supporting a Third World concern or supporting a Jewish one?
To what extent has the group been prepared to deal with such situations?
How have the decision(s) made affected the workings of the group?

F. To what extent has the group achieved unity in its analysis of racism and/or anti-Semitism?
What kinds of compromises have been made in relation to these issues which have facilitated ongoing work?
What kinds of compromises could not be worked out?
If a group has achieved some level of unity, how has it been attained?
Have members who disagreed left or been discouraged from participating?
Are shared politics stated explicitly in a position paper?
Have you or anyone else felt pressure to adhere to these positions?
If so, how has that been addressed?

G. How has the group's unity—or lack of unity—in its analysis of anti-Semitism and/or racism affected decisions about which groups to work with in coalition?
Are there specific analyses which the group—or individuals within it—feel must be shared by other members of a coalition?
How have these expectations affected coalition work?

H. What have you gained from working in a group or coalition in which participants had similar backgrounds and politics?
What have you gained from working in a group or coalition in which participants had backgrounds and politics different from your own?

NOTES

Throughout the article I describe actual incidents involving racism and/or Jewish oppression in which I participated or which were reported to me by participants. When these are not a matter of public record, I have changed specifics to protect the identities of the individuals involved while not altering the basic nature of the political issues raised.

I. Origins

[1] I use the terms "anti-Semitism" and "Jewish oppression" interchangeably. I see "Jew-hating" as a particularly virulent form of anti-Semitism which is sometimes supported by religious or political ideology.

I use the term "anti-Semitism" to refer specifically to the oppression of Jews. While an argument against such usage has been made on the grounds that Arabs are also Semitic people, historically the word relates to Jews alone. First used in 1873 by Wilhelm Marr, "anti-Semite" was immediately picked up in Germany and elsewhere by Jew-hating individuals and groups who used it as a positive description of their politics, much as we might use the term "feminist." In the following 75 years, millions of Jews were killed as a consequence of the racist ideology called "anti-Semitism." In making this semantic distinction, I am not arguing for the continued invisibility of Arab people or for continued indifference of non-Arabs to Arab oppression.

[2] "Ashkenas is the Hebrew word for Germany, but in actual usage 'Ashkenazic Jews' refers to those Jews (and their descendants) who have lived in either Western or Eastern Europe (except some Sephardic communities within this area)" (Abraham D. Lavender, "Appendix," *A Coat of Many Colors: Jewish Subcommunities in the United States,* ed. Lavender [Westport, CT: Greenwood Press, 1977], p. 317).

[3] For a discussion of the role of anti-Semitism in the Rosenberg case and the response of the Jewish community to it, see Victor S. Navasky, *Naming Names* (New York: Viking, 1980); and Vicki Gabriner, "The Rosenberg Case: We Are All Your Children," in *Chutzpah: A Jewish Liberation Anthology,* ed. Steven Lubet, Jeffry (Shaye) Mallow, et al (San Francisco: New Glide Publications, 1977), pp. 173-180. *The Rosenberg File* by Ronald Radosh and Joyce Milton reveals that after the verdict, an Associated Press reporter found the word "Jude" written on a piece of paper at the seat of the jury foreman ([New York: Holt, Rinehart & Winston, 1983], p. 530).

[4] See the articles by Black and Jewish men in Nat Hentoff, ed., *Black Anti-Semitis.   nd Jewish Racism* (New York: Schocken Books, 1969); Robert G. Weisbord and Arthur Stein, "The New York School Crisis and Its Aftermath," *Bittersweet Encounter: The Afro-American and the American Jew* (New York: Schocken Books, 1970), pp. 161-205; Paul Cowan, "Housing in Forest Hills: But Not Next Door . . . ," *The*

Tribes of America (Garden City, NY: Doubleday, 1979), pp. 113-131; and an account of the brutal beating of Black teen-ager Victor Rhodes by Hasidic Jews in June Jordan, "In the Valley of the Shadow of Death" (1978), *Civil Wars* (Boston: Beacon Press, 1981), pp. 150-162.

[5]For perspectives on these issues, see Itzhak Epstein, "Open Letter to the Black Panther Party," *Jewish Radicalism: A Selected Anthology,* ed. Jack Nusan Porter and Peter Dreier (New York: Grove Press, 1973), pp. 64-71; and Albert S. Axelrad and Robert E. Goldburg, Huey Newton, Morris U. Schappes, and George Wald, *The Black Panthers, Jews and Israel* (New York: Jewish Currents, 1971).

[6]Elly Bulkin, "Racism and Writing," *Sinister Wisdom 13* (Spring 1980), pp. 3-22. See also H. Patricia Hynes, "On 'Racism and Writing'," *Sinister Wisdom 15* (Fall 1980), pp. 105-109; letters from Louise Mullaley, Marguerite Fentin, and Andrée Collard, *Sinister Wisdom 16* (Spring 1981), pp. 90-93; and my response in issue 16, p. 94.

II. Extensions

[1]Beverly Smith with Judith Stein and Priscilla Golding, eds., "'The Possibility of Life Between Us': A Dialogue Between Black and Jewish Women," *Conditions: Seven* (1981), p. 45.

[2]Of her four novels, see especially Sinclair's *Wasteland* (1946), whose characters include Debby, a white, strongly Jewish-identified lesbian, radical and writer; and *The Changelings* (1955), which focuses on the relationship between two young adolescent girls, one Jewish, the other Black.

[3]Theresa Haynie, "Music Fest: Struggle and Solidarity," *Plexus* (November 1981), pp. 19, 20.

[4]"'The Possibility of Life Between Us'," p. 44.

[5]I use the term "non-Jewish women of color" because of the absence of another, less awkward phrase which does not deny the existence of women of color who are Jewish. Abraham D. Lavender says that "the American Jewish community is 99 percent white" (p. 3); in his overview of Black Jews, he states that "the estimated number [of Black Jews] nationally ranges from 12,000 (excluding quasi-Jewish black cults) to 100,000" (p. 15). Citations are from *A Coat of Many Colors: Jewish Subcommunities in the United States,* ed. Lavender (Westport, CT: Greenwood Press, 1977).

[6]"Sepharad is the Hebrew word for Spain, but 'Sephardic Jews' refers in a broader sense to those Jews (and their descendants) who lived in Spain and Portugal in the Middle Ages. After being forced out of the Iberian Peninsula by the Inquisition, they settled in France, Holland, England, Italy, Greece, Turkey, Israel, North Africa, the Americas, and

a few other localities. 'Sephardic Jews' . . . also refers to those Jews (and their descendants) who have lived in countries of the Middle East and North Africa since the ancient expulsions from Israel" (Lavender, p. 316). Sephardic Jews have been estimated as 2½ percent of the Jewish population of the United States (150,000 of 5,921,000) and 60 percent of Israeli Jewry (World Sephardic Federation); there are an estimated 2 to 2½ million Sephardic Jews in the world (Yeshiva University-Sephardic Studies Department) out of a total of 13 million.

[7]I am grateful to Rita Arditti for criticism which led me to consider the issues I raise in this and the preceding paragraphs. In a letter of October 11, 1983, she wrote: "My main problem has to do with the expression 'Jews of color.' I have to say that I still do not know what that means. It seems to me a broad term that derives from the North-American division between white people in this country and blacks. I do not know who invented the term, but when I first saw it, in Jewish feminist papers, I was surprised. I do not like it at all and I will try to explain why. First of all, it seems to lump together all the Jews who are not 'white'? And who are 'white Jews'? Are Ashkenazi Jews white? How about Sephardic Jews from Italy, are they white and Sephardic Jews from Turkey or Morocco Jews of color? I can tell you that my family (Sephardim from Turkey, Ladino-speaking) would be very surprised to be called 'Jews of color' and certainly they would not understand what you mean. So, who has the power of naming here? Are Jews from Ethiopia 'Jews of color'? And Chinese and Indian Jews? Is that what you mean? In short, it seems to me that the categories of 'white Jews' and 'Jews of color' are NorthAmerican categories that imitate some of the racist divisions of this culture. . . . And finally, just to confuse you further, what would you call the Jews from LatinAmerica, 'color,' 'white,' or what? In Argentina, for instance, about 25% of the community is Sephardic, with a very broad spectrum, like Jews from Syria, Turkey, Spain, Italy, etc., and the rest are Ashkenazis, mainly from Russia, Poland and Germany . . . Plus, there has been quite a lot of mixing."

[8]References to anti-Jewish incidents in the U.S. come from the 1982 Anti-Defamation League report cited in Gerald Stillman, "Polling Anti-Semitism," *Jewish Currents* (July-August 1982), p. 9. A 14.9 percent decline in 1981-82 from the 1980-81 figures is reported in "Anti-Semitic Incidents Found to Drop in Year," *New York Times*, January 11, 1983, p. A17; a decline of 19 percent from the 1982 figures is reported in "Anti-Semitic Incidents Down Sharply in 1983," *New York Times*, January 18, 1984, p. A21.

[9]The quote about the *Davka* issue, published in Los Angeles, and the reference to *Ezrat Nashim* are from "Introduction," Susannah Heschel, ed., *On Being a Jewish Feminist: A Reader* (New York: Schocken Books, 1983), p. xv. The special *off our backs* is the February/March 1972 issue. The two Jewish women's conferences are described in Maralee's "A Beginning," *Chutzpah 5* (Summer 1973), p. 5 and "First Midwest

Jewish Women's Conference," *Chutzpah 6* (Winter 1974), p. 1. An expanded version of the *Response* issue, edited by Elizabeth Koltun, was published as *The Jewish Woman: New Perspectives* (New York: Schocken Books, 1976). The establishment of the Jewish Feminist Organization is described in Anne Lapidus Lerner, "'Who Hast Not Made Me a Man': The Movement for Equal Rights for Women in American Jewry," *American Jewish Yearbook* (1977), reprinted as a pamphlet by the American Jewish Committee, p. 7; and in Maralee, "Jewish Women Join Forces," *Chutzpah 7* (Fall 1974), pp. 1, 12. "From Fears to Hope," an article on the Jewish Lesbian Gang by Katz, appeared in *Chutzpah 8* (1975), pp. 2, 7. Susan Schechter writes about the Jewish women's statement in "Solidarity and Self-Respect: Coming Out Jewish at the Socialist Feminist Conference," *Chutzpah: A Jewish Liberation Anthology*, pp. 57, 59.

10 Sara Evans, *Personal Politics: The Roots of Women's Liberation in the Civil Rights Movement and the New Left* (New York: Vintage, 1979).

11 The Combahee River Collective, "A Black Feminist Statement," *Capitalist Patriarchy and the Case for Socialist Feminism*, ed. Zillah R. Eisenstein (New York and London: Monthly Review Press, 1979), p. 365.

12 Jan Clausen, review of *This Bridge Called My Back, Conditions: Eight* (1982), p. 135.

III. Threads

1 Lucy S. Dawidowicz, "Jewish Identity: A Matter of Fate, a Matter of Choice," *The Jewish Presence: Essays in Identity and History* (New York: Harcourt Brace Jovanovich, 1978), p. 5.

2 Dawidowicz, "Can Anti-Semitism Be Measured?" *The Jewish Presence*, p. 196.

3 The "Judenrat" was "a Jewish council . . . established in each community to carry out the instructions of the Einsatzgruppen," the Nazis' special duty groups (SD) or mobile killing squads (Lucy S. Dawidowicz, *The War Against the Jews: 1933-1945* [New York: Bantam, 1975], p. 155).

4 First published in Russia in the opening years of the twentieth century, the Protocols, forged by Tsarist officials, revealed an alleged conspiracy by Jews to take over the world.

5 Cheryl Clarke, personal communication, December 1983.

6 See John Higham, *Strangers in the Land: Patterns of American Nativism, 1860-1925* (New York: Atheneum, 1966) and Thomas F. Gossett, *Race: The History of an Idea in America* (New York: Schocken

Books, 1965). Between 1890 and 1920, over 250,000 Arab immigrants came to the United States. In response to attempts during the century's first decade to keep all but Anglo-Saxons from entering the country and to an Alabama congressional representative's 1907 comment, "I regard the Syrian and peoples from other parts of Asia Minor as the most undesirable" of immigrants, Dr. H.A. El-Kourie "wrote a short essay entitled 'Facts Establishing That the Semitic is the Equal of Any Race and Superior to Many.' The writings detail the positive attributes of the Syrian immigrants and the positive role the Semitic race and its descendants—'the Syrians, Hebrews, German Jews, Russian Jews, Bedouins, and Sedentary Arabs'—had played in history" (Alan Dehmer, "The Politics of Survival: Birmingham, Alabama," *Taking Root/Bearing Fruit: The Arab-American Experience*, American Arab Anti-Discrimination Committee (Washington, DC: ADC, 1984), p. 37.

[7]Arthur D. Morse, *While Six Million Died: A Chronicle of American Apathy* (New York: Hart Publishing Company, 1967), p. 263.

[8]Connecticut Education Association, Council on Interracial Books for Children, and National Education Association, *The Ku Klux Klan and the Struggle for Equality: An Informational and Instructional Kit* (New York: CIBC, 1981), p. 7.

[9]Hannah Arendt, *The Origins of Totalitarianism* (New York and London: Harcourt Brace Jovanovich, 1951), pp. 185, 206.

[10]See Michi Weglyn, *Years of Infamy: The Untold Story of America's Concentration Camps* (New York: Morrow, 1976) and Ken Adachi, *The Enemy That Never Was: A History of the Japanese Canadians* (Toronto: McClelland & Stewart, 1976).

[11]Helen Epstein, *Children of the Holocaust: Conversations with Sons and Daughters of Survivors* (New York: G.P. Putnam's Sons, 1979).

[12]Quoted in Rita Arditti, "Sephardic Jewry," *Sojourner* (July 1983), p. 3.

IV. Separations

[1]Documents relating to the early settlement of Sephardic Jews are included in Morris U. Schappes, *A Documentary History of the Jews in the United States: 1654-1875* (New York: Schocken Books, 1950, 1971).

[2]Lucy S. Dawidowicz, *The Holocaust and the Historians* (Cambridge: Harvard University Press, 1981), p. 28. Dawidowicz goes on to point out that in the U.S., "the Jews have been conspicuous by their absence in the history books."

[3]Nathan C. Belth, *A Promise to Keep: A Narrative of the American*

Encounter with Anti-Semitism (New York: Schocken Books, 1981), p. 1.

[4]Quoted in Gordon Fellman, "Redefining the Sides, Reclaiming the Other Zionism," *genesis 2* (September/October 1982), p. 6.

[5]Stillman, p. 13.

[6]Norman Cohn, "The Myth of the Jewish World Conspiracy: A Case Study in Collective Psychopathology," *Commentary* (1966), p. 5. In *The Course of Modern Jewish History,* Howard Morley Sachar notes that "Ukrainian guerilla bands . . . committed no less than 493 pogroms during the year 1919, and had killed upward of 70,000 Jews" ([New York: Dell, 1958, 1977], p. 302).

[7]Stillman, p. 12. See also Dawidowicz, "Can Anti-Semitism Be Measured?" *The Jewish Presence: Essays in Identity and History* (New York: Harcourt Brace Jovanovich, 1978), pp. 193-215.

[8]Irena Klepfisz, "Anti-Semitism in the Lesbian/Feminist Movement," *Nice Jewish Girls: A Lesbian Anthology,* ed. Evelyn Torton Beck (Watertown, MA: Persephone Press, 1982; reprinted and distributed by Crossing Press, 1984), p. 48.

[9]"Link Seen Among Heavily Armed Rightist Groups," *New York Times* (June 11, 1983), pp. 1, 5.

[10]The Alliance Against Women's Oppression objects to the *"vast amounts* of time and energy [which] are *consumed* in workshop sessions devoted to such questions as: relating to non-Jewish lovers; the Southern Jewish experience; eliminating internalized anti-semitism; Judaism before Patriarchy; and reclaiming our Jewish identities" (my emphasis) in "The Jewish Feminist Movement—Limitations of the Politics of Identity," in a pamphlet, *Zionism in the Women's Movement—Anti-Imperialist Politics Derailed* (San Francisco: AAWO, 1983). In "Taking Our Stand Against Zionism and White Supremacy," Women Against Imperialism similarly indicates that concern in the women's movement with Jewish oppression is excessive (*off our backs,* July 1982, p. 20). This statement was reprinted widely in feminist periodicals. Also see Sandy Katz, Shelley Kushner, Louise Brotsky, "Zionism/Racism" (letter), *Big Mama Rag* (December 1981), p. 3; Lori Bradford, "'Sisters United' Is Racist," *Big Mama Rag* (April 1982), p. 4; Elly Bulkin, "Anti-Semitism" (letter re Bradford's article) and Bradford's response, *Big Mama Rag* (June 1982), p. 3.

[11]Published responses include Anna and Elizabeth, "Jews and Zionism: Fighting Anti-Semitism and Imperialism," *Matrix,* Vol. 3, No. 13 (July 1982), pp. 10-14; and Di Vilde Chayes, "An Open Letter to the Women's Movement," *off our backs* (July 1982), p. 21. Dated April 22, 1982, Di Vilde Chayes' statement, reprinted widely in feminist periodicals, was signed by Evelyn Torton Beck, Nancy K. Bereano, Gloria Z. Greenfield, Melanie Kaye/Kantrowitz, Irena Klepfisz, Bernice Mennis,

and Adrienne Rich. Publication of the statements by Women Against Imperialism and Di Vilde Chayes was followed by a number of letters, some supportive or critical of one of the two statements, others critical of both. See especially the letter from Janet Gottler in *Gay Community News* (June 19, 1982), p. 4; letters from Rachael Kamel, Morgan Firestar, Sarah Schulman, Rebecca Lesses, Rina Nissim, Bat Deborah, and Chaia Lehrer in *off our backs* (October 1982), pp. 28-30; and letters from Diane Fichtelberg and Sara Miles in *off our backs* (December 1982), p. 25. Also see the letter in response to the Women Against Imperialism statement from PM, JR, and Barbo in *Matrix,* Vol. 4, No. 4 (October 1982), pp. 4-5.

The Alliance Against Women's Oppression statement has thus far been responded to by Jewish Women for a Secular Middle East (xeroxed response, October 1983).

12Aviva Cantor Zuckoff, "The Oppression of American Jews," *Jewish Radicalism: A Selected Anthology,* ed. Jack Nusan Porter and Peter Dreier (New York: Grove Press, 1973), p. 30.

13Evelyn Torton Beck, "Why Is This Book Different from All Other Books?" *Nice Jewish Girls,* p. xxii.

14Information and quote about the Bete Yisroel is from Dan Ross, *Acts of Faith: A Journey to the Fringes of Jewish Identity* (New York: St. Martin's Press, 1982), p. 158; reference to closing of their Jewish schools is from David Rosenberg, "Fate of Falashas Still in Question," *genesis 2* (May/June 1983), p. 7; quotation about Jewish "disappeared" in Argentina is from Wendy Greenfield, "Mourning and Hope in Argentina," *genesis 2* (May/June 1983), p. 8.

Ross notes that Ethiopia's Black Jews "prefer to call themselves *beta esra'el*—'House of Israel'," rather than the more commonly used term "Falasha," which "means 'exile' or 'stranger'" (p. 146). They were not recognized as Jews by Israel's rabbinate until the early Seventies and not allowed entry to Israel under the Law of Return until 1975.

15Cherríe Moraga, "La Güera," *This Bridge Called My Back: Writings by Radical Women of Color,* ed. Moraga and Gloria Anzaldúa (Watertown, MA: Persephone Press, 1981; reprinted and distributed by Kitchen Table: Women of Color Press, 1984), p. 29.

16See Naomi Levine and Martin Hochbaum, ed., *Poor Jews: An American Awakening* (New Brunswick, NJ: Transaction Books, 1974) and Dorothy Rabinowitz, *The Other Jews: Portraits in Poverty* (New York: Institute of Human Relations Press, 1972); the impact of the current economic situation on Jews is discussed in "New Group of Jewish Poor Surfacing, Study Reveals," *The Jewish Week* (April 1, 1983), p. 9.

17Levine and Hochbaum, "Introduction," *Poor Jews,* p. 2.

18Evan M. Bayer and Gary A. Tobin, *Jewish Economic Dependency and Dislocation,* American Jewish Committee statement submitted to Committee on Ways and Means, U.S. House of Representatives (November 18, 1983), p. 2.

[19] Bernice Mennis, "Repeating History," *Nice Jewish Girls,* p. 91.

[20] Census Bureau statistics, Council on Interracial Books for Children, *Fact Sheets on Institutional Racism* (New York: CIBC, 1982), p. 3. See also Barbara Myerhoff, *Number Our Days* (New York: Simon & Schuster, 1978).

[21] Renée Franco, personal communication, August 1983.

[22] Arthur Liebman, *Jews and the Left* (New York: John Wiley & Sons, 1979), p. 603.

[23] Liebman, p. 603.

[24] Steven M. Cohen writes: "Conventional wisdom has long held that the Jews' cultural heritage was the key factor responsible for their remarkable success in this country (Glazer and Moynihan, 1970; Sowell, 1981). According to this view, the traditional heritage prized education, Jews were possessed of enormous drive and ambition, and they were adept at commerce and handling money. In contrast some have offered explanations which focus on certain structural features as the principal reasons for American Jewish mobility. They cite economic conditions and opportunities open to Jews when they arrived in the United States, and the occupational skills and financial resources they brought with them from the Old Country" (*American Modernity & Jewish Identity* [New York and London: Tavistock Publications, 1983], pp. 76-77). The latter position is developed in Sherry Gorelick, *City College and the Jewish Poor: Education in New York, 1880-1924* (New York: Schocken Books, 1982) and Stephen Steinberg, *The Ethnic Myth: Race, Ethnicity and Class in America* (Boston: Beacon Press, 1981).

[25] Will Maslow, *The Structure and Functioning of the American Jewish Community* (New York: American Jewish Congress, 1974), p. 9.

[26] The percentage of families below the federally-designated poverty level dropped slightly between the 1970 and 1980 censuses. In some cases percentages vary significantly within each group, so that the average below the poverty level among Asians and Pacific Islanders, 10.7 percent, is much below the percentage for Vietnamese.

[27] Baldwin, "Negroes Are Anti-Semitic Because They're Anti-White," *Black Anti-Semitism and Jewish Racism,* ed. Nat Hentoff (New York: Schocken Books, 1969), pp. 7-8.

[28] "The Possibility of Life Between Us," p. 40.

[29]Bertram W. Korn, *American Jewry and the Civil War* (New York: Atheneum, 1970), p. 122. Korn devotes a chapter to the repercussions of Grant's order, pp. 121-155.

[30]Korn discusses Jewish attitudes toward slavery and Northern and Southern responses to Judah P. Benjamin. Also see Schappes.

[31]Belth, pp. 64, 67.

[32]Wendell Rawls, Jr., "After 69 Years of Silence, Lynching Victim Is Cleared," *New York Times*, March 8, 1982, p. A12.

[33]For the news story about the one previous lynching of a Jew, see Schappes, "Double-Lynching of a Jew and a Negro," pp. 515-517: in Tennessee in 1868, S.A. Bierfield, Russian Jew, Radical Republican, "friendly with the Negro population," and his Black clerk, Lawrence Bowman, were lynched by the Klan. Belth describes Frank's murder as "the only lynching of a Jew in the nation's history" (p. 59). (In his study of the period from 1860 to 1925, Higham mentions the lynching of a number of Italians, singly and in groups as large as 11, including one situation reminiscent of the Bierfield murder: the Louisiana lynching, after a minor quarrel, of "five Sicilian storekeepers [who] disturbed the native whites because the Italians dealt mainly with the Negroes and associated with them nearly on terms of equality" [p. 169]).

[34]Belth, p. 61.

[35]Leonard Dinnerstein, *The Leo Frank Case* (New York and London: Columbia University Press, 1968), p. 16.

[36]Morris U. Schappes, "1913 Eye-Witness Confirms Leo Frank's Innocence," *Jewish Currents* (May 1982), p. 24.

[37]Belth, p. 37.

[38]Carey McWilliams, *North from Mexico: The Spanish-Speaking People of the United States* (New York: Greenwood Press, 1948, 1968), p. 113.

[39]Barbara Cameron, "'Gee, You Don't Seem Like An Indian From the Reservation'," *This Bridge Called My Back*, p. 50.

[40]Combahee River Collective, "Eleven Black Women: Why Did They Die?" (Cambridge, MA: Combahee River Collective, 1979).

[41]"Urban League in Los Angeles Asks Police Chief Suspension," *New York Times*, May 12, 1982, p. A24.

[42]The first of three young white men convicted in the murder of Turks has already been released. Convicted on misdemeanor assault charges, he served seven months in prison.

V. Left Leanings

[1] Ruth Seid, personal communication, March 3, 1983.

[2] *Wasteland* was awarded the 1946 Harper Prize and was translated into six languages. Seid's other two novels are *Sing at My Wake* (1951) and *Anna Teller* (1960). She is currently at work on a novel.

[3] Rukeyser writes about the Scottsboro Trial in "The Trial," first published in *Theory of Flight* (1935); the poem appears also in *The Collected Poems of Muriel Rukeyser* (New York: McGraw-Hill, 1978), pp. 28-30. The reference to the "tabu . . . bed of forbidden things finally known" is from "The Transgress," *The Speed of Darkness* (New York: Random House, 1968), p. 5. Rukeyser writes about performing civil disobedience in the title poem of *Breaking Open* (New York: Random House, 1973), pp. 105-134. "To be a Jew in the twentieth century," first published in *Beast in View* (1944), appears in *Collected Poems*, p. 239.
For a discussion of lesbian themes in the opening poems of *The Speed of Darkness*, see Elly Bulkin, "Introduction: A Look at Lesbian Poetry," *Lesbian Poetry: An Anthology*, ed. Elly Bulkin and Joan Larkin (Watertown, MA: Persephone Press, 1981; reprinted and distributed by The Gay Presses of New York, 1984), pp. xxiv-xxv. Shortly before her death, Rukeyser agreed to be on the lesbian literature panel at the 1978 convention of the Modern Language Association, but was prevented from participating because of illness.

[4] Tillie Olsen, "I Want You Women Up North To Know," *Feminist Studies*, Vol. 7, No. 3 (Fall 1981), pp. 367-369; originally printed in *The Partisan* (March 1934). Olsen's report, "The Strike," originally published in *Partisan Review* (September-October 1934), appears in *Years of Protest: A Collection of American Writings of the 1930's*, ed. Jack Salzman with Barry Wallenstein (New York: Pegasus, 1967), pp. 138-144. The two stories I refer to are "O Yes" (1956) and "Tell Me a Riddle," from the fiction collection *Tell Me A Riddle* (New York: Dell, 1961). The quotation is from "Tell Me A Riddle," p. 111. See also Deborah Rosenfelt, "From the Thirties: Tillie Olsen and the Radical Tradition," *Feminist Studies*, Vol 7, No. 3 (Fall 1981), pp. 371-406; and Naomi Rubin's interview with Olsen, "A Riddle of History for the Future," *Sojourner* (July 1983), pp. 4,18.

[5] The Harlem unemployment statistic comes from Mark Naison, *Communists in Harlem during the Depression* (Urbana: University of Illinois Press, 1983). p. 116. The statistics on Jewish CP membership are from Arthur Liebman, *Jews and the Left* (New York: John Wiley & Son, 1979), p. 59.

[6] Liebman, p. 502. Liebman notes the inconsistency of CP policies, which "at the same time, . . . allowed the Yiddish Workers University to function even though the curriculum was conducted in Yiddish

and included Jewish history" (p. 502). For a fuller discussion of these issues, see Liebman's section, "The Communist Party and Zigzagging on Jewish Issues," pp. 501-510.

[7]Irving Howe, *World of Our Fathers,* abridged (New York: Bantam, 1980), p. 352; Liebman, p. 502.

[8]Naison, p. 324.

[9]For discussions of the impact on Jews in the CP of the Nazi-Soviet Pact, see Howe, pp. 354-356; and Liebman, pp. 507-510.

[10]See Robert Shaffer, "Women and the Communist Party, USA, 1930-1940," *Socialist Review,* No. 45 (May-June 1979), pp. 73-118.

[11]Naison, pp. 18, 19. Elsewhere, Naison describes the public trial for white chauvinism of August Yokinen, a CP member; publicized nationally by the Party, the trial was even reported in the *New York Times* (pp. 47-49).

[12]Liebman, p. 68.

[13]Robert G. Weisbord and Arthur Stein, *Bittersweet Encounter: The Afro-American and the American Jew* (New York: Schocken Books, 1970), p. 147. The three-part article, "Semitism in the Black Ghetto" by Eddie Ellis, first appeared in the January 1966 issue of the *Liberator.*

[14]Harold Cruse writes, "The expansion in scope and quality of the Negro civil rights movement has brought to the surface the residual anti-Semitism that has always existed among Negroes, a group attitude which the Jews themselves are at least partially responsible for fostering" (*The Crisis of the Negro Intellectual* [New York: William Morrow & Company, 1967], p. 170).

[15]Weisbord and Stein, p. 148.

[16]Weisbord and Stein, p. 117. Chrisman's review, "The Crisis of Harold Cruse," is from the November 1969 issue of *The Black Scholar.*

[17]Rabbi Jay Kaufmann, "'Thou Shalt Surely Rebuke Thy Neighbor'," *Black Anti-Semitism and Jewish Racism,* ed. Nat Hentoff (New York: Schocken Books, 1969), pp. 50-51.

[18]See Vincent Harding, *There Is A River: The Black Struggle for Freedom in America* (New York: Harcourt Brace Jovanovich, 1981) for a history of Black revolt that began before the captives were removed from Africa.

VI. The Male Enemy/The Left Enemy

[1] Anne Braden, "A View from the Fringes," *Southern Exposure*, Vol IX, No. 1 (Spring 1981), p. 71.

[2] Rima Shore, "Sisterhood—And My Brothers," *Conditions: Eight* (1982), pp. 98-99.

[3] Radical feminist theory has affected far more women than those who would define themselves as "radical feminists." Women who would characterize themselves as lesbian-feminists or lesbian separatists, for example, have been greatly influenced by radical feminist thought. Originally, in the very late Sixties and early Seventies, "radical feminists" were women like Shulamith Firestone who sought to develop a materialistic analysis which would regard women's oppression as seriously as Marx had regarded economic oppression. Later, radical feminists tended to focus more on the psychological aspects of oppression. The term "radical feminist" is sometimes used today to identify a woman who is radical *and* a feminist, not one whose feminism is liberal or mainstream. In her discussion of radical feminist theory, Hester Eisenstein discusses "three elements of continuity" in radical feminist theory: "(1) a divorce from the left and from Marxism; (2) a focus on psychology at the expense of economics; and (3) a false universalism in the analysis of gender" (*Contemporary Feminist Thought* [Boston, G.K. Hall & Co., 1983], p. 125).

[4] Combahee River Collective, "A Black Feminist Statement," *Capitalist Patriarchy and the Case for Socialist Feminism*, ed. Zillah R. Eisenstein (New York: Monthly Review Press, 1979), pp. 365-366.

[5] Audre Lorde, "An Open Letter to Mary Daly," *This Bridge Called My Back: Writings by Radical Women of Color*, ed. Cherríe Moraga and Gloria Anzaldúa (Watertown, MA: Persephone Press, 1981; reprinted and distributed by Kitchen Table: Women of Color Press, 1984), p. 97.

[6] Kalpana Ram, "Sexual Violence in India: A Critique of Some Feminist Writings on the Third World," *bitches, witches & dykes*, (May 1981), p. 13.

[7] Ram, p. 13.

[8] Mary Daly, *Gyn/Ecology: The Metaethics of Radical Feminism* (Boston: Beacon Press, 1978), p. 298.

[9] Daly, pp. 311-312.

[10] Mary Kurtzman, "Demystifying Plath," *New Women's Times Feminist Review* (July/August 1982), p. 20.

[11] See Jil Clark, "Andrea Dworkin on Her Writing, the Holocaust,

Biological Determinism, Pornography, and S&M," *Gay Community News* (July 19, 1980), p. 10; and Dworkin, *Right-Wing Women* (New York: Perigee, 1983), pp. 107-146.

[12]Dworkin, *Pornography: Men Possessing Women* (New York: Perigee, 1981), pp. 144, 145.

[13]Melanie Kaye/Kantrowitz, "Some Notes on Jewish Lesbian Identity," *Nice Jewish Girls: A Lesbian Anthology*, ed. Evelyn Torton Beck (Watertown, MA: Persephone Press, 1982; reprinted and distributed by The Crossing Press, 1984), pp. 28-44; Paula Gunn Allen, "Beloved Women: Lesbians in American Indian Cultures," *Conditions: Seven* (1981), pp. 67-87.

[14]Elana Dykewomon, "The Fourth Daughter's Four Hundred Questions," *Nice Jewish Girls*, p. 159.

[15]Sara Evans, *Personal Politics: The Roots of Women's Liberation in the Civil Rights Movement and the New Left* (New York: Vintage, 1979); Robin Morgan, "Goodbye to All That" (1970), *Going Too Far: The Personal Chronical of a Feminist* (New York: Random House, 1977), pp. 115-130; and Marge Piercy, "The Grand Coolie Damn," *Sisterhood Is Powerful: An Anthology of Writings from the Women's Liberation Movement*, ed. Robin Morgan (New York: Vintage, 1970), pp. 421-438.

[16]Dworkin quotes Jesse Jackson and Jim Douglass, a "male pacifist," in *Right-Wing Women*, pp. 74, 99. By expanding her definition of the left to include "the Democratic Party, establishment home of many Left groups" (p. 99), Dworkin is able to condemn "the left" for the anti-abortion actions of Jimmy Carter and Joseph A. Califano, Jr.

[17]Dworkin, *Right-Wing Women*, p. 104. In this statement, Dworkin assumes that all of these men are heterosexual. Other recent anti-left statements by feminists include Kathleen Barry, "'Sadomasochism': The New Backlash to Feminism," *Trivia* (Fall 1982), pp. 77-92; and Ellen Frankfort, *Kathy Boudin and the Dance of Death* (New York: Stein and Day, 1983). See also Susan Saxe's review of Frankfort's book, "A Piece of the Rope," *off our backs* (April 1984), pp. 20-21. For a critique of anti-feminism in the left which does not confuse the entire left with some of its parts, see Andrea Cammarata, Nancy Langer, Sarah Schulman, Libby Smith, Shawn Towney, Janna Dieckmann, and Maxine Wolfe, "The Pro-Family Left: Whose Family? Which Left?" *Reproductive Rights Newsletter*, Vol. 5, No. 1 (March 1983), pp. 15-18.

[18]Chrystos, "Nidisheňŏk (Sisters)," *Maenad*, Vol. 2, No. 2 (Winter 1981), p. 23.

[19]Adrienne Rich's writing illustrates both this earlier feminist anti-leftism and a more recent reconsideration of those politics. In "Power

and Danger: Works of a Common Woman" (1977), she wrote: "For many of us, the word 'revolution' itself has become not only a dead relic of Leftism, but a key to the deadendedness of male politics: the 'revolution' of a wheel which returns in the end to the same place; the 'revolving door' of a politics which has 'liberated" women only to use them, and only within the limits of male tolerance" (*On Lies, Secrets and Silence: Selected Prose, 1966-1978* [New York, W. W. Norton, 1979], p. 248). After a trip to Nicaragua, Rich wrote:

> In the late sixties and early seventies many U.S. feminists, myself included, voiced frustration and disillusionment with the Marxist Left which seemed incapable of recognizing and addressing women's oppression as women. We insisted that our chains were not only economic but mental, embedded in that domestic or 'private' sphere where men of all classes dominate women. I believe we were right; no ideology which reduces women simply to members of the working-class or the bourgeoisie, which does not recognize how central feminism must be to the revolutionary process, can be taken seriously any longer. But also, in the past decade "radical feminists," "socialist feminists," "lesbian feminists" have been pulling at each other, stretching each other's minds, eavesdropping on each other, learning from each other, more than we often admit. Women of color have often been the catalyst for these connections, and the chief exponents of the evolving consciousness.
>
> Feminists have, and rightly, judged harshly of a socialism that leaves women still accepting a secondary role, and working two fulltime jobs instead of one as a measure of their liberation. But to stop with that judgment, to forget that revolution is itself in evolution, is to abandon politics for lifestyle. No historical process is ever totally repetitive or totally new.
>
> —"A Footnote on 'Being There': Being Here," *off our backs* (October 1983), p. 11.

[20]Bat Deborah, *off our backs* (October 1982), p. 30.

[21]Nora Levin, *While Messiah Slept: Jewish Socialist Movements, 1871-1917* (New York: Schocken Books, 1977), p. 166. See also Paul Buhle, "The Roots of Jewish Labor: Will the Vision Be Renewed?" *genesis 2* (February 1983), pp. 8-9.

[22]Arthur Liebman, *Jews and the Left* (New York: John Wiley & Sons, 1979), p. 506.

[23]Ellen Willis comments: "Anti-semitism is something in the culture that, like sexism, transcends conventional political boundaries and the spectrum from Right to Left. It really has to do—often on a very deeply unconscious level—with perceiving Jews as aliens and as dangerous, potentially very powerful aliens, aliens who are out to take over, subvert, to pursue their own ends at the expense of everybody else. And I think that on the Left and on the Right this takes various forms. On the Right it takes the form of equating Jews as communists, Jews as revolutionaries, Jews as being out to burrow into the culture and subvert all the old traditional values and take it over. On the Left it takes the form of

calling Jews exploiters and allied with established authority, maybe they are secretly the real power behind the scenes, even more important than the established authorities themselves." (Martha Ackelsberg, Paul Cowan, Jack Newfield, and Ellen Willis, "Pride, Prejudice, and Politics: Jewish Jews on the American Left," *Response*, No. 43 [1982], p. 13).

[24] Deb Luger, "Anti-Semitism Is Alive & Thriving in Denver, Colorado and Throughout the US," *Big Mama Rag* (Feburary 1984), p. 11.

[25] All African Peoples Revolutionary Party, *Israel Commits Mass Murder of Palestinian & African Peoples*, pamphlet (Washington, DC).

[26] Levin, p. ix. See also Jack Nusan Porter and Peter Dreier, "Introduction: The Roots of Jewish Radicalism," *Jewish Radicalism: A Selected Anthology* (New York: Grove Press, 1973), pp. xv-liv.

[27] Steven Lubet and Jeffry (Shaye) Mallow, "That's Funny, You Don't Look Anti-Semitic: Perspective on the American Left," *Chutzpah: A Jewish Liberation Anthology*, ed. Lubet, Mallow, et al (San Francisco: New Glide Publications, 1977), p. 52. See also Ackelsberg, Cowan, Newfield, and Willis, pp. 3-39; Morris U. Schappes, "The Jewish Question and the Left—Old and New" (1970), *A Third Decennial Reader*, ed. Louis Harap (New York: Jewish Currents, 1977), pp. 178-200; Arthur Liebman, "Anti-Semitism on the Left?" forthcoming in *Ambiguous Encounter: Anti-Semitism and Jewish-Gentile Relations in American History*, ed. David Gerber (Urbana: University of Illinois Press, 1985); and "The A.D.L. and Reality" by Ilana DeBare and Paul Blickman, and "The A.D.L. and Reagan" by Stan Steinreich, both in *Shmate No. 7* (1983).

[28] Irena Klepfisz, "Resisting and Surviving America," *Nice Jewish Girls*, p. 107.

[29] Louis Marton, "Why I&P?" *Israel & Palestine*, No. 100 (October-November 1983), p. 2.

VII. Breaking a Cycle

[1] Melanie Kaye/Kantrowitz, "Anti-Semitism, Homophobia, and the Good White Knight," *off our backs* (May 1982), p. 30.

[2] Hope Landrine, "Culture, Feminist Racism & Feminist Classism: Blaming the Victim," *off our backs* (November 1979), p. 3. Several letters from Jewish women about the article appeared in the January 1980 issue: by Helene Rosenbluth, Paula Tobin, Sylvia Kohan, Simone Wallace, and Ellen Ledley; Chaya Gusfield, Elia Sheva Dreyfuss, Zimma, Nora Krauss, and Madeline Poplin; and Lynne S. Brandon (p. 28).

[3] Women Against Imperialism, "Taking Our Stand Against White Supremacy," *off our backs* (July 1982), p. 20.

[4]Kaye/Kantrowitz, p. 30.

[5]Kaye/Kantrowitz, p. 31.

[6]Kaye/Kantrowitz, p. 31.

[7]Necessary Bread Affinity Group, "Necessary Bread Disarmament Statement," *Feminist Studies,* Vol 8, No. 3 (Fall 1982). Necessary Bread consisted of Dorothy Allison, Elly Bulkin, Cheryl Clarke, Jan Clausen, Jewelle Gomez, Barbara Kerr, Cherríe Moraga, Carroll Oliver, Mirtha Quintanales, and Barbara Smith.

[8]Di Vilde Chayes, "An Open Letter to the Women's Movement," *off our backs* (July 1982), p. 21.

[9]Combahee River Collective, "A Black Feminist Statement," *Capitalist Patriarchy and the Case for Socialist Feminism,* ed. Zillah R. Eisenstein (New York: Monthly Review Press, 1979), p. 366.

[10]Alice Walker, letter of May 9, 1982, *Ms.* (Feburary 1983), p. 16; reprinted in Walker, *In Search of Our Mothers' Gardens: Womanist Prose* (New York: Harcourt Brace Jovanovich, 1983), p. 354.

[11]Mab Segrest, "Mama, Granny, Carrie Bell: Race and Class, A Personal Accounting," *Conditions Ten* (1984).

[12]My wording here draws on Samuel Johnson's statement: "Sir, a woman preaching is like a dog's walking on his hind legs. It is not done well; but you are surprised to find it done at all" (*Boswell's Life of Johnson,* Vol. 1, p. 287). In "Black Women on Black Women Writers: Conversations and Questions," Linda C. Powell says: ". . . it's been my experience that what's been operating in the women's community is that whole thing that if a black woman speaks the language and is nice around white folk, 'the dancing dog' is in operation. She can speak at conferences. She can write reviews. And even if she's mediocre, it's not bad for a negro. Occasionally, they hit pay dirt" (*Conditions: Nine,* 1983, p. 101).

[13]"Medea Media's Hotterline . . . ," *Feminist Bookstores Newsletter* (November 1981), p. 15.

[14]For a discussion of an earlier period in which a problem for Jewish feminists was "not presence but visibility," see Elinor Lerner, "American Feminism and the Jewish Question, 1890-1940,"forthcoming in *Ambiguous Encounter: Anti-Semitism and Jewish-Gentile Relations in American History,* ed. David Gerber (Urbana: University of Illinois Press, 1985). An earlier version of this paper was presented at the 1983 National Women's Studies Association Conference.

[15]"A Nice Jewish Girl: Evi Beck," interview by Fran Moira, *off our*

backs (August-September 1982), p. 10.

[16]Letty Cottin Pogrebin, "Anti-Semitism in the Women's Movement," *Ms.* (July 1982), p. 69.

[17]In her article "Anti-Semitism in the Women's Movement," Annette Daum finds a "note of despair" in Pogrebin's closing statement: "It is for decent persons to come forward and sound that note of hope, either through self-repair or through declarations of abhorrence of anti-Semitism. We Jews can't get rid of anti-Semitism by ourselves." "Taken to its logical conclusion," Daum writes, "no action should have been required regarding equality for women except to wait for decent men to repair themselves. The same principles of consciousness-raising used so successfully in the women's movement can and should be applied to the problem of anti-Semitism within the movement" ("Anti-Semitism in the Women's Movement," *Pioneer Women,* September-October 1983, p. 22).

[18]Beck, pp. 9, 10.

[19]Gloria Z. Greenfield, "Shedding," *Nice Jewish Girls: A Lesbian Anthology* ed. Evelyn Torton Beck (Watertown, MA: Persephone Press, 1982; reprinted and distributed by The Crossing Press, 1984), p. 8.

[20]Pogrebin, p. 70.

[21]Walker, p. 16.

[22]Irena Klepfisz, "Anti-Semitism in the Lesbian/Feminist Movement," *Nice Jewish Girls,* p. 50.

[23]Cherríe Moraga, "A Long Line of Vendidas," *Loving in the War Years/lo que nunca pasó por sus labios* (Boston: South End Press, 1983), p. 135.

[24]I disagree with the inclusion of Carole Clemmons Gregory's "Love Letter" in Pogrebin's list of anti-Jewish examples. In the poem, Gregory is transferring Black identity to Old Testament characters, a common Afro-American literary device, rather than commenting on interactions between Blacks and Jews.

[25]For another instance of focusing on people of color in such a way as to imply greater responsibility on their part for anti-Semitism, see Selma Miriam, "Anti-Semitism in the Lesbian Community: A Collage of Mostly Bad News by One Jewish Dyke," *Sinister Wisdom 19* (1982), pp. 50-60, my response, *Sinister Wisdom 21,* pp. 108-113; and Selma Miriam's reply in the same issue, pp. 115-118.

[26]Pogrebin, p. 70.

[27]Barbara Smith, "Introduction," *Home Girls: A Black Feminist Anthology,* ed. Barbara Smith (New York: Kitchen Table: Women of

Color Press, 1983), p. xliv.

28Greenfield, p. 8.

29Cherríe Moraga, Julia Perez, Barbara Smith, Beverly Smith, "Racism and Anti-Semitism" (letter), *Gay Community News*, March 7, 1981, p. 4. See also Rosario Morales' article on the workshop, "Double Allegiance: Jewish Women and Women of Color," *A Working Conference on Women and Racism: New England Women's Studies Association Newsletter* (May 1981).

30*Jazz Spotlite News* (1981-1982), p. 133.

31Lawrence Bush, "WABC, Blacks and Jews," *Jewish Currents* (February 1983), p. 7.

32*The Black American* has published such articles as George Nicholas' "Jewish 'Hit Squad' Targets Dissidents," which refers to the Institute of Historical Review, a white organization dedicated to proving that the Holocaust didn't happen, as "a small, serious center of scholarship" (Vol. 20, No. 20, pp. 28, 38); and Keith Stimely's "Zionists Duck Chance to Prove 'Holocaust'," which outlines the Institute for Historical Review's "inability" to find someone to claim its $50,000 reward by demonstrating that "gas chambers for the purpose of killing human beings existed at or in the Auschwitz Concentration Camp during World War II" (Vol. 21, No. 57). Both articles appear to be reprints. Although my copies of these articles don't have dates on them, these articles appeared between 1981 and 1983.

33Klepfisz, p. 49.

VIII. Semite Vs. Semite/Feminist Vs. Feminist

*I.F. Stone, "Holy War," *The Israeli-Arab Reader*, ed. Walter Laqueur, 2nd edition (New York: Bantam, 1969, 1971), p. 310.

1As a result of the June 1967 War, Israel occupied the Sinai Peninsula, Golan Heights, West Bank, Gaza Strip, and East Jerusalem. Since then the Sinai has been returned to Egypt and the Golan Heights (previously Syrian territory) has been annexed by Israel. There are 1.2 million Palestinians living in the Israeli-occupied West Bank and Gaza Strip. A recent study, "The West Bank Data Project: A Survey of Israel's Policies," concludes that "annexation of the West Bank now seems only a matter of time." The report, directed by former deputy mayor of Jerusalem Meron Benvenisti, noted that West Bank Palestinians "live under 'temporary military occupation,' lack the right to vote and are 'deprived of basic civil rights'." (Bernard Gwertzman, "Study Sees Israel Staying in Arab Areas," *New York Times*, April 25, 1984, p. A3). Before he became Prime Minister, Yitzhak Shamir denied any need to annex the West Bank and the Gaza because "they are part of Greater Israel, and what is part of your country you do not annex" (quoted in *Jerusalem*

Post, April 3, 1983; reprinted in *Israel & Palestine,* April-May, 1983, p. 18).

[2]Miriam Socoloff, Leo Schlosberg, and Jeffry (Shaye) Mallow mention this restriction on the Law of Return in "Why We Write About Gay Liberation," *Chutzpah: A Jewish Liberation Anthology,* ed. Steven Lubet, Jeffry (Shaye) Mallow, et al (San Francisco, New Glide Publications, 1977), p. 28.

[3]Israeli Arabs, Palestinians who are Israeli citizens, constitute 17 percent of the Israeli population. A special four-part series by David K. Shipler on Israeli Arabs and Israeli Jews appeared in the *New York Times,* December 27-30, 1983.

[4]Although the term "Sephardic Jews" is sometimes used to designate all "non-Ashkenazi" Jews, I use the term "Oriental Jews" here to designate Jews from Asia and Africa who face special discrimination in Israeli society. These terms are discussed in Shlomo Swirski, "The Oriental Jews in Israel: Why Many Tilted Toward Begin," *Dissent,* Vol. 31, No. 1 (Winter 1984), p. 77. "Adot Ha-Mizrach," tribes of the East, is the term preferred by Nava Mizrachi ("Adot Ha-Mizrach," *off our backs,* March 1984, p. 12). Dena Attar, daughter of an Iraqi Jew, uses the term "Arabic Jew" ("An Open Letter on Anti-Semitism and Racism," *Trouble and Strife,* Winter 1983, p. 14).

[5]Swirsky notes that from 1919 to May 1948, 12 percent of Jews who immigrated to Palestine came from Moslem countries.
"From 1948 to 1956, a total of some 450,000 Jews arrived in Israel from Asia and Africa—compared to 360,000 Jews from Europe and America" (p. 79).

[6]This information is from Kenneth Brown, "Iron and a King: The Likud and Oriental Jews," *MERIP Reports* (May 1983), p. 10. David K. Shipler published a three-part series on "divisions between Israel's two Jewish cultures," in the *New York Times,* April 6-8, 1983.

[7]The Israeli Declaration of Independence, issued in 1948 but never legally adopted, proclaimed that Israel "will foster the development of the country for the benefit of all inhabitants; it will be based on freedom, justice and peace as envisaged by the prophets of Israel; it will ensure complete equality of social and political rights to all its inhabitants irrespective of religion, race or sex; it will guarantee freedom of religion, conscience, education and culture." Israel has no Constitution or Bill of Rights. (Information from the American-Israeli Civil Liberties Coalition "Statement of Purpose," November 1982).

[8]Di Vilde Chayes, "An Open Letter to the Women's Movement," *off our backs* (July 1982), p. 21. Letty Cottin Pogrebin,"Anti-Semitism in the Women's Movement," *Ms.* (June 1982), p. 65. "Marcia Freedman on Israeli Feminism," interview by Tacie DeJanikus, *off our backs*

(March 1983), p. 20. I.F. Stone, "The Other Zionism," (1978), *Underground to Palestine* (New York: Pantheon, 1946, 1978), pp. 237-260; also see Simha Flapan's chapter "The Bi-Nationalists," *Zionism and the Palestinians* (New York: Barnes & Noble, 1979), pp. 163-189.

[9]Edward W. Said, *The Question of Palestine* (New York: Vintage, 1979), p. 57. Malea Kiblan is quoted in "Palestinian Question," *off our backs* (May 1983), p. 12. Helen Samhan, "The Veil of Misunderstanding: Arab Women and Stereotyping," *ADC Reports*, No. 19 (Summer 1983), p. 37; this is the text of a speech Samhan gave at the 1983 National Women's Studies Conference. Yerachmel Domb, "Neturei Karta," *Zionism Reconsidered*, ed. Michael Selzer (New York: Macmillan Co., 1970), p. 43. Shasi, *Report to Friends Abroad—No. 2*, mimeographed sheets (November 1977). Jewish Women for a Secular Middle East, "Response to Alliance Against Women's Oppression Paper, 'Zionism in the Women's Movement'," mimeographed reply (October 1983). All African Peoples Revolutionary Party, *Israel Commits Mass Murder of Palestinian & African Peoples*, pamphlet (Washington, D.C.).

[10]Uri Avnery, "Arafat and Peace" (interview), *New York Times* (July 13, 1982), p. 25.

[11]Raymonda Hawa Tawil, *My Home, My Prison* (New York: Holt Rinehart & Winston, 1979), p. 200. In "Israel: What's Our Line," the Chutzpah collective wrote: "Perhaps after living side by side in separate nations for some time, a bi-national state would be desired by both groups" (*Chutzpah No. 7*, Winter 1974, p. 1).

[12]The reference to Nasser is from Fawaz Turki, *The Disinherited: Journal of a Palestinian Exile* (New York and London: Monthly Review Press, 1972, 1974), p. 30. The quote about the destruction of Israel is from Libya's representative to the United Nations, March 24, 1976 at the 1897 meeting of the Security Council; it is quoted by Rabbi Marc H. Tanenbaum in his preface in Judith Herschcopf Banki, "*The UN's Anti-Zionism Resolution: Christian Responses* (New York: American Jewish Committee, 1976), p. 11.

[13]Azizah al-Hibri is quoted in "Issues Concerning Arab Feminism," *off our backs* (August-September 1983), p. 9. New Jewish Agenda supports "the Jewish people's right to national self-determination in the State of Israel"; "National self-determination for the Palestinian people"; mutual recognition; "withdrawal by Israel from territories occupied since June 5, 1967"; and "guarantees for Israeli security" (New Jewish Agenda National Platform, November 1982).

[14]"Anti-Zionism=Anti-Semitism?!" (dialogue), *Chutzpah No. 8* (1981), pp. 11, 21.

[15]Chaia Lehrer, "Polarization" (letter), *off our backs* (October 1982), p. 30.

[16]Big Mama Rag Collective, "Where We're At," *Big Mama Rag* (July 1983), p. 2.

[17]Alliance Against Women's Oppression, *Zionism in the Women's Movement: Anti-Imperialist Politics Derailed* (San Francisco: AAWO, 1983), p. 4.

[18]See Said's discussion of European colonialist ideas, pp. 56-82.

[19]The reference to "modern political Zionism" is from Walter Laqueur, *A History of Zionism* (New York: Schocken Books, 1972), p. 84. Howard M. Sachar quotes Nordau in *A History of Israel: From the Rise of Zionism to Our Time* (New York: Knopf, 1982), p. 163.

[20]Sachar, p. 163.

[21]Amos Elon, *The Israelis: Founders and Sons* (New York: Penguin, 1971, 1981), p. 156.

[22]For discussions of Great Britain's actions, sometimes supportive of Jewish settlement, sometimes impeding it, often playing Arabs and Jews off against each other, actively interfering in early attempts at Jewish-Arab cooperation, see Flapan, and Aharon Cohen, *Israel and the Arab World* (Boston: Beacon Press, 1970, 1976). The Balfour Declaration is quoted in Laqueur, *The Israeli-Arab Reader,* p. 18.

[23]Quoted in Ian Lustick, *Arabs in the Jewish State: Israel's Control of a National Minority* (Austin: University of Texas Press, 1980), p. 28.

[24]Lustick, p. 53.

[25]The 1950 Absentees Property Law defined as "absentee" "Arabs in the Galilee or in the mixed cities who for one reason or another were not 'at their usual place of residence' when Jewish forces took control"; their property was taken over by the government (Lustick, p. 173). According to Sachar, these regulations "authorized the confiscation of nearly 40 percent of the land belonging to legal Arab residents of Israel" (p. 387). Sachar notes the seizure of property from Jews who left Arab states following the 1947-1949 war (p. 396ff.); although this is sometimes used to show that the injustices on both sides were equal, the fact remains that it was the Arab states, *not* the Palestinians, who benefited from the seizures of property, while Israel did benefit from its own actions. The 1958 Israeli Prescription Law "amended the older Ottoman law so that Occupiers of unregistered land were required to demonstrate unchallenged possession, not for ten years as had been the rule, but for twenty-five. Under the terms of this law Arabs were forced to produce records from the British Mandate period," most of which had been lost during the war (Lustick, p. 176).

[26] The reference to the 90 percent of Israeli land that is state-owned

is from Shulamit Aloni, "Colonial Laws in the Service of the Israeli Government," *New Outlook* (January/February 1983), p. 44.

[27] Aloni, p. 43.

[28] Aloni, pp. 43-44.

[29] Begin's comment is from a speech to the Knesset. Amnon Kapeliuk, "Begin and the 'Beasts'," *New Statesman*, June 25, 1982.

[30] Eitan's statement was made in reference to stone-throwing by Arab youths. From David K. Shipler, *New York Times*, April 14, 1983; quoted in Noam Chomsky, *The Fateful Triangle: The United States, Israel and the Palestinians* (Boston: South End Press, 1983), p. 130n.

[31] Kahan Commission of Judicial Inquiry, "Inquiry in Jerusalem: Dismissals Are Suggested," *New York Times*, February 9, 1983, p. A20.

[32] Abdul Sattar El-Sayad, "The Jews and the Koran," *Arab Theologians on Jews and Israel* (Geneva: D.F. Green, 1974); quoted in *"Israel and the Palestinians,"* Chutzpah Supplement, *Chutzpah No. 9 & 10* (1975), p. 15/7-S.

[33] S. D. Goitein, *Jews and Arabs: Their Contacts Through the Ages* (New York: Schocken Books, 1955, 1974), p. 66.

[34] Goitein, pp. 87-88.

[35] Goitein, p. 67.

[36] In no way comprehensive, this list of anti-Jewish acts in Arabs lands was compiled from Goitein and from Itzhak Ben-Zvi, "Eretz Yisrael under Ottomon Rule, 1517-1917," *Jews: Their History*, ed. Louis Finkelman (New York: Schocken Books, 1949, 1970), pp. 399-486.

[37] Morris U. Schappes, *A Documentary History of the Jews in the United States, 1654-1875* (New York: Schocken Books, 1950, 1971), pp. 201, 200.

[38] Ben-Zvi mentions the Jerusalem blood libel but gives no information about it (p. 468).

[39] Albert Memmi, "Questions for Colonel Kaddafi," *Jews and Arabs* (Chicago: J. Philip O'Hara, 1975), p. 32.

[40] Arnold Forster and Benjamin R. Epstein, *The New Anti-Semitism* (New York: McGraw-Hill, 1974), p. 159.

[41] Forster and Epstein, p. 160.

[42]Forster and Epstein, pp. 158-159.

[43]Di Vilde Chayes, p. 21.

[44]"Jewish & Arab Women's Dialog," *off our backs* (January 1983), pp. 6-7, 27.

[45]George Orwell, "Marrakech" (1939), *A Collection of Essays* (Garden City, NY: Doubleday, 1954), pp. 186-193.

[46]Elon, pp. 22-23.

[47]The Arab community near Atlantic Avenue is discussed in Alan Dehmer, "On Freedom's Shores: Brooklyn, New York," *Taking Root/ Bearing Fruit: The Arab-American Experience*, American-Arab Anti-Discrimination Committee (Washington, D.C.: ADC, 1984), pp. 47-52.

[48]Janice Terry, "Images of the Middle East in Contemporary Fiction," *Split Vision: The Portrayal of Arabs in the American Media*, ed. Edmund Ghareeb (Washington, D.C.: American-Arab Affairs Council, 1983), pp. 315-325.

[49]Frank Litsky, "A Kicker Challenging Danelo," *New York Times*, July 19, 1983, p. A17.

[50]Murray J. Rossant, "Baron Guy de Rothschild: Starting Over in America," *New York Times Magazine*, December 5, 1982, p. 45.

[51]Leo Schlosberg, review of *The Disinherited, Chutzpah No. 7* (Summer-Fall 1974), p. 12; reprinted in slightly revised form in *Chutzpah: A Jewish Liberation Anthology*, ed. Steven Lubet, Jeffry (Shaye) Mallow, et al (San Francisco; New Glide Publications 1977), p. 121.

[52]For a discussion of this issue, see Yvonne Haddad, "Arab Muslims in America: Adaptation and Reform," *Taking Root/Bearing Fruit*, pp. 101-105.

[53]Rosemary Sayigh uses Tawil as an example of someone "without organizational roots, easily discounted by the [Palestinian] mainstream as Western-oriented and bourgeois" ("Encounters with Palestinian Women under Occupation," *Journal of Palestine Studies*, Summer 1981, p. 4).

[54]"Out of Egypt: A Talk with Nawal El Saadawi," by Tiffanny R. Patterson and Angela M. Gilliam, *Freedomways*, Vol. 23, No. 3 (1983), p. 190. Saadawi was arrested in 1981 by Anwar Sadat for "criticizing puritanical Islamic notions of pre-marital virginity" (Don Schanche, as quoted in Irene L. Gendzier, "Foreward," *The Hidden Face of Eve: Women in the Arab World* by Nawal El Saadawi [Boston: Beacon Press, 1981], p. xvi, 4n.).

[55]"Out of Egypt," p. 190.

[56]Leila Ahmed, "Western Ethnocentrism and Perceptions of the Harem," *Feminist Studies,* Vol. 8, No. 3 (Fall 1982), pp. 521-522.

[57]Ahmed, p. 531.

[58]Leila Ahmed, "Feminism and Feminist Movements in the Middle East, A Preliminary Exploration: Turkey, Egypt, Algeria, People's Republic of Yemen," *Women's Studies International Forum: Special Issue, Women and Islam,* ed. Azizah al-Hibri, Vol. 5, No. 2 (1982), p. 153.

[59]Etel Adnan, *Sitt Marie Rose,* trans. Georgina Kleege (Sausalito, CA: The Post-Apollo Press, 1978, 1982).

[60]"Report: Women Against the Invasion," mimeographed flyer, April 1983. Women Against the Invasion later changed its name to Women Against the Occupation.

[61]Sayigh, p. 4.

[62]Ingela Bendt and James Downing, *We Shall Return: Women of Palestine* (Westport, CT: Lawrence Hill & Co., 1980, 1982), p. 5.

[63]Bendt and Downing, p. 18.

[64]Bendt and Downing, pp. 25-26.

[65]Annette Daum, "Anti-Semitism in the Women's Movement," *Pioneer Women* (September-October 1983), p. 22.

[66]Joanne Yaron quoted in "Regina Schreiber," "Copenhagen: One Year Later," *Lilith,* issue 8 (1981), p. 35. "Regina Schreiber" is a pseudonym used because of "the controversial and painful nature of this topic " (p. 30).

[67]Pogrebin, p. 70. On returning to live in the U.S. after years of living in Israel, Marcia Freedman has said: "I feel much more vulnerable as a woman than as a Jew in this society . . ." ("Marcia Freedman on Israeli Feminism," p. 20).

[68]Elinor Lerner, "American Feminism and the Jewish Question: 1890-1940," forthcoming in *Ambiguous Encounter: Anti-Semitism and Jewish-Gentile Relations in American History,* ed. David Gerber (Urbana: University of Illinois Press, 1985).

[69]Pogrebin, p. 48.

[70]Pogrebin, p. 49.

[71] Pogrebin, p. 49.

[72] Schreiber, p. 32.

[73] Schreiber, p. 32.

[74] Sayigh, p. 4. Prior to making this statement, Sayigh notes about the 1980 Copenhagen Conference: "... with Palestinian Women tabled on the official agenda, the General Union of Palestinian Women (GUPW) sent a delegation armed with data on the "Case," but little on women. Whether this way out of the dilemma was due to a principled stand, or to insufficient preparation, it missed a rare opportunity to present a world audience with researched information about Palestinian women: their conditions, educational levels, employment, health problems, participation in national struggle, social, political, and cultural activities" (pp. 3-4).

[75] National Coalition of American Nuns, quoted in Schreiber, p. 32.

[76] Schreiber, p. 32.

[77] Information reprinted in *Maariv* (Israel), November 28, 1983, and in *Israel & Palestine Supplement: Report on Palestinians under Israeli Rule*, Vol. VI, No. 127 (November 1983), p. 9.

[78] Pogrebin, p. 48.

[79] "Amnesty International was sufficiently disturbed by the seriousness and persistence of allegations of ill-treatment, and by the inadequacy of the Israeli authorities' published replies to these allegations to seek, in June 1979, further clarification from the authorities of the procedures and safeguards currently in effect to protect the rights of persons in custody ... "(*Report and Recommendations of an Amnesty International Mission to the Government of the State of Israel, 3-7 June 1979* [London: Amnesty International, 1980], p. 13). The report concludes that procedures in the Occupied Territories "in some respects facilitate violations of prisoners' basic human rights. The Attorney General ... has not relieved Amnesty International's concern that the procedures now in effect neither provide sufficient protection to suspects in custody nor enable a factual assessment of allegations of ill-treatment" (p. 71). The report contains a number of detailed allegations of torture and other human rights abuses. A 1984 article by David K. Shipler, "Testing the Limits of Israeli Civil Liberties," describes the mistreatment of a Jewish man suspected of being part of an anti-Arab terrorist ring, who, according to his mother, was hooded and shackled, despite his asthma (*New York Times*, May 6, 1984, p. E5).

[80] Pogrebin, p. 49.

[81] Tawil, p. 131.

[82]The Israelis wanted to find out from Oudeh where ammunition was stored. When Oudeh did not cooperate, they demolished her family's house. (See Amnon Kapeliuk, "Collective Punishment on the West Bank," *New Outlook*, April 1982, pp. 7-10, 49). The Amnesty International Report on Israel says that it "recognizes the obligation of a government to protect its citizens from the dangers of violence. However, in fulfilling this obligation every government must do so in a manner compatible with respect for and protection of the fundamental human rights of all people under its jurisdiction" (p. 47).

[83]Tawil, p. 133.

[84]Tawil , p. 250.

[85]Women Against the Occupation, "Palestinian Women in Prison" (letter), *off our backs* (January 1984), p. 20.

[86]Schreiber, p. 32.

[87]Pogrebin, p. 65.

[88]Pogrebin, p. 65.

[89]David K. Shipler, "Israel Steps Up Drive Against P.L.O. on West Bank," *New York Times*, July 11, 1982.

[90]Maxim Ghilan, "The Antagonists," *Israel & Palestine* (December 1982), p. 13. Ghilan reports on the issuance of a statement, "The Palestinians Want Peace," by Anwar El Khatib, deposed Arab mayor of East Jerusalem, Rashed Shawa, deposed mayor of Gaza, Bethlehem Mayor Elias Freij, Hebron Mayor Mustafa Natsche, and ex-Mayor of Ramallah Nadim Saroo: "an appeal in favor of mutual recognition of the PLO, 'our legitimate representative,' and Israel." Shawa is also quoted in an interview in the Israel news weekly *Ha-Olam Ha-Zeh* as saying, "we want to live with you in peace. We want to have a Palestinian state alongside the state of Israel" (interview of May 12, 1982; reprinted in *Trenton Times*, July 18, 1982). Mayor Natsche and the city council of Hebron were dismissed from their positions by the Israelis on July 10, 1983.

[91]Pogrebin, p. 62.

[92]Alice Walker, *Ms.* (February 1983), p. 16.

[93]Americans for Peace and Democracy in the Middle East ad, *New York Times*, June 19, 1983, op ed page.

[94]Samhan, p. 28.

[95]Annette Daum, "Anti-Semitism in the Women's Movement," *Pioneer Women* (September-October 1983), p. 23. Rita Giacaman recent-

ly mentioned a study by Meron Benvenisti on infant mortality statistics (80-100 per 1,000 live births) which contradicts the mortality statistics claimed by the Israeli military (90 per 1,000 live births). Giacaman's own study of a West Bank rural village indicates a mortality rate of 90 per 1,000 live births. Giacaman presented this data at a talk in New York City on March 4, 1984 sponsored by New Jewish Agenda; it was part of a national tour Giacaman, a faculty member at Bir Zeit University, did with Tamara Berger, an Israeli Jew.

[96]Tawil, p. 189.

[97]Tawil, pp. 189-190.

[98]*Al Hamishmar* (Israel), June 2, 1980; reprinted in *Najda* (September/October 1980), p. 6.

[99]Nawal El Saadawi notes: "Arab women are now permitted to vote in most Arab countries. Exceptions are to be found especially in the Gulf countries like Kuwait, Saudi Arabia, etc." She places this information in perspective by saying, "Arab women still remain politically weak despite the fact that in many countries they have been accorded the right to vote. It is clear that the crucial issue is not that of obtaining political rights such as the vote, but what is done with such rights. Within patriarchal class societies women are prevented from becoming an active political force by a multitude of barriers and pressures exercised by the ruling classes and by men" ("Women and Islam," *Women's Studies International Forum: Special Issue, Women and Islam,* p. 206).

[100]Laqueur, p. 227.

[101]Laqueur, p. 213.

[102]Samham, p. 37.

[103]Edmund Ghareeb, "A Renewed Look at American Coverage of the Arabs: Toward a Better Understanding?" *Split Vision,* p. 193.

[104]See, for example, the reference to a connection between European anti-Semitism and Christian Arab communities in Tina Naccach, "What Does the Middle East Have to Do with Feminism?" interview by Jan Adams and Rebecca Gordon, *Lesbian Contradiction,* issue 1 (Winter 1982-1983), p. 12. Before describing some of the persecution suffered in Iraq by her Jewish father, Dena Attar mentions a "new myth," that "Jews were never oppressed in Arab countries, but always co-existed happily with their Moslem neighbours; therefore women who challenge this picture of our recent past are being racist" ("An Open Letter on Anti-Semitism and Racism," p. 14).

[105]Melanie Kaye/Kantrowitz and Irena Klepfisz, "Jewish Activism in the Lesbian-Feminist Movement," *Jewish Currents* (March 1984), p. 17.

[106] Cluster bombs, which open in midair or explode on impact to emit hundreds of bomblets over an area several hundred feet in diameter, were reportedly used by the Israelis in areas with large civilian populations. They were sold to the Israelis by the U.S. government on the grounds that they be employed only against fortified military targets. (Charles Mohr, "'78 Pact Said to Limit Israeli Use of Cluster Bombs," *New York Times*, June 30, 1982).

[107] Jacobo Timerman, *The Longest War: Israel in Lebanon* (New York: Vintage, 1982), p. 121.

[108] Kaye/Kantrowitz and Klepfisz, p. 17.

[109] Alliance Against Women's Oppression, p. 4.

[110] See Chomsky for an extensive discussion of the U.S. role in the Israeli-Palestinian conflict; and Esther Howard, "Israel: The Sorcerer's Apprentice," *MERIP Reports* (February 1983), pp. 16-25, on the relation between U.S. policy and Israeli arms sales.

[111] Turki, p. 29.

[112] Robbi Keist, "The Emergence of Palestinian Nationalism," *Chutzpah: A Jewish Liberation Anthology*, p. 116; information from *The Palestinians: People, History, and Politics*, ed. Michael Curtis (New Brunswick, NJ: Transaction Books, 1975).

[113] Edward W. Said, Ibrahim Abu-Lughod, et al, *A Profile of the Palestinian People* (Chicago: Palestine Human Rights Campaign), p. 6.

[114] Turki, p. 53.

[115] Turki, p. 37.

[116] A special issue of *MERIP* (Middle East Research & Information Project) *Reports* deals with the split in the PLO in the aftermath of the Israeli invasion of Lebanon (No. 119, November-December 1983).

[117] Elias Freij, *Al Hamishmar* (Israel), September 9, 1983; reprinted in *Israel & Palestine Supplement: Report on Palestinians under Israeli Rule*, p. 5.

[118] See, for example, Sachar, pp. 266, 333. The Deir Yassin massacre is discussed in great detail in anti-Zionist histories and is barely mentioned in Zionist histories. For a discussion of the difficulty of learning about this event from Zionist sources, see Irwin Pollock, "Deir Yassin," *Israel Horizons* (May/June 1983), pp. 32-33.

[119] Quoted in Amnon Kapeliuk, "Arafat the Diplomat," *New York Times*, January 4, 1984, p. A19.

120 American-Israeli Civil Liberties Coalition, *New York Times,* September 26, 1982, p. E7. The ad expressed "anger, revulsion, and deep sadness" at the Sabra-Shatila massacre.

121 Christie Balka, Arden Handler, Claudia Kraus, Janet Tobacman, Sherry Weingart, Debbie Zucker, "Discussing the Middle East" (letter), *off our backs* (June 1982), p. 27.

122 The *Spare Rib* collective decided "not to publish letters which some of us considered pro-zionist" (*Spare Rib*, June 1983, p. 26). U.S. discussion of this controversy has included Alice Henry, "British Feminists Clash Over Anti-Zionism," *off our backs* (June 1983), pp. 11, 22; Reva Landau, "Iraq's Anti-Semitic History" (letter), *off our backs* (October 1983), p. 26; and Di Vilde Chayes, "On the Need for Jews to Be Heard" (letter), *off our backs* (August-September 1983), p. 33.

123 Timerman, *New Yorker,* October 18, 1982, pp. 89-90; reprinted in slightly revised form in *The Longest War*, p. 47.

124 Ruth R. Wisse, "Bearing False Witness," *Commentary*, Vol. 75, No. 3 (March 1983), p. 77.

125 Janet Gottler, letter, *Gay Community News*, June 19, 1982, p. 4.

126 Rachael Kamel, letter, *off our backs* (October 1982), p. 28.

127 Shelly Ettinger, "Middle East," *Gay Community News*, November 27, 1982, p. 5; Ann Gluck, letter, *Gay Community News*, December 11, 1982, p. 4.

128 See Timerman, and Andrea Behr, "Nazi Language Applied to Israel," *Shmate*, Vol. 1, No. 3 (September/October 1982), p. 13.

129 Nihal, in "Jewish & Arab Women's Dialog," p. 27.

130 New Jewish Agenda members have been "excommunicated" by three Conservative rabbis for supporting Palestinian autonomy (and lesbian and gay rights).

131 Naccach, p. 12.

132 Samhan, p. 28.

133 Information on these demonstration are from recent issues of Israeli newspapers, reprinted in the periodicals *Israleft* and *Israel & Palestine Supplement: Report on the Palestinians under Israeli Rule;* and from reports in *Israel & Palestine* and *New Outlook*.

134 *Israel & Palestine* (February 1983) contains an extremely useful annotated list of Israeli peace forces. The statement of purpose of one

group not listed there, East for Peace, an organization of Oriental Jews, is included in *New Outlook* (March/April 1984), p. 35.

135 "Jewish Arab Forum Against Racist Agitation" describes the response to MENA (*New Outlook,* January 1984, pp. 36-37). The National Meeting of Jews and Arabs Against Racism and For Coexistence attracted 1,000 people in Nazareth (Wendy Leibowitz, "This Is An Arab and A Jewish Problem," *New Outlook,* March/April 1984, p. 36). Other information cited here is from the periodicals listed in note 133. Sponsored by New Jewish Agenda and the American Friends Service Committee, Mordechai Bar-On, once a close aide to Defense Minister Moshe Dayan, and former mayor of Halhul Mohammed Milhem did a month long U.S. speaking tour early in 1984. Palestinians and Israelis at a Harvard symposium agreed that direct talks should begin on the basis of "mutual and simultaneous recognition of both nations' right of self-determination" (Walid Khalidi, "An Arab: Talk with Palestinians," *New York Times,* March 9, 1984, p. A29).

IX. Openings

1 Barbara Myerhoff, *Number Our Days* (New York: Simon & Schuster, 1978), p. 80.

2 Mab Segrest, "Mama, Granny, Carrie Bell: Race and Class, A Personal Accounting," *Conditions: Ten* (1984).

3 Melanie Kaye/Kantrowitz, "Anti-Semitism, Homophobia, and the Good White Knight," *off our backs* (May 1982), p. 30.

4 Bernice Johnson Reagon, "Coalition Politics: Turning the Century," *Home Girls: A Black Feminist Anthology,* ed. Barbara Smith (Kitchen Table: Women of Color Press, 1983), p. 359.

5 Audre Lorde, "Between Ourselves," *The Black Unicorn* (New York: W. W. Norton, 1978), p. 112.

6 Adrienne Rich, *Sources* (Woodside, CA: The Heyeck Press, 1983), p. 33.

7 See the questions on anti-Semitism in Irena Klepfisz, "Anti-Semitism in the Lesbian/Feminist Movement," *Nice Jewish Girls: A Lesbian Anthology,* ed. Evelyn Torton Beck (Watertown, MA: Persephone Press, 1982; reprinted and distributed by The Crossing Press, 1984), pp. 50-51; and Tia Cross, Freada Klein, Barbara Smith, and Beverly Smith, "Face-to-Face, Day-to-Day—Racism CR," *All the Women Are White, All the Blacks Are Men, But Some of Us Are Brave: Black Women's Studies,* ed. Gloria T. Hull, Patricia Bell Scott, and Barbara Smith (Old Westbury, NY· The Feminist Press, 1982), pp. 52-56.

RESOURCES

The following are addresses of many of the organizations and alternative periodicals and presses which have published work that has been useful to me in putting together this article.

Alliance Against Women's Oppression, The Women's Building, 3542 18th Street, San Francisco, CA 94110

American-Arab Affairs Council, 1730 M Street, N.W., Washington, DC 20036

American-Arab Anti-Discrimination Committee, 1731 Connecticut Avenue, N.W., Washington, DC 20009

American Jewish Committee, 165 East 56th Street, New York, NY 10022

American Jewish Congress, 15 East 84th Street, New York, NY 10003

Amnesty International, 304 West 58th Street, New York, NY 10019

Claremont Research Center and Publications, 160 Claremont Avenue, New York, NY 10027

Conditions, P.O. Box 56, Van Brunt Station, Brooklyn, NY 11215

Council on Interracial Books for Children, 1841 Broadway, New York, NY 10023

The Crossing Press, 22D Roache Road, Freedom, CA 95019

Feminist Studies, Women's Studies Program, University of Maryland, College Park, MD 20742

Freedomways, 799 Broadway, New York, NY 10003

Gay Community News, 62 Berkeley Street, Boston, MA 02116

genesis 2, 99 Bishop Allen Drive, Cambridge, MA 02139

International Jewish Peace Union, P.O. Box 5672, Berkeley, CA 94705

Israel Horizons, 150 Fifth Avenue, New York, NY 10011

Israel & Palestine, Magelan, B.P. 130-10, 75463 Paris Cedex 10, France

Jewish Currents, 22 East 17th Street, New York, NY 10003

Journal of Palestine Studies, P.O. Box 19449, Washington, DC 20036

Kitchen Table: Women of Color Press, P.O. Box 908, Latham, NY 12110

Lawrence Hill & Co., 520 Riverside Avenue, Westport, CT 06880

Lesbian Contradiction, 1007 North 47th, Seattle, WA 98103

Lilith, 250 West 57th Street, New York, NY 10019

MERIP (Middle East Research & Information Project), P.O. Box 1247, New York, NY 10025

Monthly Review Press, 155 West 23rd Street, New York, NY 10011

Najda, P.O. Box 7152, Berkeley, CA 94707

New Jewish Agenda, 64 Fulton Street, New York, NY 10007

New Outlook (Israel), U.S. office: A.I.E.S., 295 Seventh Avenue, New York, NY 10001

off our backs, 2423 18th Street, N.W., Washington, DC 20009

Palestine Human Rights Campaign, 20 East Jackson, Chicago, IL 60604

Pioneer Women, 200 Madison Avenue, New York, NY 10016

The Post-Apollo Press, 35 Marie Street, Sausalito, CA 94965

Reproductive Rights Newsletter, 17 Murray Street, New York, NY 10007

Response, 610 West 113th Street, New York, NY 10025

Shmate, P.O. Box 4228, Berkeley, CA 94705

Sinister Wisdom, P.O. Box 3252, Berkeley, CA 94703

Sojourner, 143 Albany Street, Cambridge, MA 02139

South End Press, 116 St. Botolph Street, Boston, MA 02115

Southern Exposure, P.O. Box 531, Durham, NC 27702
Spare Rib, 27 Clerkenwell Close, London EC1, Great Britain
Touble and Strife, 30 Bradenell Avenue, Leeds 6, Great Britain
Women's Studies International Forum, Pergamon Press, Headington Hill Hall,
    Oxford 0X3 0BW, Great Britain

ABOUT THE AUTHORS

ELLY BULKIN, b. 1944, The Bronx. Elly Bulkin is an Ashkenazi Jew who lived nearly all of her life in New York City. With her daughter off at college, she now lives in Albany, New York. She is a founding editor (1976-84) of *Conditions,* a feminist magazine of writing by women with an emphasis on writing by lesbians. Editor of *Lesbian Fiction* and co-editor of *Lesbian Poetry,* two 1981 anthologies (Gay Presses of New York, P.O. Box 294, Village Station, New York, NY 10014) she has published articles in *College English, Feminist Studies, Radical Teacher, Sinister Wisdom,* and *Women's Studies Quarterly.* Active in the local and national work of New Jewish Agenda, she was part of the collective which wrote "Coming Out, Coming Home: Lesbian and Gay Jews and the Jewish Community," an NJA brochure. She helps edit *Gesher/Bridge,* a Jewish-feminist publication sponsored by NJA's National Feminist Task Force. She is finally writing her first book of her own.

MINNIE BRUCE PRATT, b. 1946, Selma, Alabama. Minnie Bruce Pratt is a white Southerner, born and raised in Alabama, now living in Washington, D.C. She has published two books of poetry, *The Sound of One Fork* and *We Say We Love Each Other* (Spinsters/Aunt Lute Book Company, P.O. Box 410687, San Francisco, CA 94141), and has worked on the editorial collective of *Feminary: A Feminist Journal for the South,* which emphasized the lesbian vision. Her work has appeared in *Conditions, IKON, New England Review/Bread Loaf Quarterly, Sinister Wisdom, Southern Exposure,* and elsewhere. She teaches part-time in the Women's Studies programs of the George Washington University and the University of Maryland-College Park, and is the mother of two grown sons.

BARBARA SMITH, b. 1946, Cleveland, Ohio. Barbara Smith has worked in a variety of progressive movements since the early 1960s and has been active in the Black feminist movement since 1973. She has co-edited and edited three major anthologies about African American women: *Conditions: Five, The Black Women's Issue* with Lorraine Bethel (Conditions, P.O. Box 56, Van Brunt Station, Brooklyn, NY 11215); *All the Women Are White, All the Blacks Are Men, But Some of Us Are Brave: Black Women's Studies* with Gloria T. Hull and Patricia Bell Scott (The Feminist Press, 311 East 94th Street, New York, NY 10128) and *Home Girls: A Black Feminist Anthology* (Kitchen Table: Women of Color Press, P.O. Box 908, Latham, NY 12110). She is a co-founder of Kitchen Table: Women of Color Press, the only publisher for women of color in the U.S., and has served on the board of the National Coalition of Black Lesbians and Gays since 1985. She is currently completing a collection of her own fiction.

Other titles from Firebrand Books include:

A Burst Of Light, Essays by Audre Lorde/$7.95

Diamonds Are A Dyke's Best Friend by Yvonne Zipter/$9.95

Dykes To Watch Out For, Cartoons by Alison Bechdel/$6.95

The Fires Of Bride, A Novel by Ellen Galford/$8.95

Getting Home Alive by Aurora Levins Morales and Rosario Morales/$8.95

Good Enough To Eat, A Novel by Lesléa Newman/$8.95

Jonestown & Other Madness, Poetry by Pat Parker/$5.95

The Land Of Look Behind, Prose and Poetry by Michelle Cliff/$6.95

A Letter To Harvey Milk, Short Stories by Lesléa Newman/$8.95

Living As A Lesbian, Poetry by Cheryl Clarke/$6.95

Making It, A Woman's Guide to Sex in the Age of AIDS by Cindy Patton and Janis Kelly/$3.95

Mohawk Trail by Beth Brant (*Degonwadonti*)/$6.95

Moll Cutpurse, A Novel by Ellen Galford/$7.95

The Monarchs Are Flying, A Novel by Marion Foster/$8.95

More Dykes To Watch Out For, Cartoons by Alison Bechdel/$7.95

My Mama's Dead Squirrel, Lesbian Essays on Southern Culture by Mab Segrest/$8.95

Politics Of The Heart, A Lesbian Parenting Anthology edited by Sandra Pollack and Jeanne Vaughn/$11.95

Presenting...Sister NoBlues by Hattie Gossett/$8.95

A Restricted Country by Joan Nestle/$8.95

Sanctuary, A Journey by Judith McDaniel/$7.95

Shoulders, A Novel by Georgia Cotrell/$8.95

The Sun Is Not Merciful, Short Stories by Anna Lee Walters/$7.95

Tender Warriors, A Novel by Rachel Guido deVries/$7.95

This Is About Incest by Margaret Randall/$7.95

The Threshing Floor, Short Stories by Barbara Burford/$7.95

Trash, Stories by Dorothy Allison/$8.95

The Women Who Hate Me, Poetry by Dorothy Allison/$5.95

Words To The Wise, A Writer's Guide to Feminist and Lesbian Periodicals & Publishers by Andrea Fleck Clardy/$3.95

You can buy Firebrand titles at your bookstore, or order them directly from the publisher (141 The Commons, Ithaca, New York 14850, 607-272-0000).

Please include $1.75 shipping for the first book and $.50 for each additional book.

A free catalog is available on request.